Hugh Mackay is a social researcher and the author of sixteen books – ten in the field of social analysis and ethics, and six novels. He is a Fellow of the Australian Psychological Society and has been awarded honorary doctorates by Charles Sturt, Macquarie, New South Wales and Western Sydney universities. In 2015, Mackay was appointed an Officer of the Order of Australia. He lives in the Southern Highlands of New South Wales.

www.hughmackay.net.au

Other books by Hugh Mackay

Non-fiction
Reinventing Australia
Why Don't People Listen?
Generations
Turning Point
Media Mania
Right & Wrong
Advance Australia . . . Where?
What Makes Us Tick?
The Good Life
The Art of Belonging
Beyond Belief

Fiction
Little Lies
House Guest
The Spin
Winter Close
Ways of Escape
Infidelity

The Art of Belonging

Hugh Mackay

PAN

First published 2014 in Macmillan by Pan Macmillan Australia Pty Limited
This Pan edition published 2016 by Pan Macmillan Australia Pty Limited
1 Market Street, Sydney, New South Wales, Australia, 2000

Reprinted 2016

Cataloguing-in-Publication entry is available
from the National Library of Australia:
http://catalogue.nla.gov.au

Typeset in Bembo by Midland Typesetters, Australia
Printed by McPherson's Printing Group

Extract on page 50 © Inga Clendinnen, taken from *Agamemnon's Kiss*,
published by The Text Publishing Co Australia

The author and the publisher have made every effort to contact copyright holders for material used in
this book. Any person or organisation that may have been overlooked should contact the publisher.

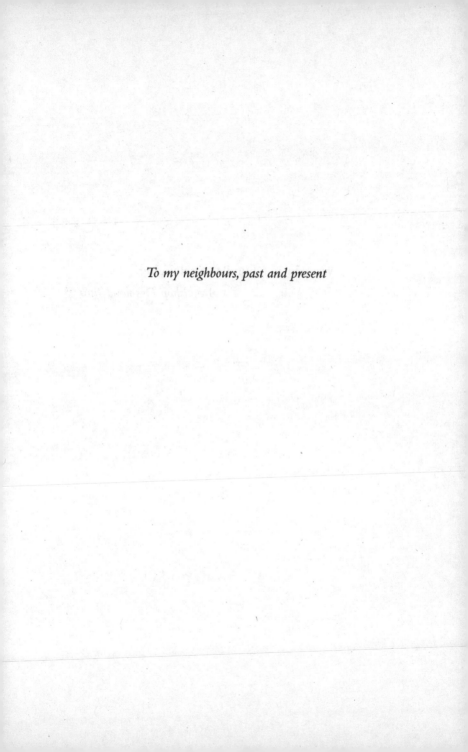

To my neighbours, past and present

We exist in a bundle of belonging.

Archbishop Desmond Tutu

Contents

INTRODUCTION

Independent and interdependent, all at once

This is a book about what happens when humans live in close proximity to each other. 'In close proximity' is, of course, a description of our natural habitat – just take a look at how most of us choose to live: in cities, suburbs, towns and villages. We are, by nature, social creatures who congregate; it's in our cultural DNA. We are not good at surviving in isolation. We rely on communities to support and sustain us, and if those communities are to survive and prosper, we must engage with them and nurture them. That's the beautiful symmetry of human society: we need communities and they need us.

It is our species' reliance on communities that explains why we've evolved to be so good at cooperating with each other. We are also, for quite different evolutionary reasons, self-interested and competitive. That may well be our deepest quandary: we are individuals with an independent sense of personal identity *and* we are members of groups, with a strong sense of social identity fed by our desire to connect and to belong. It's not an easy alliance because these two sides of our nature often seem to be in conflict, and that war within us helps to explain why there is so much conflict between us.

We hear a lot about the two sides of human nature – our Dr Jekyll and Mr Hyde; our left and right brain; our rational and emotional sides; our femininity and our masculinity. Most of these distinctions are pretty arbitrary and, as research probes further into what makes us tick, they begin to seem less sharp and to ring less true. What is clear is that we are complex creatures, each of us located at different points along many different dimensions of personality, temperament, gender and physicality, and a great deal of what's going on in our brains is inaccessible to us, let alone consciously controlled by us.

But the tension between our independence and our interdependence may be one of the most useful explanations of why we so often feel conflicted and confused about what we should do. We know we should treat each other respectfully and with kindness: after all, that's the basis of any civil society. But sometimes we just want to get our own way, regardless of the negative impact of our behaviour on others. We know we should sometimes restrain our impulses and appetites – material, sexual and otherwise – in order to be true to ourselves or to serve the common good, but sometimes our avarice, our greed or our addictions get the better of us and we overeat, overspend or overreach in some other way. Altruism – the noblest expression of our interdependence – is in our nature, but we are all driven by self-interest as well.

One of the many reasons why team sports have such a deep hold on our psyches is that they so vividly exemplify this tension between our competitive and our cooperative natures. For a team to play well, it must not only be committed to beating its opponent, its members must also be prepared to cooperate with each other – sometimes sacrificing personal glory for the greater good of the team. This is why 'man of the match' is such a ludicrously inappropriate concept: it glorifies the performance of one player when the very essence of team sport is that each member contributes to the team's overall success.

There's a very effective business model that encapsulates the tension between independence and interdependence: the insurance industry. We each pay our insurance premium – for our house, car, health, or even our life – in order to protect ourselves and our dependents in the event of an accident or disaster. We recognise that we might go through life without ever having to make a claim, yet we continue to pay – partly because we know this is a reasonable gamble against fate, but also because we understand the system: if we each pay our small premium, there will be enough in the kitty to help those who do suffer some hardship via theft, accident, illness or the death of a breadwinner. Winston Churchill once said: 'If I had my way, I would write the word "insure" upon the door of every cottage and upon the blotting book of every public man, because I am convinced, for sacrifices so small, families and estates can be protected against catastrophes which would otherwise smash them up forever.' Though insurance appeals to our self-interest, it also relies on our cooperative nature. No wonder people are so outraged when insurance companies appear to be rigid and insensitive in responding to claims, or when their senior executives appear to be plundering the organisation via what looks to the community like excessive remuneration: both kinds of behaviour fly in the face of the cooperative values on which the insurance model is based.

The credit union movement was founded on the same principle of interdependence. We are naturally keen to borrow and save money at attractive rates of interest, but we may be able to do this and help others do the same by forming a cooperative alliance with them, in which we agree to pool our resources for the benefit of members rather than shareholders.

∼

It's the contest between our individual and social natures that leads many of us to speculate about an ideal way of living that would allow us to strike a better balance between the two. So we harbour fantasies about an ideal *place* that would make it easier for us to live well; a place where we could be true to our values and live as we think we should; a place where we could 'please ourselves' while also being part of a functioning community.

For many people, that imagined ideal is a somewhat smaller place than where they are living now. If you live in a large city, you might imagine that life would be easier in a small one. There's some evidence to support that idea, by the way: when sociologists, psychologists, urban planners, economists and others try to determine the world's most 'liveable' cities, they rarely pick the big ones. Copenhagen (population: 700,000) is a current favourite. And it seems inarguable that smaller apartment blocks work better for their residents than high-rise versions, and small towns are typically (but not always) safer and friendlier than large towns.

But so what? Towns and cities are organic systems that tend to keep growing unless there are natural boundaries (in which case, like Manhattan, they might just shoot straight up). It's hard to impose artificial limits to their growth. You might well argue that a city of one million would be 'better' to live in than a city of twenty million, but it's a somewhat pointless argument, now that so many horses have bolted. The truth is that twenty million people live in each city of twenty million and only one million people live in each city of one million, though there are more of the latter than the former. Are the residents of either kind of city expressing a preference, or is this, like so much of the rest of human existence, an accident? (How many real 'decisions' do we make?)

It makes no sense to think of humans as essentially rational creatures: we are driven more by the heart than the head, and we are driven even more inexorably by circumstance and family background. So most of us don't find ourselves living in some ideal place that we've carefully researched and chosen on rational grounds – though I do recall a man who did just that, when he was trying to decide where in Australia to retire. His choice of the Tasmanian city of Launceston received a lot of publicity. This did not, by the way, lead to a rush of people moving to Launceston, because it's never that simple, is it? Our work takes us to certain places and not others, family ties bind us, and friendship circles spring up in the most unlikely places and make their emotional claims on us.

And what happens then? Those ties, those networks, those circles become a resource; part of who we are. They answer our need for psychological security. That's why the answer to the eternal question *Who am I?* must be weighed against the answer to an even deeper question: *Who are we?* As I suggest in chapter 1, we are writing each other's stories, as much as we are writing our own.

For many urban dwellers, the word that best captures the idea of a supportive, cohesive community is that charming word 'village' (see chapter 2). We sometimes indulge in lush fantasies about a village where, because of the very nature of the place, our life's dreams might come true: a rustic little hamlet where everyone knows everyone, where doors can be left unlocked, where kids make billycarts and race them on safe roads instead of crouching over video games in darkened rooms. A place where we could grow our own fresh food, organically, in a viable vegetable patch; where there's a quaint village school with an eccentric but loveable teacher; where the neighbours would be friendly and free with advice about everything from snake repellent to pump repairs; where we could finally indulge our secret wish to become a wood-turner, a weaver or a poet.

Most of us are never going to do it, though there are hundreds of little villages out there offering cheap housing and yearning for a population boost. Perhaps we have an inkling that it might not be as rosy as the fantasy suggests. (Perhaps we've dwelt a little too long on the implications of those references to snake repellent and pump repairs.) It might not be as convenient or comfortable as where we live now. That quaint little school may turn out to be either under-resourced or long since closed, necessitating an hour's drive to the nearest town or the wrench of having to wave your kids off to boarding school. Those backyard vegetables might not survive the first grasshopper plague or drought (or both at once) and if they did, you might find yourself with a glut of lettuces and no spuds, or feel guilty about not supporting those who struggle to make a living from growing fruit and vegetables commercially.

There's no harm in our occasional daydreams about such places. But, to be harshly practical, wouldn't most of us prefer to satisfy the urge to be part of a close-knit community without having to sacrifice the comforts of an urban existence?

The good news – and it's the central message of this book – is that you can have both. The *idea* of the village can be realised wherever you live. However urbanised your situation, it's usually possible to create a spirit of community, and when you do, that place will come to feel like home to you in just the way you imagine a traditional village might. (Not always: you'll encounter some people in the book who couldn't make it work and had to move to a more congenial neighbourhood.)

In most of the important ways, the dream of village life is really a dream about security – both physical ('I'm safe here') and emotional ('I belong here'). Once we have fulfilled that dream, wherever we may be, we will find it easier to reconcile the personal and the social sides of our nature. We will also become less defensive and more ready to accept some moral responsibility for the wellbeing of others. You can see it happening every day, all over the world: people popping next door to do some babysitting or to feed a pet, to take a meal to a sick neighbour or to lend a hand with a bit of heavy lifting. When we feel as if we belong somewhere, this kind of thing comes naturally to us. That's what 'social creatures' means.

The place where we live matters, to the extent that we all need to know we have a secure roof over our heads, and we naturally prefer to live in a place we find comfortable and convenient – and, if we're lucky, aesthetically pleasing. But 'home' is a far richer and more complex concept than the house or street you live in. In the end, it's more about the people than the place; more about belonging than acquiring; more about engaging than cocooning. That's why, when we experience the little miracle of connection with a community, we hear ourselves say, 'I feel at home here.'

~

The Art of Belonging is a work of social analysis, and a fictional Australian suburb called Southwood is our laboratory. Southwood could equally be a suburb in many other parts of the world, such as Western Europe and North America, but it happens to be set in Australia. More precisely, it is set entirely in my imagination, though the raw material used in its creation comes from my experience as a 'hands-on' social researcher, sitting in the living rooms of Australia, listening to people telling their stories.

No one likes to be thought of as 'typical', yet everything we do reveals something about human nature that is common to us all. The citizens of Southwood are unique individuals, of course, but they are also members of a community that is, in many ways, like human communities everywhere. In fact, all of us are both unique *and* typical. That's why, as you move through the book, you'll find the distinction between the social analysis and the stories of Southwood becoming less distinct. To get to the whole truth about who we are, we need a combination of the researcher's big picture *and* the miniatures of individuals' private lives.

I hope you enjoy meeting the people of Southwood: I'm sure you'll recognise some of them.

1

Community magic

The Southwood Community Association's executive committee is in session, with Councillor Dom Fin in the chair. This used to be called the Southwood Progress Association, until a property developer called Hank Thyssen gained control of it and came up with a series of proposals he thought could be justified in the name of 'progress', but which everyone else found repugnant. Like his proposal to drain Southwood Ponds and turn the area into a race track for dirt bikes, with Thyssen himself holding the concession. Or his plan to close part of Railway Parade and turn it into a plaza with market stalls controlled by his wife's company. Or his idea for a design competition to encourage international architects and urban planners to submit ideas for a massive redevelopment of Southwood Central. 'We don't have to award a contract to any of them, but we might attract some fresh thinking and get some useful ideas,' Hank Thyssen thought.

That was the point at which the mayor of Southwood, Mary Kippax, stepped in. Supported by everyone on the council except Mrs Thyssen, she decided to abolish the Progress Association and replace it with a Community Association of eight members, elected annually, each member representing a particular constituency – sporting clubs, youth organisations, service clubs, churches and charities, the business chamber, schools and adult education groups, the creative and performing arts, and the historical society.

The centenary of Southwood is rapidly approaching, and the Community Association is pondering ways of celebrating the occasion. Dom Fin, the deputy mayor, is responding to a suggestion from the representative of the churches.

'Thank you for the thought, Pastor Jim, but really . . . cart before the horse. Know what I mean? We're not sufficiently advanced to take up your offer of a festival service out there at Southwood East church. We haven't yet really decided what form the festival is going to take. We haven't even decided if there's going to be a festival and, if there is, whether we're going to call it a festival. Know what I mean?'

Jim Glasson, the elderly minister of the Southwood East Community Church, slumps in his chair, fighting familiar feelings of frustration. He couldn't help noticing Dom's use of the phrase 'out there', as if Southwood East, a mere ten minutes away, was too remote from the action to be a suitable venue for a festival service. Jim recalls the Southwood of old, when he was growing up here and churchgoing was pretty close to the norm. Mainly Protestant, back then. But the combination of a sharp drop in church attendance all over Australia and the emergence of Roman Catholics as the dominant denominational group, thanks to an influx of Italian, Spanish and Vietnamese migrants, has eroded support for churches like Jim's.

Jim looks around the table at his fellow committee members, but they are all avoiding eye contact – even Judith MacGregor, one of his own parishioners who, in this context, is representing the Southwood Players. Judith is widely expected to run for council at the next local government election. Jim worries that she might be overcommitted.

Now Judith is speaking: 'Well, let me say, for the record, that I think there *should* be a festival, we should *call* it a festival, and we should start planning right now. I can see a street parade, a historical pageant – perhaps some re-enactment of the pioneering days of Southwood – a choral festival with some interpretive dance . . . what is it, Marcus?'

Judith has become conscious of a groan from the other end of the table. Marcus Li, the representative of the education sector, has his hands over his face.

'Marcus?' Dom Fin says kindly. He admires Judith's energy but does not find her an easy person to deal with and is wary of her increasingly evident hunger for power.

'Please, please, please . . . no re-enactments. Please! Haven't we all had enough of re-enactments?' Marcus Li appeals to the group for support.

It comes from an unlikely source: Geraldine O'Brien, the chair of Southwood Historical and Heritage Society (that cumbersome name the result of a merger between two falling memberships). 'I couldn't agree more. We must do our best to save ourselves from public embarrassment. I don't mind if the Players want to stage some well-proven period piece, but I would draw the line at untrained local people – or schoolchildren, even worse – dressing up and taking part in some tedious ceremony that we imagine will inspire us all to think fond thoughts of the real estate company that developed Southwood in the first place. There's nothing particularly noble or heroic about our origins, Judith. Pioneers? No way. We were just another suburb created by a smart developer who saw an opportunity and grabbed it. What's to re-enact?'

Judith MacGregor is smiling patiently in the direction of Dom Fin, as if she's merely indulging all this peripheral talk. 'Chair, if I may?'

Dom nods.

'Forget I ever mentioned re-enactment. I'll wash my mouth out. I was simply throwing out ideas.'

'Yes, well throw that one out,' says a barely audible male voice – probably the man from the soccer club, Judith thinks.

'As I was saying, perhaps a music-hall type evening, perhaps a display of fashions over the hundred years of our history. Fireworks, dancing, floral displays, street parties, vintage cars of the period, old photographs, books . . .'

'*Books?*' Marcus Li is on red alert once more.

Dom Fin intervenes. 'Thank you, Judith. I think we get the idea and we're grateful to you for coming up with such an extensive list of possibilities. Others might want to come up with some more . . . er, original ideas, too. Perhaps it's time to wrap this up and we can take these thoughts back to our various organisations for discussion. There's not a lot of time. If we're going to stage something in the spring, we need to decide whether to focus on a particular weekend, or perhaps a week, like Southwood Centenary Festival Week – I'm just putting that out there. Or people might prefer to spread it out over a longer period. We meet again in a month. Thank you, all.'

As they are leaving the meeting, Marcus Li and Jim Glasson fall into step beside each other and Marcus says: 'Can I have a word with you, Jim?'

'Of course,' Jim replies, 'let's have a cup of coffee.'

They find a corner table at E.K., where Southwood's best coffee is served, and settle in. 'What is it?' says Jim, intrigued by this approach from Marcus, a man with a good reputation for his work as deputy principal at Southwood High, and the moving spirit behind a new community garden for refugees.

'I'm not a great committee man, I've decided,' Marcus replies. 'I'm used to making decisions and getting on with it. Not that I don't consult with my colleagues before I decide something, but I'm not sure I've got time for all this wheel-spinning that goes on in meetings like the one we've just endured. What's the point?'

Jim sips his coffee and looks into the face of the younger man. Energetic, impatient, creative . . . just the kind of talent

Southwood needs, he thinks. 'I'll tell you what I've found, over the years. When it comes to boards and committees associated with volunteer work, process is everything. In some ways, the process of making a decision is more important than the decision itself. Does that sound crazy? I'll tell you why I say that: these people are all volunteers, which means they have good hearts. Oh, they might be ambitious, but mostly they're here to make the world a better place – or this neck of the woods, anyway. So they need to be heard. They think very seriously about these things; this might be the one place where they feel they really can make a difference. A surprising number of people don't feel like that about their paid work, I've found. So when they get involved in some community project, they want to shine. They want to contribute. So they tend to insist on having their say, even if it's been said by someone else already, as you saw in that meeting just now. Yes, it may take a bit longer to arrive at a decision – and sometimes we never get there and someone just has to take the ball and run with it.'

'I guess I'll have to change into a different gear when I come here.'

'Exactly. Well put.'

'By the way, Jim – do you mind if I call you Jim? – you looked a bit grumpy when Dom stomped on your offer. Is there a bit of history I need to know?'

'No, not really. I made the offer in good faith, no pun intended, but I guess it was a bit pushy. Dom knows I'm always on the lookout for ways of putting our little operation on the map. Just indulge an old bloke, will you?'

Marcus smiles. 'Thanks for the coffee. My shout next time.'

Come and hover with me in a helicopter above Southwood. What do you see? At first glance, it looks pretty formless, doesn't it? Just another vast suburban sprawl. Could be anywhere, really.

Red roofs as far as the eye can see, interrupted by occasional green or blue tiles, with patches of grey in the newer areas. In Southwood, 'newer' means they were built thirty or forty years ago, when the emerging architecture of domestic housing demanded open-plans inside and anything but red on the roof. (There was also a bold attempt to reintroduce corrugated iron to the suburbs – not only for roofs but water tanks – but that initiative failed to impress Southwood Council.)

Southwood has no riverbank or harbour's edge to mark its boundary, no mountains – not even much undulation, apart from a prominent hill to the north-west. A few arterial roads stand out boldly from the rest of the streets; a four-lane highway sweeps past its western side; a railway line; a series of small lakes surrounded by houses laid out in an unconventional array, like clusters, quite different from the inexorable grid pattern that chops the rest of Southwood into more traditional blocks. A crisscross of electricity wires running from pole to ugly pole. A large retail precinct. A scattering of slightly taller buildings – offices, perhaps, or apartments – but no towers. Cars everywhere.

It almost looks like a caricature of a suburb; a stereotype. Standard three-bedroom housing stock dominates, sliced and diced, row upon row, so similar as to appear homogeneous from this height. Streets, mostly straight, lined with an assortment of parked vehicles, including trailers, boats and a few cars without wheels, up on blocks. Unrelieved by much vegetation, though there are thousands of front lawns and backyards down there, many with swimming pools, and a few playing fields and parks dotted about.

We know from our pre-flight briefing that about 75,000 people live here. Because we can't make out any natural boundaries, it's hard to know where Southwood begins and ends, or how large the area is – about 30 square kilometres, we were told, but unless you're a geographer, that doesn't convey much. Perhaps it's easier to grasp that there are about 30,000 dwellings in Southwood, most of them detached house-and-gardens, but there's a steadily growing supply of medium-density housing, too – low-rise flats and some modern approximations of terrace houses, now called 'townhouses' to add a touch of grandeur to a low-cost option.

It's not as crowded as an inner-city residential area with its teeming street life; not as spread out as some suburbs on the outer rim of the metropolitan area that strive to maintain a semi-rural identity, with occasional paddocks where children's ponies graze, brightly painted barns housing luxury cars rather than hay, gravel drives, lofts and mini-orchards. Southwood used to boast that kind of thing, though in rougher and more authentic form than the newer, more cultivated versions. But that was a hundred years ago. Now, although there's an echo of its heritage in the area called Southwood Fields, it has become unambiguously, uncompromisingly, unfashionably . . . suburbia: there's no other name for it.

And what's wrong with that?

The suburbs – disparagingly, 'the burbs' – get a bad rap, which is unfair to the billions of people around the Western world who live in them. *Most* of us live in them, because it's affordable, convenient and pleasant. Yet suburb dwellers are constantly being told their lives would be richer and more rewarding if only they would sell up and move to an apartment or a terrace closer to the action – where 'action' is defined as inner-city living. Or, at the other end of the spectrum, they are urged to 'go bush' – which might mean those semi-rural areas on the metropolitan rim, or it might mean moving to a regional town or village where it is assumed that life is simpler, people are nicer, communities function more effectively and mental health will be restored. Get onto acres somewhere and become self-sufficient!

Depending how far out you go, there may be other complications not always spoken about: drought, flies, mosquitoes, deadly spiders and snakes; intractable unemployment; an economy in thrall to commodity prices; limited access to medical, educational and financial services; higher rates of obesity, suicide and alcohol addiction; more respiratory disease due to a combination of pollens and a haze of agricultural chemicals. (In fact, most people will stay right where they are, in the suburbs, while cheerfully embracing the symbols meant to evoke rural culture and frontier myths: blue jeans, rugged boots on city pavements, plaid shirts fit for a bit of hunting and gathering at the supermarket or the hardware store, and a growing preference for SUVs that shout or, more often, whisper, 'off-road'.)

If you're not prepared to swap that dreary suburban existence for inner-city stimulation or bucolic charm, then get yourself to the coast and feel as if you're permanently on holiday. You might have to adapt to the unique problems of saltwater rust, the influx of tourists in summer, the threat of rising ocean levels and the increased incidence of storm surges (plus the standard problems faced by non-urban communities), but it will be worth it for those sea breezes and the ozone in your lungs.

Stop!

Nowhere is perfect. Moving to this or that place won't transform your life – many people who make the sea-change eventually move back to the comfort and familiarity of the suburb where their friends and neighbours sustained them more than they had realised. Which would most of us prefer: to be lonely in a beauty spot, or nurtured by a thriving community in a visually dreary suburb? We all know the answer to that (though, naturally, we'd prefer to have a bit of both, thanks). People rarely advocate suburban living for its clever compromise, combining semi-urban convenience with more space to breathe and a garden to tend. The suburbs are more often ridiculed for being neither urban *enough* nor tranquil, spacious and beautiful *enough*.

Yet if we were to swoop low over Southwood – low enough to glimpse the lives being lived under all these red roofs; low enough to sense what's really going on here – we'd get a very different impression. Southwood, like every place of human habitation, is a rich and complex cultural phenomenon. Yes, it's one of those much-maligned suburbs; but aren't the suburbs where most poems are written, most cups of sugar borrowed, most flowers grown, most dreams fulfilled, most passions stirred, most sexual relationships consummated, most babies conceived, most marriages celebrated? It's the suburbs where most parents feel those primitive surges of joy, swelling like silken banners in the heart. The suburbs are where faith is most often tested by experience, and where the most painful lesson of all – that love's work is hard work – is usually learnt. Suburbs are where the joy of sex is most often experienced (and its disappointments most often faced), where most intimations of mortality are first detected, and where a feeling of contentment – yearned for, yet unexpected – most often descends on people.

This is not because suburbs are better or worse places to live than anywhere else. All those things happen in country towns, too; they happen in inner-city terraces and apartments, in caravan parks and fishing villages. But the suburbs have the numbers.

Which is to say: most *life* happens in the suburbs.

Kendall Street, in Southwood Fields, had been a close community in the 1970s, full of families with young children. As the children grew up and moved elsewhere, some of the residents sold the family home and moved to apartments or to smaller houses closer to the city. Some moved interstate to be near their grandchildren. Others stayed to watch a new generation of families arrive and begin the cycle all over again.

When a young Vietnamese couple, Jason Ng and his heavily pregnant wife Victoria, moved into number 8, their next-door neighbours on both sides welcomed them, but Victoria and

Jason were both working and there had not been much time to connect with other people in the street before their baby was born. They had both come to Australia as students and then been granted permanent residency, so they had no family in Australia.

When their baby died in his cot, aged three months, the young couple felt their world had collapsed.

They were devastated by shock and grief. They called their parents – Victoria's in Hanoi and Jason's in Bien Hoa – and both mothers agreed to come out, though it would take a little time to organise. Sympathetic friends dropped in, rendered speechless by sadness.

The appearance of the ambulance had triggered an immediate reaction in Kendall Street. The next-door neighbours had insisted on bringing Victoria and Jason into their home for a cup of tea and something to eat. Those neighbours had been phoned by various other people in the street enquiring what had happened.

Over the following days, a stream of local people came to the house to introduce themselves and offer support. One did some shopping; one mowed the lawn; several prepared simple meals and dropped them in, ready for heating.

At first, Victoria and Jason, inconsolable, didn't know whether they wanted to be left alone or embraced by these kindly strangers. But the trickle of visitors came anyway – no one stayed for long, but people felt it was important to make sure everything possible was being done for the bereaved couple. When it was decided that a service would be held in the funeral director's chapel, the street turned up and packed the place out.

Weeks passed. Waves of grief still engulfed the young couple without warning, but they gradually embraced the idea that life could go on; must go on. They were comforted by the kindness of their neighbours. When the two mothers finally arrived, they met several of the families in Kendall Street and were assured that Victoria and Jason would never feel alone or neglected here.

～

Tragedies and disasters often have the effect of bringing a community closer together (see chapter 9). But, whatever our circumstances may be, the natural human tendency is to seek the security of being woven into the social fabric.

Like most species, we humans are great congregators. See how we cluster into suburbs like Southwood. If we were to fly in our helicopter away from the city and hover over a regional town or a rural village, we'd be struck by the same thing. Most people choose to live in close proximity to each other.

Yes, there are hermits and isolates who hate companionship and really need to be alone or just with a partner or a dog, but most of us hanker after the herd. There are people whose work forces them into social isolation – but mostly they'll go into a town somewhere when their week's work is done, seeking companionship, connection, community.

That magical word *community* conjures up the deepest truth about us: that we are social creatures by nature. We belong in social settings. We like being around other people. We work with colleagues, often in tight-knit groups. We play together. We drink together (who *chooses* to drink alone except a bruised soul or a drunk?). We like to eat in company with others (so if we live alone, we'll often eat out – see chapter 4). We go to meetings. We join clubs and choirs and committees. We go to church for social as well as spiritual reasons (see chapter 5). We like to congregate in small groups that satisfy our herd instinct. We need networks – our families and our friends – to be accessible *in the flesh*, and not just online or acknowledged in an exchange of Christmas cards.

The great myth of materialism (and its most pleasing illusion) is that we are defined by the objects we possess, including not only our cars and clothes but our houses. The truth about us is quite different. In fact, we are defined by community: we belong to each other in ways we can never 'belong' to a house or a car, a pair of shoes or a piece of jewellery. Those things belong to us, but that's a one-way street unless we have surrendered so utterly to materialism that we've actually become slaves to our desire to possess. Materialism seduces us as successfully as it does by appearing to confuse subjects and objects: we – you and I, living persons – are subjects, but the things we possess are mere objects. This blurring of the distinction between subjects and objects gets us into terrible trouble in other ways, too: if we commodify people, treating them as objects to be possessed or manipulated, we diminish both them and ourselves in the process. *Place* – a house, a street, a suburb or town – matters so deeply to us not because it is a precious object in itself but because it symbolises the fact that we belong to a family, or a community.

We become deeply attached to particular places because of the life we associate with them. The most lavish house in the world will ultimately seem pointless and empty – except as the equivalent of a velvet-lined cave that provides shelter – unless it works as a symbol of our connectedness. This is why the true meaning of 'home' has little to do with bricks and mortar. Indigenous people's attachment to the land – expressed as a quasi-mystical sense of place – points to the *social* significance of those places, their meanings for a tribal group, their cultural and ancestral significance, *not* their significance as a pile of rocks or a running stream, per se.

We are not only defined but actually sustained by our social networks. We thrive on being part of a community – whether that's familial, social, residential, intellectual, cultural, political, religious, professional or vocational. In the end, it makes no real sense – no biological sense, no psychological sense – for us to dwell on our identity as individuals. That's not who we are. We're tribal. We're social. We're communal. We need to *belong*.

But here's the rub: communities don't just happen. We have to create them and build them. That means participating in the life of the community – socially, commercially, culturally. It means, among other things, paying our fair share of the taxes that fund the infrastructure the community relies on. (In fact, arranging your affairs so you can avoid paying tax in the place where you live is a powerful declaration of a desire *not* to belong.) After all, communities don't automatically survive – history is littered with examples of towns that died; neighbourhoods that ceased to function as communities and became dangerous, hostile places; communities that lost their cultural soul, or their commercial heart; entire civilisations that crumbled. Yes, we're sustained by our communities, but they don't have a life of their own: we must nurture them. For communities to survive, we must engage with them and attend to them.

If the deepest truth about us is that we are social creatures by nature, then it follows that social isolation is unhealthy for us. A less-than-optimal dose of regular social contact can have a deleterious effect on our wellbeing, our mental acuity and our outlook of life: nothing keeps us on our toes like random, unplanned conversations. Reduced Social Interaction (let's call it the *other* kind of RSI) carries a hefty penalty, and online contact doesn't quite measure up as a substitute (see chapter 7).

That's why being deliberately excluded from a community – banished, excommunicated – is the toughest punishment of all. Even being accidentally excluded – by carelessness or thoughtlessness on the part of our neighbours, for instance, or being overlooked when a work colleague is inviting everyone but us out to lunch – can induce feelings not only of isolation, but of alienation and even worthlessness.

Allowing our neighbourhoods and communities to disintegrate is not only foolish: it diminishes our very nature as humans. Our primary responsibility to our species is not merely to reproduce, but to create and nurture these fragile yet precious communities that sustain us. For all their tensions and difficulties, for all their inevitable rifts and rivalries, communities give us the juices we need if we are to realise our full potential as human beings.

Whether in Southwood or any of the millions of other densely settled suburbs around the world, or in cities and towns, or in villages clinging to the coast, nestled in the hills or dotting the wide plains, we are at our best when we belong. Belonging is one of the deepest sources of human fulfilment. Welcoming someone into a group is therefore one of the most warmly appreciated of the gifts we can offer each other. Knowing I belong implies that I am taken seriously; I am connected; I am supported.

Part of the magic of communities is that, however imperceptibly, they shape us to fit them. That applies as much to a neighbourhood as to a political party, a church, a school, a workplace, a club or a choir. Any community we belong to – any setting where we gradually come to feel 'at home' – will make a rich contribution to the story of who we are. None of us is born a blank slate: we have too much genetic inheritance to claim such a thing. But the story that gradually unfolds on that slate is mostly written by others, not by us. We are the authors of each other's stories through the influence we have on each other, and the way we respond to each other. Each of our stories is unique, but the subtext is universal – it is about finding the answer to just one question: *Where do I belong?*

Not all our impulses are directed towards building up the community, and not all neighbourhoods encourage or foster the spirit of community. We humans are caught in the crossfire between two conflicting sides of our evolutionary heritage: we are selfless and cooperative by nature, because we need to maintain the communities that sustain us; yet we are also selfish and competitive by nature, because we are driven by the need to ensure our personal survival and that of our families. We are both nurturers and fighters.

It might not feel like a war within us, but the tension is ever-present. The outcome depends on which side of our nature we choose to nurture, to reinforce, to encourage; which inner army we choose to feed. Each of us is capable of behaving nobly; each of us is equally capable of ugly, insensitive behaviour. Some circumstances bring out the best in us; some provoke the worst. Our restraining moral sense is community-based; our recklessness is usually all our own work (though gangs can be reckless, too). We are both nice and nasty. All of us.

Selfish impulses can damage the spirit of a community, such as when we become obsessed with accumulating wealth at the expense of others; when the drive for success overwhelms our moral scruples, or when the desire for power or status erodes our willingness to respect other people's rights and needs; when our aggressive tendencies are let off the leash in the form of prejudice against 'otherness'; when we give way to jealousy, rage, greed or sexual predation.

At one of Southwood's most 'desirable' addresses – Liesl Crescent, Southwood Rise – lives Angie Koutsoukas, forty-two, married, no children. She is a public relations consultant in a city firm. Her next-door neighbour is Bill Ritchie, fifty-five, married, two daughters aged twenty-eight and twenty-five, neither living at home.

Angie's husband, Michael, knows his wife is deeply unsatisfied. He suspects she actually despises him and his work (he's a mid-level corporate lawyer). He, in turn, finds it hard to take her work seriously, and he assumes she realises that. But he knows she loves their house, their cars, their exotic holidays and their easy access to the cultural life of the city. Their personal life is chilly but civil. Michael holds out the hope that, one day, Angie might rediscover the passion for him she once appeared to feel. He adores her, and he can't help noticing that many other men adore her, too.

Bill Ritchie's wife, Petra, has a fulfilling professional life as a teacher at one of Southwood's seven primary schools. She knows her husband is bored with their marriage, but that's part of a bigger problem: she senses that he's bored with his work, too (he's a solicitor in a suburban practice twenty minutes' drive from Southwood). He's clearly bored with their almost non-existent social life, short of male friends and disappointed that his sister has moved interstate and doesn't keep in touch with him. (She occasionally phones Petra but rarely asks to speak to Bill.)

Petra often finds Bill standing at their front window, staring into the street, or sitting at his study desk, gazing out the window at nothing but the side of the Koutsoukases' house, barely three metres away. She has wondered if he's depressed, but has concluded the problem really is simple boredom. Yet he snarled at her when she suggested inviting some of her colleagues and their partners for a Sunday barbecue, and he sneered when she proposed enrolling together in one of the courses being offered at the library, so she has given up trying to provide the stimulation she believes he needs. He tells her he doesn't need friends.

The Koutsoukases and the Ritchies do not socialise with each other, nor with anyone else in their street. It's a street where people come and go by car. There's very little footpath traffic, and the few children who live in Liesl Crescent are driven everywhere by their parents. Though both the husbands are lawyers, this hasn't drawn them together. They nod in acknowledgement when they see each other, and occasionally exchange a few words when they are putting out the garbage or watering the garden, but nothing more. The wives chat to each other in the polite way of neighbours who feel no warmth towards each other. They would all say they were lucky to have 'nice' neighbours, and they take a certain pride in the fact that they actually know each other, since many people in Southwood Rise and elsewhere in Southwood say they don't even know their neighbours' names. Petra and Angie would never meet for coffee at the weekend, though Petra occasionally does with other women in Southwood.

Bill Ritchie is consumed by lust for Angie Koutsoukas. When he gazes out his study window, he sees more than the side of a house: he sees the window of Michael and Angie's bedroom and, on a few recent occasions, he has seen Angie preparing for bed through the partially-open slats of a venetian blind angled to his advantage. If it happens much more, he will be tempted to conclude that Angie knows what she is doing.

Neither Angie nor Bill feel they belong where they are. They don't feel comfortable, content or fulfilled. They both look beyond their marriages and their neighbourhood for some half-imagined source of fulfilment that eludes them. Angie feels some connection with the people she works with, and with some of her clients: that's a kind of community, but the members of it keep changing. Bill's workplace is more stable, but his relationships with his colleagues are confined almost entirely to the professional level. He doesn't discuss sport or music or politics with them. He doesn't enquire after his colleagues' kids, or volunteer anything about his own. He lunches alone. He fantasises endlessly about Angie and some imaginary paradise where they will end up together, yet he barely knows her. They have exchanged only a dozen sentences in the year they have been living next door to each other, but each of those fleeting encounters has been, for Bill, electrifying. And from the warmth of Angie's smile and the intensity of their eye contact, he senses it might be the same for her.

~

All over Southwood, there are people who appreciate the sustenance and the discipline – and sometimes even the chaos and distractions – of being part of a functioning community. Those are the people who know how to engage, but not everyone does. Some residents of the district don't even realise what treasures are on offer. In single-person households, in two-person households, and even in many three- or four-person households, the need for connection with a social network runs deep, but is not always recognised for what it is: the answer to one of our most insistent human yearnings.

It almost goes without saying that the people who are drawing most deeply on the resources of Southwood are those who are contributing most to it. Those who are nurtured by their neighbours and by the life of the community are those who, consciously or not, are themselves nurturing the life of that community. Those who think the place has no soul haven't yet realised it might be their own soul that's missing.

In primitive tribal societies, there is nowhere to hide from the community: it's everywhere; there's nowhere else to be but in it, part of it. Nor is there anywhere to sulk or smoulder if you belong to a large and rowdy household; you might need to go out occasionally to find some peace, but you're inextricably part of the dynamic life of the domestic herd. In smaller households, people often do hide from each other, because the emotional temperature is too high; the focus – particularly on the one or two kids – is too intense. Being part of a larger community protects us from that intensity and relieves us of the burden of having to take too much responsibility for each other's wellbeing.

'It takes a village to raise a child', yes, and we ignore that wisdom at our children's peril. If we insulate the child from the village and try to do all the raising on our own, when will the child learn about complexity, diversity, ambiguity? How will the child learn to meet the challenge of difference? Schools are helpful socialisers, but they are only one part of the 'village': the neighbours we never chose are a crucial factor in the process of developing the resilience and the tolerance we will need if we are to learn how to fulfil our destiny as social creatures.

It's not only children: it takes a village to keep an adult sane and sensible, too. The French Catholic existentialist Gabriel Marcel (1889–1973) claimed that the reality of our personal existence could only be fulfilled through our engagement with communal life. Marcel believed – and who would disagree? – that if we position ourselves (or are forced) outside a community, we tend to become obsessed with ourselves and our own needs. Self-absorption, self-pity and self-indulgence are the sure signs of a person not engaged with a community.

The US psychotherapist Carl Rogers (1902–87) had precisely the same view. He found that when his patients came to a full realisation of who they were, it always included the sense that they were essentially social creatures who belonged in groups, who needed networks, and who thrived on being part of a community.

The Australian social analyst, Richard Eckersley, has put the point rather more metaphysically in 'Redefining the Self' – the sidebar to a paper titled 'Whatever Happened to Western Civilization?' (*The Futurist,* November–December 2012):

> When I was at school we were taught that the atom was made up of solid particles, with electrons whizzing around the nucleus like planets orbiting the sun. Now, we think of the atom as more like a fuzzy cloud of electrical charges. Similarly, we currently think of the self as a discrete, biological being with various needs it seeks to satisfy. Like atoms combining into molecules, we form and dissolve bonds with other separate selves to create and terminate relationships. Sociologists talk of modern society as [comprising] 'atomized' individuals.
>
> What if we were to see the self not as a separate physical entity, but as a fuzzy cloud of relational forces and fields? This would be a

self of many relationships, inextricably linking us to other people and other things and entities. Some are close and intense, as in a love affair or within families; some are more distant and diffuse, as in a sense of community or place or national or ethnic identity; and some may be more subtle, but still powerful, as in a spiritual connection or a love of nature.

. . . Transforming how we see the self in this way – as a fuzzy cloud of relationships – would change profoundly how we see our relationships to others and to the world . . . It brings us closer to how indigenous people see the self, and represents one way that scientific and spiritual views can be compatible.

In an era of rampant individualism, we have often lost sight of our nature as social creatures. Seeing ourselves in the way Eckersley suggests might help us recognise our inescapable interconnectedness and that, in turn, might encourage us to accept our responsibilities to the communities that sustain us. The neighbourhood can be a magic place, but the magic comes *from* us, as well as *to* us.

Community and morality

In cities, towns and suburbs all around the Western world, the same concern is being aired: do we look out for each other as much as we used to? Are neighbourhoods functioning as well as they did in the past?

Some of this might be good old-fashioned nostalgia, but there's a sufficiently persistent pattern of concern to warrant some investigation. And the starting point is to recognise that the two most common complaints about 'decline' in Western societies are inextricably linked. First: *Our communities are not functioning as well as they once did.* Second: *Our shared values are not as clear or strong as they once were; the idea of 'right and wrong' is more slippery than it used to be.* How can you separate those two things? The moral sense is, after all, a social sense: we develop our moral codes and systems out of the experience of learning how to get along with other people – first in the family, then in the classroom and the playground, and finally in the wider community. It's not the values we're taught that shape our true morality: it's what works in practice.

Cohesive communities produce coherent moral systems. So communities are not just places where we can belong; they are also places where we learn to tell right from wrong and distinguish good from bad. Communities are our moral teachers and, when they're working well, they're also our moral guardians.

It's a funny thing – the kids that cause most trouble in Southwood Fields are the ones we don't see much, the ones we don't really know. I remember when I was growing up in a country town, everybody seemed to know everybody and that put a sort of pressure on you when you were a kid. A good sort of pressure, though. Made you realise that things you might want to do – silly things – had consequences for other people, and those other people might be someone your mum and dad knew.

We got into various scrapes – what kid doesn't? – but you always knew people were keeping a bit of an eye on you. 'Oh, you're Eric's boy, aren't you?' So then you were identified, tagged; it was a bit like carrying your ID around with you.

To some extent it's the same around here. There are some kids you recognise, or you've seen them with their parents, or you know where they live. And that helps. Not that you want to be spying on kids all the time, but it's often for their own good. If you can see they're in a jam of some kind, you know who they are and where to take them.

In some parts of Southwood, you never see the kids outside – or not in the street, anyway. Their parents drive them everywhere and you'd never get to know them unless you happened to have kids around the same age. I think that's a pity. How can they feel part of the place if they don't know their own neighbours?

Of course, it's not just kids. We all rely on each other a bit, don't we? To keep an eye on things? And there's no doubt you're more likely to do the right thing by people you know. I often think that about graffiti – there's a bit of that up at Southwood Central. Would those kids be doing that to someone they know? Would they be doing it if they knew we knew who they were and who their parents were?

I just don't get the feeling that people care about each other as much as they used to.

Want to hear the worst example of what I'm talking about? Just a few blocks away from here, still in Southwood Fields, an old man died in his house. This was not a man I knew, and it didn't happen in my street, but we all heard about it. He died in his house and no one noticed for two weeks. Two weeks! Can you imagine that? I'm not talking about trying to imagine the stench when the police finally went in and found him. I'm talking about the fact that no one noticed he wasn't around. No one noticed the newspapers piling up on his front step, or the mail spilling out of his letterbox. I don't think it would happen in our street – we're all pretty alert if someone is sick, or hasn't appeared for a day or two. You knock on the door or phone them, just to say, 'Haven't seen you around – I just wanted to make sure you're alright. Is everything okay?' No one's going to be bothered by that. It's alright for people who've got family and that, but a surprising number of people live on their own around here, especially older people or people licking their wounds after a break-up. They're the ones you've got to look out for.⁹

Morality is only ever about one thing: how we treat each other. In *The Good Life* (2013) I expressed it like this:

Morality can never be a solo performance. You can be comfortable on your own; you can be rich on your own; you can have bright ideas or tinker with inventions on your own; you can sail around the world or cross the Sahara on your own (though if you get into trouble, you might be glad to know other people who think your survival matters); you can even be happy on your own. You can lead a blameless, exciting or passionate life on your own, but you can't lead a good life on your own, because morality is about our interactions with each other. It makes no sense to consider the good life in isolation.

When communities fragment or disintegrate, the one certain casualty is their moral standards. That's why we are generally at our worst, morally speaking, when we live in segregated or divided societies – such as the years of South Africa's policy of apartheid or the US's racial segregation – or when the fabric of a community is frayed. (William Golding's great novel *The Lord of the Flies* is, in essence, the story of what happens when the constraints of a cohesive society are removed.) If you think morality is in decline, the first and most logical place to look for an explanation would be to the life of our neighbourhoods and communities: *are* they in danger of fragmenting, or is this all a myth?

Take a dispassionate look at the state of contemporary Western society and you will certainly identify some trends that might be expected to erode the cohesiveness of neighbourhoods. Changes in our patterns of marriage and divorce would be one factor: if marriage is becoming a less stable institution, this may well threaten the stability of local communities. High rates of marriage breakdown imply high rates of family disruption and that implies some fracture of social networks.

Unless we manage it very carefully, it's obvious that children can suffer when their family falls apart. Imagine how it must be, at a young age, to find yourself suddenly caught up in the disruptions of regular access visits that unplug you from one parent, one home and one micro-community and plug you into another, sometimes with acrimonious exchanges between your parents at the changeover. In Australia, about half a million children are involved in these regular back-and-forth movements between their separated parents' homes. Not all of those are traumatic or even unpleasant for the children involved, but all of them are disruptive.

Some children who grow up with this kind of instability will learn to take comings and goings in their stride, and might become more socially and emotionally adaptable as a result. Others might react quite differently – feeling insecure and hesitant about forming close relationships because of a lurking fear of further emotional upheaval. Some will be grateful to their parents for managing a difficult situation sensitively, and for continuing to love and nurture them in a way that protected their feeling of emotional security. Others may resent parents who had seemed to place their own needs above the needs of their children.

As time passes, all these reactions will be carried into the adult community – some as resources and some as emotional baggage. They will become part of the social fabric.

Here's another potentially fragmenting factor: low birthrates. The low birthrate in most Western countries (well below the replacement level of 2.1 babies per woman) has an inevitable impact on communities, since kids are often the social lubricant that facilitates contact between their parents.

Many other factors may be contributing to the trend: the rise of the two-income household – generally welcomed as a sign of the liberation of women from domestic oppression – means that, in most households, both partners are absent from their local neighbourhood by day and busy with domestic matters at weekends. The increasing mobility of the population means we are less likely to stay in one home for a lifetime – or even for a long time – than our parents and grandparents were, which might make us feel less committed to the long-haul business of nurturing relationships within the local neighbourhood. Almost universal car ownership reduces public transport use and local footpath traffic – both effects tend to reduce the accidental encounters that traditionally helped to maintain social contact between neighbours. And increased reliance on information technology draws us into online communities that may distract us from our connections with the local neighbourhood (see chapter 7).

That's by no means a comprehensive list, but there are clearly many reasons to suspect that Western social cohesion has been under threat. Which means we need to compensate; we need to try harder to maintain the all-important local connections that fuel the life of the local community; we need to acknowledge the symbiotic relationship between community and morality. If our suburbs were to become mere dormitories, with no cohesive *communal* life of their own, our moral sensitivity would indeed be under threat. If we were only to connect with people we like or who share our interests, that might be comfortable for us, but how healthy is it for the continuing development of the noblest human values, like tolerance, patience, compassion, kindness and respect? The way we respond to people who are *unlike* us is the best test of our moral integrity.

A fashionable dystopian vision of the future is of a place where the sense of community has been corrupted by greed, vanity and selfishness; where the idea of 'neighbourhood' no longer counts; where garbage piles up in unkempt streets; where law enforcement has become an impossibility because the local citizens have lost interest in taking any responsibility for each other's wellbeing; where gunshots are often heard in the night; where there are bars on every window and locks and bolts on every door; where people come and go by car and never connect; where there's an air of deep insecurity and mistrustfulness, sometimes amounting to menace; where online communities are the prime source of connection and emotional support.

Some pessimists think we're halfway there already. It's true that some parts of the world's big cities have gone through somewhat dystopian episodes. It's true that crime sometimes takes over a neighbourhood and the police seem powerless to control it. It's true that, in many streets of many cities, neighbours don't know each other and appear to show no interest in doing so. It's true that the domestic security industry is booming – deadlocks, alarms, CCTV cameras, electronically operated gates, window bars, all the way up (or down) to 'gated communities' with boom gates and armed guards.

But who welcomes that kind of development? Who thinks that's a good way for humans to live? Who doesn't think that, if some of those developments were to become major trends, we would have a huge social problem on our hands? Who would welcome the idea of our cities becoming a series of ghettos disconnected from (and perhaps impenetrable to) each other? Who wouldn't rather live in a friendly and safe street than an unfriendly and unsafe one? Who wouldn't like to live in a street where, if we were going away, we could leave the key to our house with a trustworthy neighbour?

The good news is that there are countless towns and suburbs like Southwood around the world, where the residents do nurture their local community and take some pride in its health. So the challenge is: how do we preserve that way of life, and extend it to neighbourhoods where isolated people are at risk of being paralysed by fear and insecurity?

Part of the answer lies in the quality of urban design and, in particular, the creation of more imaginative and socially attuned living spaces with increasing emphasis on public rather than private space – including well-designed 'hubs' (see chapter 5).

Another answer is to focus more on the development of contemporary versions of the well-proven model of medium-density housing that eschews unsustainable house-and-garden developments at one end of the scale and inhospitable high-density housing at the other.

But even in cities, towns and suburbs that don't enjoy the benefits of enlightened design, there are hopeful signs that we understand the threat posed by fragmenting communities. Many of us are paying more attention to our local neighbourhoods. We are coming out of our shrinking households to find new ways of herding (see chapter 3). The tide may well be turning for communities and that's good news not only for our social nature, but for our moral nature too.

2

'The village' comes to town

If you lived in New York, you might tell people from elsewhere that you're a New Yorker, and you might identify proudly with the Big Apple. But if you're with another New Yorker, you'll each identify with your own village – Upper East Side, Greenwich Village, the Bronx, Queens, Manhattan, the West Village. In many ways, those urban villages are subcultures, rather like separate little buckets of culture that only occasionally slop over into a common pool called 'New York'.

That's how it is in every city in the world.

In London, the question is whether you belong in Soho, Westminster, Notting Hill, Mayfair, Highgate, Hampstead ... 'Everything you could want in a village is here,' boasts an estate agent's pitch for houses in Hampstead. 'The hills and lanes, the old gas lamps, the pubs, the funfair on the heath. There are fishmongers, butchers, French bakers, an eclectic range of restaurants, the Everyman cinema where food is delivered to your sofa seat, summer concerts and exhibitions at Kenwood on Hampstead Heath.'

Rural villages in many countries have diminished or died, but the *idea* of the village – the dream of belonging to a village – persists. And so the village has come to town. In contemporary Western society, the most appealing features of 'the village' as we fondly remember or imagine it are increasingly found in pockets of cities too large to have a single identity of their own.

Sydney has been explicitly reimagined by its lord mayor as 'a city of villages'. There, as in all large cities, the villages have distinct cultural identities: witness the difference between Newtown and The Rocks, or Ultimo and Kings Cross. Well beyond the inner-city villages, there are many different perceptions of what living in any particular city means. Suburban areas also have their identities, each with a set of unique connotations. Sydneysiders, for example, understand the broad cultural distinctions between the Eastern Suburbs, the North Shore, the St George district, the Western Suburbs (not to be confused with the Inner West), the Northern Beaches, the (Sutherland) Shire and so on, but even within each of those broad categories they are acutely aware of the nuances: if you lived in Point Piper or Vaucluse, you wouldn't want people interpreting *your* 'Eastern Suburbs' as implying Bondi Junction or Kingsford. And if you were from Pymble or Wahroonga, you might be quite careful to specify 'Upper North Shore' so as not to be confused with those who live 'lower down' in places like Chatswood or Waverton.

A village, in the popular imagination, is a place where people know, trust and look out for each other; where neighbours have struck that delicate balance between open friendliness and an appropriate respect for each other's privacy; where it is possible to imagine (if perhaps never quite to achieve) a gentler, more relaxed pace of living . . . a 'simpler' life, where we have opportunities to spend time with our neighbours, if not in the street, then in local cafes and bars.

So persistent and pervasive is the dream of village life, we attach that magic word 'village' to everything we can: highly sophisticated shopping malls; new housing estates whose developers wish to project the warm and friendly associations of 'village' onto the cold vista of sealed roads with not a person in sight and not a sod yet turned; any shop you can think of in any setting at all – the Village Antiques, the Village Wi-Fi Cafe, the Village Medical Centre (but very few village blacksmiths, these days). What else would you call cluster housing for retirees but a 'retirement village'? The very name conjures up the idea of a welcoming community where you will quickly find your feet and not mourn, for too long, the loss of the home and neighbourhood you've left behind. Even high-rise apartment blocks and office towers are sometimes referred to as 'vertical villages' as architects and interior designers take big strides towards the creation of spaces intended to feel a bit like a village, with coffee shops, child-minding areas, seating and eating areas, rooftop gardens, and recreational and exercise areas dotted throughout the building.

These attempts are generally more successful in commercial than residential applications. In high-density apartment buildings, residents are less inclined to socialise with each other: the very density of the habitation increases our desire for personal privacy rather than shared space, which is why anecdotal evidence suggests that the higher the density, the less likely people are to make eye contact (let alone conversation) in a lift or a carpark, and why high-density housing is often associated with social tensions, including suspicion and even hostility between the occupants. Many residents of such buildings prefer to go elsewhere for recreation, eating and socialising. It's *medium*-density living that better facilitates the urge to connect with a community.

The subtitle of this book says 'It's not where you live, it's how you live', implying that we can nurture the life of any local community, even if it doesn't have the classic qualities – particularly the geographical features – we associate with ideal villages or towns. You can make a community work like a village in a suburb like Southwood, or in the various localities which comprise that suburb, just as you can in the inner city or on the outer fringes of a metropolitan area.

But not everyone can feel as if they *belong* everywhere. Not everyone can slot comfortably into every social setting. Sometimes, you simply can't join the dots in a way that includes you. There is such a thing as cultural incompatibility.

'Look, I don't want to sound snobbish about this, but the simple fact is you can't talk about Southwood as if it's just one big amorphous lump. Up here in Southwood Rise, it feels like quite a different place from the other parts of Southwood. Southwood East, certainly. Or even Old Southwood. Well, that isn't its official name, but we all tend to call it Old Southwood – quite affectionately, I might add. That was the original part of the suburb, developed almost a hundred years ago, I understand, and there are some very charming places there, some lovely old Federation houses I wouldn't mind living in myself. There's been a lot of renovation going on, which is good, I suppose, although not all of it as tasteful as you might wish. I'm sure the people who live there are very charming, too, some of them. It's an older demographic than ours, of course, although they tell me a few young families are starting to move in and liven the place up a bit – prices are just that bit cheaper down there, of course, so it's a good place for young couples to start off.

Frankly, if I didn't live in Southwood Rise, I doubt if I'd be living in Southwood at all. I'd be in Kentwell or Lewis. Or perhaps an apartment in the inner city. We do talk about doing that, eventually. But this is lovely, for the time being. We have everything we need here. We both work, so we don't spend much time socialising, except people often do have drinks parties on weekends. You tend to see the same people, over and over, but that's inevitable in a small community, and we're pretty much of one mind up here – when it comes to politics, at least – so it's all pretty civilised.

I go into Southwood Central for serious grocery shopping. Otherwise, I just stick to the local village. We have everything we need here. Bruno's coffee is to die for, Bruno himself is just delightful, and his little cafe is packed on weekends. There's a very acceptable deli run by a lovely little French couple, and the Vintage Crop stocks most of what we want for day-to-day quaffing – Morgan buys our serious wine on our annual swing through vineyard country. We even have a bookshop in the village, though I think it's a bit of a struggle for them – so many of us just browse in the shop, which is lovely, and then buy what we want online. I couldn't survive without my iPad – don't know how I ever did. Or my iPhone – it's the last thing I look at before I go to sleep and the first thing I look at when I wake up . . . poor Morgan. Anyway, I see the bookshop is diversifying into gifts – that's usually the beginning of the end, I find. It would be a pity if they folded; a bookshop adds such character to a place, I always feel.

So does our fruiterer. You pay through the nose, of course, but the quality is definitely there. And they do a very stylish lunch on weekends – we often pop in there on our way back from the boys' sport. Oh yes, the school situation. We let them go to the local primary school in the early years. I had no complaints about that. They could practically walk to and from, although one of us mostly drove them. But when Jasper got to year five . . . I don't know. We just felt it was time to get them into something a bit more . . . reliable? We weren't sure about Southwood High. Bit of a mixed reputation. Values, you know, and discipline. We think that's very important. And it's paid off. They are both very happy at St Paul's, so we feel that was the right decision. It's not too crushingly religious, but they do insist on the boys doing the right thing. Very big on manners and courtesy. I approve of that. Morgan drops them off each morning and they find their own way home by bus. Well, that makes them sounds a bit like neglected children – it's not quite like that. St Paul's runs a minibus right here into the village and they usually buy a fresh juice at the fruit shop and then walk the two blocks home.

The housekeeper is always there to make them some afternoon tea and get the dinner on. She's from Old Southwood, come to think of it. A lovely Italian woman who has had reams of kids of her own, so she understand little boys. I'm not sure I do!

Our next-door neighbours are fine, by the way. They never give us any trouble – apart from their dog that's one of those yappy little things. Sometimes we have to bang on the side fence to tell them to shut it up. The people on the other side keep pretty much to themselves, although we do share a gardener. But, as I say, it's all very civilised around here.'

Not everyone in Southwood Rise feels quite as enthusiastic about it as that resident. Ken and Margie Isherwood moved back to the city from their rural property when Ken's back gave out. They had wanted to buy something in Southwood Fields, which is the very place where Ken's grandfather used to run cows before the swelling tide of urban development engulfed him, but they couldn't find anything suitable and settled for a large house on the Rise, Southwood's solitary hill, overlooking the Fields.

At first, everything seemed perfect. Margie quickly found a job in administration at the local hospital and Ken, a keen Rotarian, linked up with the Southwood Central club. His back prevented him from doing anything too strenuous, but Rotary gave him the opportunity to become involved in some volunteer work, which he loved.

They both assumed that, in a suburb like Southwood, it would all be pretty friendly and laid-back. It gradually dawned on them that Southwood Rise was a little ghetto of privilege that actually made them feel rather uncomfortable. They were virtually ignored for the first few months, although the neighbours on one side invited them in for a drink one Friday evening and introduced them to some other people from the street. After that, there was a lot of friendly waving from cars, but no actual speech and no further socialising.

Gradually, invitations to drinks parties began to arrive – sometimes by phone and once by a written note so formal in style that Margie seriously doubted whether she owned anything suitable to wear. They'd been caught out at their first drinks party when the host had said 'just wear old clothes', so they did. Everyone else appeared to be seriously dressed up, which made them wonder later whether, in Southwood Rise, 'old clothes' meant 'something you've worn at least once before' . . . or perhaps even 'vintage'.

The conversation often turned to politics and it was assumed that Ken and Margie, being from 'the bush', would be firmly located at the extreme right of the political spectrum. In fact, their background and their attitudes were more liberal than that – Ken's father had been a paediatrician who worked only in public hospitals, and Margie's mother was a feisty social democrat and women's libber who had raised her daughter to be independent-minded on all subjects, including politics. A few times, early on, they expressed views that dissented from the run of the conversation and were met with frosty stares.

After a while, Ken decided it was safer to stick to cricket and football, and Margie fended off invitations to meetings of the local Liberal Party branch. Everyone was polite, but the Isherwoods struggled with a feeling of incompatibility.

Margie believed fiercely in the need to connect with her local community. She and Ken invited several of their hosts back for a barbecue lunch one Sunday, and the story of that event quickly passed into their family's folklore as a complete disaster. Margie decided to say what she thought about the asylum-seeker question – she was in favour of onshore processing and allowing asylum seekers access to the job market – and the woman standing next to her, whom Margie had been finding unbearably stitched-up, prejudiced and supercilious, had simply turned her shoulder towards Margie and formed a new circle that excluded her. (*In my own home*, Margie had said to a friend on the phone later that evening.)

Ken, meanwhile, standing nearby with the men (having tried in vain to integrate the sexes), was equally determined to say what he really thought about the state of the public school system. Eyebrows were raised, a couple of the men made mildly supportive remarks along the lines of 'yes, it's important to have a viable public school system for those who wish to avail themselves of it' and then the men, too, wandered off into a corner of the back garden where they were presumably trying to cope with their incredulity.

Left on their own, Ken and Margie drifted unobtrusively across their back deck, hoping it would look as if they were heading for the kitchen. Once out of sight, they crept upstairs and fell on their bed, helpless with stifled laughter. Resisting the temptation to stay there until everyone had gone, they finally ventured back down the stairs and rejoined their guests in the garden, refilling drinks and remaining disengaged from the conversation. No one appeared to have missed a beat. The guests stayed until five o'clock and then apologised for having to leave so abruptly, having suddenly realised they were all expected *that very minute* at a drinks party nearby.

As they left, the woman who had so expertly given Margie the cold shoulder paused at the front door, offered her fingertips to be shaken by Ken, and gave Margie an appraising look. Her thin lips were pursed and there was a frown of unmistakeable disapproval. Without even attempting to lower her voice, she said to Margie, 'I'm not sure you're really comfortable here, are you, dear?' She subsequently wrote Margie and Ken a thank-you note that praised the house and garden and made no reference to their hospitality. ('I'm not sure you're really comfortable here, are you, dear?' quickly became a running joke within the Isherwood family circle. From then on, any time anyone in the family expressed displeasure, anxiety or concern about anything at all, someone would always respond: 'I'm not sure you're really comfortable here, are you, dear?')

Apart from having experienced a disabling combination of humiliation and fury, Margie used the whole incident to convince Ken that they should start looking for a house in Old Southwood, or even in Southwood Ponds, where one of her colleagues from the hospital worked.

'I never thought I could feel so out of place. Fancy feeling like such a misfit – almost an alien – in your own *home*. I'm disappointed in myself, Ken. I honestly thought I could fit in anywhere. Look at all those terribly right-wing National Party functions we went to in the country . . . they were never anything like this. Do you think we should stay put, and just ignore the neighbours?'

They agreed that 'ignoring the neighbours' was not an option, being contrary to everything they believed in about living in a community. Having returned to the city from rural life, they had actually looked forward to becoming part of a more closely-settled local neighbourhood. But now they were forced to acknowledge that there are such things as culture gaps that can only be bridged if both parties want to make it happen.

'The worst part about all this,' Margie said as they lay in bed on the night they agreed to buy a house in Southwood Ponds, 'is that I really believe communities are good for us. We need to make adjustments. We should be able to get on with all kinds of people.'

Ken's response left her puzzled and sad: 'There are such things as closed communities, Marg. They really should have a boom gate at the end of Liesl Crescent. There's already one there, in their minds. And if that's the way they feel, is that really a community you'd *want* to belong to?'

Sometimes, *moving on* is a good idea

Many young people feel the sense of 'not *wanting* to belong here' very keenly. An urge to leave the area where we grew up (even if only temporarily and symbolically) is not uncommon and may be healthy for us – perhaps to put some necessary distance between us and our parents as a way of asserting our independence, perhaps to experiment with different ways of living, perhaps to find a milieu that seems more culturally stimulating, more challenging or more compatible with our changing values.

Creative artists as wildly disparate as James Joyce and Barry Humphries felt it necessary to leave Dublin and Melbourne respectively in order to spread their creative wings. They then used their home towns as constant reference points – Joyce both to caress and condemn from the safe distance of Paris; Humphries to mock from London. J.D. Salinger, author of *The Catcher in the Rye*, felt similarly compelled to leave New York in his early thirties and spend the rest of his life in rural New Hampshire, writing in a concrete bunker near his house in the woods. Yet his writing never left New York: ever after, he wrote only of the highly urbanised lives of the members of his fictional Glass family.

Less dramatically, many young adults treat the experience of living in a new and different social environment as essential to their emotional development. The so-called 'gap year' (between secondary and tertiary education) has become a fashionable rite of passage: whether it takes the form of third-world volunteering, travel, temporary paid employment or immersion in a foreign language and culture, its purpose is to break away from the bonds of home and family in search of the unfamiliar.

'International experience' is regarded as valuable in fields as diverse as business, academia and the arts precisely because of the benefits thought to accrue from living in a place where you *don't* belong. Experiencing what it is like to be 'other', to be an outsider, can play an important role in sharpening our sense of social identity, as well as teaching us to appreciate how things are done by people unlike us. Robert Joss, US banker and a former CEO of Australia's Westpac bank, has hypothesised that societies like the US and the UK benefit from young people moving away from home to attend university because this contributes to a greater maturity, flexibility and independence of mind than might be typical of the products of stay-close-to-home cultures like Australia.

While it remains true that we can learn to fit in almost anywhere, it is equally true that we don't always want to. A feeling of cultural incompatibility can be tolerated for a while but, in the end, we may come to feel that 'if I stay here, I'll end up like them', and that prospect can be enough to make us pack our bags.

Disputes with neighbours can make us feel as if 'this is not the place for me'(see chapter 8), most obviously when the dispute involves a clash of values, rather than mere differences in tastes and preferences. And some communities – harsh boarding schools, churches run by abusive priests, exploitative workplaces, stifling neighbourhoods, dysfunctional families – either drive us away (if we are free agents), or lead us to feel trapped (if we are not free to leave). Even if we get away, we may never quite escape the emotional scars, since the experience of *bad* community strikes at the heart of our identity as social creatures.

Yet we all need to feel as if we belong *somewhere*, and the process of learning how to fit into a particular geographical neighbourhood – and then to do it again and again as our circumstances propel us from place to place – is one of life's most challenging lessons.

In the US and Australia, people move house, on average, once every six years – a figure boosted by the relatively higher mobility of younger people. (After the age of fifty, most people would expect to move only once or twice more in their lifetime.) In general, the rich move more frequently than the poor (though renters move more frequently than owners, which complicates that picture). Motives for moving include a need for more (or less) space, an aspiration to move 'up' or a need to move 'down', a desire to escape – from parental pressure, from an unpleasant or dysfunctional neighbourhood, or even from persecution – or a simple wish for the stimulation of change. One way or another, there's a lot of migration going on – between suburbs, between cities, between urban and rural areas, between countries – and that's a sign of the restlessness of modern populations.

Many people eventually return either to the area where they grew up or to a similar neighbourhood (or, like Joyce and Salinger, continue to write about it) simply because our formative experiences of community etch such powerful messages on our hearts that we can't, in the end, resist them.

The local neighbourhood is special

Most of us belong to several communities at once, based on where we live, where we work, our professional associations, the extended family, friendship circles, looser networks of old friends who have to cross a city or a country to meet each other by appointment, religious congregations and common-interest groups (music, drama, sport, education) that bring people together for an hour or two each week.

All those are authentic, legitimate communities and they all fuel our sense of identity and emotional security. Yet the neighbour-hood – the place where we actually live – has a special place in the hierarchy of human communities. It's not a common-interest group; it's not held together by the bonds of friendship; it's not formed through a process of selection (such as the selection of staff for a workplace, or players for a team, or singers for a choir). It's a more-or-less random collection of people who happen to live together, but didn't know who their neighbours would turn out to be until they moved in. (Did you ever interview the neighbours before you decided to buy or rent a house or apartment? Very few people do – we mostly just hope for the best.)

It's a special case because it's the one situation in life where we are expected to get along with a diverse collection of people who happen to share the same space – a street, a block, a district – day in, day out. The neighbourhood stands on common ground – literally. It's the only setting where, over a sustained period, we have to learn how to live alongside people who may not seem to have much affinity with us; people we might not like much; people with whom we might disagree about politics, religion, aesthetics, education, child-rearing and much more. Yet here's the suburban miracle: most of the time, in most of the streets of most of the towns and suburbs of the world, people *do* get along with their neighbours. It might begin badly, it might be a little cool and restrained, it might never become much more than polite, and sometimes it might be aggressively, even violently, hostile – but, mostly, we make it work. And mostly, over time, it warms up. It is here that we learn – because we have to – that people of every kind, of every age, of every background deserve our respect. When we take each other seriously and treat each other with kindness and courtesy, the suburban miracle – the township miracle, the village miracle – happens, over and over again. At the very least, we manage to live at peace with each other. Quite often, we do much better than that.

In 'Big Louis', one of the essays in *Agamemnon's Kiss* (2006), Australian historian Inga Clendinnen describes her encounters with people sharing her experience of receiving a liver transplant:

'In the clinic I found again the radiantly chaotic world I thought I had lost when I left primary school and began a lifetime of picking and choosing friends and associates. The studious egalitarianism of the Australian national health system serves up a marvellous mix of genders, ages, classes and ethnic origins.' In a typical suburban neighbourhood, the mix might not be quite as diverse as in an organ-transplant unit, but the underlying dynamic is the same: these are not people we chose to be with, but the curious intimacy of shared space (like the even more curious intimacy of shared illness) challenges us to connect with each other, at some level.

In fact, the local community makes demands on us that no other communities do: they are the kind of sustained demands that test our values and refine our moral code. It's in the process of learning to get along with accidental neighbours that we learn the most important lessons about cooperation, sensitivity, tolerance, trust and mutual obligation. All those things come easily among friends, and even among members of common-interest groups. In a neighbourhood, we have to work at them a little harder: the greater the diversity, the greater the challenge.

Of course, neighbours don't stay strangers for long. Over time, if we are doing our duty as engaged members of a community, we will get to know them better. As we do, we might like them less or more, or trust them less or more, but we know that, simply because we are neighbours, we shall have to find a way of coexisting harmoniously. In some cases, the fact that we happen to live next door or down the street or around the corner might gradually evolve into something that feels more significant: we may become more attached, more involved; we may care more; we may share some responsibility for each other's children; we may seek each other's advice; we may borrow stuff from each other; we may console each other in times of crisis or sadness; we may become friends.

The neighbourhood community does not demand friendship: it only demands that we all recognise this as our common space, and so offer each other the kind of support that makes the place safe and secure – emotionally as well as physically. The neighbourhood demands of us that we acknowledge our responsibility to be sociable, kind and considerate, and to accept the constraints of mutual respect, so the place does not degenerate into the kind of brittle, surly chaos that happens when we attend only to our own needs, assert only our own rights, and are concerned only for our own wellbeing.

We came to Southwood Central because we could afford it, to be honest. We found an awesome little unit, just across from the railway station and above a row of shops. It was so convenient. It was a bit like living in the inner city, but without the noise and dirt, and it felt safer, too. And it was only thirty minutes on the train into work for both of us.

When Jen became pregnant, we decided we were rather attached to Southwood. We'd both been to a few of the classes at the library – we attended a series of fabulous lectures on the Middle East that opened our eyes to what was likely to happen in Syria – and we always supported the local dramatic society. It was huge fun, and surprisingly well done. And we'd made friends with another couple in the same block of units – they became pregnant at the same time as us.

Anyway, once we'd decided to stay around this part of the world, it was a matter of looking for a house. We got a lot of advice from the people we knew – some of them had grown up here – and it all pointed to Southwood Fields or Southwood East. They were the most affordable but also, just driving around, they felt like the kind of places we could slot in. There seemed to be lots of kids, good parks and sports grounds, and there were local shops in both places, but Jen said she thought Southwood Fields felt more like a village. She liked that. She also liked the fact that it really used to be a dairy farm, so the name meant something. (Jen's a bit of a romantic.) Even some of the street names come from cows: we've got Friesian, Jersey, Guernsey and Ayrshire, and there are little lanes called Daisy Place and Clover Lane. Quite cute, I suppose.

Anyway, it's been a huge success. We still wave to our little unit every time we go past, because we wouldn't have discovered Southwood if it hadn't been for that. And the street we live in is terrific. There are a few young families like us, but there are also some older people, which I really like. They're good with the kids and are friendly without being pushy at all. Jen does the weekly supermarket shopping for the old lady who lives two doors down, because she can't manage too well on her own, and you'd think we'd done some amazing thing. But it's just what you do, isn't it? She's part of the street, too, just like us. And she's been here for yonks, so she's full of stories about what the place used to be like.

We had our moments with one of the other neighbours – a cranky bastard who used to freak out whenever one of the kids ran onto his lawn – but we asked him and his wife round for a beer and that soon fixed him. Turns out he lost his only child when she was in her teens – car accident. There's always a story, isn't there?

Southwood Ponds used to be the settling ponds for the local sewerage works, before Southwood was connected to the main. The area lay dormant for years, marshy and misty in winter and swarming with mosquitoes in summer, until an enterprising developer realised its potential and undertook the major earthworks necessary to convert it into a series of ornamental ponds. He had wanted to call it Southwood Lakes – no surprises there – but was constrained by a famous Southwood mayor, Councillor Len Heywood, who insisted that 'Lakes' was (a) an exaggeration, and (b) too far removed from the origins of the place.

For some older residents of Southwood, 'The Ponds' are something of a joke. The area is still commonly referred to by people who don't live there as 'The Pongs', but its own residents love it. 'Water views in Southwood' they proudly proclaim. And the house prices there – only exceeded by the prices on Southwood Rise – soon wipe the smiles off the faces of anyone who imagines there might be bargains on offer because of the area's unappealing origins.

The cheapest houses in Southwood are in Southwood East. Although most of the medium-density housing is clustered around the railway station in Southwood Central, Southwood East also has some townhouses, a few duplex homes and some low-rise apartment blocks. A young local architect, a devotee of the German social-housing legend Bruno Taut, has received several awards for his contemporary variations on the old Victorian terrace theme. Southwood East might be the cheap end of the suburb but it's also the place where some of the most stylish and innovative examples of low-cost, medium-density housing can be found. The houses are smaller and built on narrower blocks than elsewhere in Southwood. The roads are narrow, but playgrounds and bicycle trails are plentiful and the place is humming. The residents are reaping the benefits available to people who live in places where medium-density housing is combined with plenty of public space.

Neil Bonham has lived there for ten years. Here's his take on the place:

> ❝Ah, yes, Southwood East. What would you like me to tell you about it? There's no pub here, for a start. We have to go to Southwood Central for that, and then how are we sup-posed to get home? There's no bus at night. Oh, yeah, the bloody 'designated driver' thing ... I forgot. Actually, it's not that far to walk on a fine night. We're a bit short of shops here at Southwood East, too. But there's a general-store type of thing which is good, and a newsagent and a bottle shop.

The milk bar and hamburger joint is good for the kids. We do alright.

It's a close-knit community though, I'll give you that. We're all sorts here – Irish, Italians, Vietnamese, Greeks, Turks, Poms, Indians, even a few Sudanese now. Even one or two Aussies. Not so many Chinese – they're more in the Fields and the Ponds.

We all get along. 'Course we all get along. Why wouldn't you? 'Course we give people a hard time when they first get here – that's part of the fun – but most of them give as good as they get. And you have a few drinks, or invite them over for a barbie, and there you go.

We get blamed for everything that goes wrong around the place. Goes without saying. Look at the local paper. You'd think Southwood East was a den of iniquity, full of juvenile delinquents and hard-core crims. Any vandalism up the bloody Rise? Blame the kids from Southwood East! A break-in down the Pongs? That'll be the Southwood East gang for sure.

What about when we have a break in, or someone steals one of our cars or smashes a window up Pastor Jim's church? I suppose we do that to ourselves, do we? Yeah, that'd be right. We're idiots too, are we?

Listen, this is a good area. People look out for each other here. I'm not saying we don't have blues. 'Course we do. Who doesn't? Don't tell me they don't have blues up the Rise. And Pastor Jim does a good job here with his church and that. Runs things for the kids in school holidays. He's always turning on barbecues and stuff. Has that singles club thing – we call it the swingers night. Pulls them in, though, Pastor Jim does.

It's a good Labor suburb, Southwood East. No nonsense. Feet on the ground. It's not a poor suburb, I wouldn't say, although it can be tough when people are out of a job or when 'part-time' just doesn't add up to enough hours. That's when Pastor Jim comes into his own. He organises the rest of us to help out.

You just have to be told someone's in strife – you can't help them if you don't know they need help, so Jim's worth his weight in gold in that respect. It makes me wonder, sometimes. Like, maybe every community needs a kind of pastor figure like Jim. I don't mean in a religious way, but just someone who keeps a bit of an eye out for the special case – the person who might slip between the cracks. I mean, we're all supposed to do that for each other, but Pastor Jim has a knack of sussing out the ones who need a bit of special attention. I always call him Pastor Jim, out of respect, even though I never go to his church.

I've lived all over – inner city, high-rise, you name it. I wouldn't live anywhere but here. Not now. My wife is always saying, 'It feels like home here, doesn't it?' and she's right. *Go, East!*

Councillor Heywood, the mayor who had baulked at 'Lakes' back in the 1930s, was also responsible for a building covenant limiting the height of every building in Southwood – commercial and residential – to three storeys. You could have as many basement floors as you liked, but three levels above ground was the max. No ifs or buts. Len Heywood had been very impressed by his one visit to Paris, and he had decided that, in its own modest way, Southwood would follow the Parisian low-rise model. There were to be no lifts, except for hydraulic goods lifts to be installed in every building higher than two storeys. Heywood was a firm believer in the fact that the electric lift was the scourge of modern cities, having facilitated high-rise buildings and thus the concentration of huge numbers of people into small areas, with attendant traffic and other congestion problems. Remarkably, no council since Heywood's time had ever rescinded this covenant, in spite of sustained pressure from several developers, notably Hank Thyssen. In fact, the guarantee of a low-rise built environment had become a unique selling point in favour of Southwood.

Len Heywood had a clear vision for Southwood: 'Every precinct will be a village,' he declared, and then set about ensuring that the infrastructure would match the dream. No one who knows the history begrudges him the fact that he also proposed 'Heywood Place' as the name for the plaza by the railway station.

Most of the socialising in Southwood takes place within the separate subcultures of the different villages, and their ways of socialising are quite distinct. In Old Southwood, being asked over for afternoon tea is about as intimate as it gets, except for children's birthday parties that usually involve the parents as well, and the annual street parties that have become a popular event. Southwood Rise has its drinks parties and coffee mornings. Southwood Fields tends to rely on accidental encounters on weekends that lead to a spontaneous invitation to come in for a drink – a drink that often extends well into the evening and may finally involve food and a call to a couple of other neighbours to join in.

At Southwood Ponds, things are less jaunty than in the Fields. The people are a bit older, on average, and they often meet each other as they walk by the ponds in the evening, sometimes with visiting grandchildren in tow, armed with fishing rods. Those pond-side conversations tend not to move indoors, but they are highly valued as a way of keeping in touch, with no one having to go to any trouble.

In Southwood Central, it's all eating in cafes and drinking in the pub. On Saturday nights, the Central crowd merges with the crowd from Southwood East, often to watch a game on the big screen in the main bar. Things rarely get out of hand.

Hereford Street runs like an arrow from Southwood Central to Southwood East, splitting Old Southwood in two. Whitelaw Avenue is generally regarded as the boundary between Old Southwood and Southwood East, though the transition is a bit more gradual than that and all parts of Southwood share the same postcode. At the intersection of Hereford and Whitelaw is a block of sixteen houses – once fine old homes – that have been gradually falling into disrepair, with neglected paintwork, dirty windows and overgrown gardens. They are still inhabited, mostly by university students from the Kentwell campus who can afford the rent by banding together and crowding the houses.

No one complains too much. The students are sometimes noisy, but they add colour to the area and everyone knows this is a temporary, short-term arrangement: the sixteen houses are slated for demolition.

At first, no one twigged to the fact that a developer was buying up the houses, one by one. The first residents to sell were surprised to be approached out of the blue and offered such good prices. They were quite happy to move away from busy Hereford Street, mostly to other parts of Old Southwood or down to the Ponds. Once the developer had established a significant toehold, a general offer went out to the other residents of the block, simply stating that a major development was planned for the area and offering them 10 percent above a 'reasonable market price'. Most accepted the offer with alacrity, but two held out in anticipation of the price going up as the developer became more desperate to get on with whatever this mysterious project might be.

As time passed and their neighbours' houses fell into disrepair and the low-rent students moved in, those hold-out owners realised the game was up. The character of their block had changed dramatically, and the developer was clearly in no hurry. The offer had not edged upward as they had hoped; indeed, there were rumours that the price might come down again, given the fact that no one else was ever likely to buy those houses. So they, too, sold.

Still nothing happened. The council could provide no information, since no development application had been received. The rumour mill swung into action. It was going to be a mosque, replete with towering minarets that would be seen for miles. It was going to be a flash new day-stay hospital and medical centre, with all the latest gear. It was going to be some unspecified type of 'clinic'. It was going to be developed into four residential 'pavilions' each containing fifteen one-bedroom apartments – *Not even any proper kitchens! Just a sink, fridge and microwave in a cupboard!* – so there would be sixty homes where there had once been sixteen. There was some rather hopeful talk about a branch of the library – *That would be quiet, at least* – but this was quickly dismissed, in view of the money so recently spent on the new library centre in Southwood Central. No, it was none of that. A wonderful developer was going to build a group of small but tasteful homes in landscaped gardens – it would be a retirement village, or at least an 'over-55s' development and was going to be called Southwood Village. No one should worry; it would be beautiful – even better than what was there now.

The mosque rumour had caused some restlessness. People focused on the inappropriateness of the scale and style of the building, and tried not to confuse that with any hint of religious prejudice. Even the hospital was a worry to some of the locals – they welcomed the idea of such smart facilities being close at hand, but wondered about the size of the development and the likely look of the place. In both cases, there was anxiety about the volume of traffic likely to be generated.

At last a development application went into council and the word was out. The one thing the rumour-mongers had got almost right was that it was going to be called 'Southwood Village'. In fact, the developer was even smarter than that: it was going to be called 'Old Southwood Village', and it would be a modest (three-storey, following the Heywood law to the letter) shopping mall.

The community went wild, and not with enthusiasm. Whatever happened to the retirement village? That had turned out to be a mere figment of someone's hopeful imagination. Where had the day-stay hospital idea gone? Since it had never 'come', it didn't have to 'go'. And the mosque? Some residents now supposed a well-designed shopping mall might be more acceptable than a mosque, though this was said tentatively.

It is only a development application, said the council. Nothing has been decided. There'll be community consultation before we make any determination.

And so there was. Meetings were held in the local school hall, not far from the proposed site, and in the Southwood East Community Church, with Pastor Jim Glasson beaming at another influx of non-churchgoing locals. ('Anything to get them comfortable with coming to the place.')

The tone of the two meetings was quite different. In Old Southwood, concerns were expressed about traffic and parking, about attracting 'undesirables' (nature unspecified) to the area, and about the likely impact on the nearby strip of local shops for which many residents had great affection – not always matched by patronage, since many residents of Old Southwood drove to the Southwood Central Mall. 'So would Old Southwood Village be more convenient for some of you, then?' asked the young woman who was representing the developer. That was greeted by murmurs that were hard to interpret – some were dissenting, some were reluctantly forced to agree that that might well be so, some were simply acknowledging the pluck of the young woman for putting it so bluntly.

In Southwood East, people found it hard to imagine why anyone would oppose such a development. It was quite a trek to the existing mall at Southwood Central and although this one would be smaller, it would be just down the road and people imagined it would have everything they needed. Again, there was concern about the local shops, but most people thought this new mall would be far enough away from the East shops to allow them to survive. 'Up to us, isn't it? If we use them, they'll survive,' said one pragmatic fellow.

There was great disagreement within the council. Most of the opposition was focused on 'the character of the area', the local amenity and the traffic-control plan. Most of the support was commercially motivated, though some councillors saw this as a gesture towards Southwood East, generally regarded as the most deprived part of Southwood.

Meanwhile, the owners of the Southwood Central Mall secretly appointed a public relations company to set up a so-called residents' action group that was designed to look like a spontaneous, grassroots movement in opposition to the new mall. Several long-term residents of Old Southwood responded to the notice of the first meeting of this group, and people also came from the Fields and the Ponds. The person welcoming everyone to the meeting was a stunningly attractive woman named Angie, from Southwood Rise. There were several unidentified men in suits also in attendance, and one of them chaired the meeting, introducing himself only as Geoff, and appearing to be a concerned resident, though no one recognised him. No one from the council was present.

There was strong encouragement from Geoff for the pro-position that the new development would be 'one too many' for Southwood, and that the impact on the existing local shops could be disastrous. Attempts were made to identify ways in which this new development would be environmentally damaging and this line of discussion was also encouraged by Geoff, until a woman stood up and declared that no council was more environmentally responsible than Southwood and that people should be prepared to trust the council's judgement on that question. A petition was proposed, though few people were ready to sign it there and then, and it was agreed that 'we need more information'.

Within a week of the meeting, an elaborate leaflet appeared in letterboxes throughout Southwood, reporting on the meeting in terms that those who had been there found hard to reconcile with what had actually happened. 'Residents outraged!' thundered the leaflet. 'Moves are afoot to petition council to stop this encroachment on the character and heritage of Old Southwood,' it went on. There was a photograph of the site, with a rather exaggerated drawing of 'the proposed assault on our suburb' superimposed on it. The body copy was similarly lurid, referring to a smouldering rage in the community that was about to erupt into a revolt. Dark references were made to the 'claws of commerce' being sunk into the flesh of Old Southwood.

Dan Furness, an architect, had been at the meeting. When the leaflet arrived in his Southwood Ponds letterbox, he smelt a rat and began sleuthing the origin of the leaflet. He started with the printer, clearly identified on the back page, and that led him to a public relations firm. No one there would speak to him about the project, but a feigned interest in the services offered by the firm gleaned a copy of their glossy promotional brochure, which proudly named Southwood Central Mall among their clients. That proved nothing, of course, but it convinced Dan that he was onto something.

He took the leaflet and the PR brochure to a friend in the building department of the council. She spoke to a councillor, the councillor spoke to the mayor, Mary Kippax, and the mayor rang her old sparring partner, Laurie Griff, the chairman of Southwood Central Mall's holding company. The conversation was not polite: these two had great respect for each other's fighting prowess, but there was not much affection between them.

'You know what I'm thinking, Laurie,' said the mayor.

'I'll look into it, Mary,' agreed Laurie, denying any knowledge of the link, but knowing the alternative to some careful admissions would be a public fishing expedition, led by a popular mayor and splashed across the front page of the *Southwood Gazette* – the local weekly newspaper that had defied all predictions of its imminent demise. (It's still required reading, in fact, for anyone serious about keeping in touch with local news.) Laurie knew the social media would also swing into action, tweets swarming around his head like a cloud of gnats.

Before the second meeting of the residents' action group had been called, it was all over. The news was leaked to the *Gazette* that, unknown to the board or the CEO of Southwood Central Mall, some misguided and unethical middle managers had apparently taken it into their own heads to try to fend off the threat to their business posed by the mooted development in Old Southwood. As a result, there was a surge of such hostility towards Southwood Central Mall that opposition to the development of Old Southwood Village crumbled. Residents now welcomed it as a sign of vigorous competition and a vote of confidence in the future of Southwood. They were assured by council that any approval would be hedged with strict conditions governing the aesthetics of the project, and ensuring that the development would include a medical practice and a child-care centre. All parking would be underground, with the entrance and exit controlled by traffic lights to be installed at the developer's expense. Approval was duly granted, and the residents of Old Southwood decided they were quite looking forward to getting rid of the eyesore on the corner of Hereford and Whitelaw.

Dan Furness had a couple of sleepless nights wondering whether he might have been a pawn in some devious double-cross designed to win support for one developer by discrediting the other. He decided he was being paranoid. In Southwood Ponds, he had become something of a local hero.

Beware of the lure of the exotic

Travel may broaden the mind, but it also creates the hazard of thinking that this charming little village in Umbria could be just the place for me. The people seem so warm and welcoming (unlike my rather ho-hum neighbours back home), the life seems so vibrant and everything seems so fascinating, I can see myself fitting right in here.

Not so fast. Most of us are attracted to places we visit precisely because we are visitors. We've shed our domestic responsibilities; we have money to spend (which is one reason we're so welcome); we feel free and flexible. Part of the pleasure (and the point) of holidays is that they fuel dreams of a better life: they create circumstances in which we may well feel 'this is who I really am' or 'I could really be myself in a place like this'. Holidays are meant to be therapeutic, and part of the therapy is to indulge the pleasing fantasy that, if only we lived *here*, life would come closer to our dreams of Utopia.

Foreign countries are a particular trap. Because we don't really understand the culture – and perhaps not much of the language beyond the phrasebook – it's even easier to indulge those fantasies because the place seems so enchantingly exotic, the culture so attractive, the possibilities so romantic.

In the extreme case, if you were wealthy enough, you might dream of living permanently on an ocean liner, cruising the world, popping in on an endless supply of fascinating places and never having to engage with a local neighbourhood again. You might even imagine that your fellow residents in this floating village would become your community and that there, in the lap of luxury, is where you rightfully belong, with no decisions to be made except which entertainment to attend or what to have for dinner tonight. You might rationalise this by convincing yourself that life is all about the journey, not the destination, so here you are on a floating metaphor. For a while, you might even enjoy the fact that everyone on board is rather like you – in socio-economic terms, in attitudes, in prejudices and in the desire to 'leave it all behind', where 'all' might range from family tensions to neighbourhood disputes, the futility of politics, the hassles of home and car ownership, or the inconvenience of having to shop, cook and deal with the garbage.

Suppose you did it. Eventually, such a strategy would diminish any of us by turning us, quite literally, into passengers. When we cease to be active, engaged members of heterogeneous communities that demand some compromise, concession and charity from us, we cease to be fully functioning humans. Finding your community is not a matter of scouring the world in search of the most charming spot or the most interesting and engaging community you can find and then trying to settle into it. Finding your community is about developing your capacity to make sacrifices for the common good, not about permanent exposure to the stimulation of the exotic (which, to state the obvious, ceases to be exotic once you adopt it as your own). The secret to the art of belonging is no secret at all: it is to accept that 'belonging' is not dependent on finding some Utopian setting. There is no wondrous community waiting somewhere for you to arrive so you can be embraced by the natives and imbued with the great Spirit of Belonging.

It's not where you live, it's how you live.

3

Herding

We humans are by nature herd animals, and the long history of human civilisation tells us that we are most comfortable in herds of between about five and eight people. Below five, social energy is harder to generate; above eight, the dynamic changes and it becomes a more formal setting that's less intimate and potentially more inhibiting for some members of the group.

Though our strong desire to belong to a herd can sometimes encourage an unhealthy degree of acquiescence and conformity, herding is a critical factor in developing our awareness of ourselves as social creatures. Membership of an optimally-sized herd fuels our confidence and self-respect and reassures us that we are being accepted and valued.

Five to eight people is the most efficient and practical size for a work group (in the army, the standard size of an infantry section is eight soldiers), the most productive size for a board or committee, the most realistic size for a management span of control. It's the perfect size for a dinner party: invite ten or twelve people and watch them fragment into smaller groups, or else watch one or two confident extraverts (or narcissists) dominate the proceedings. ('The life of the party' usually spells the death of conversation.) Tutorial groups work best with between five and eight students; so do discussion groups assembled for research purposes. The strongest bonding in sporting teams occurs within sub-groups like forwards and backs; in orchestras, people identify more closely with their section than with the whole group; in large choirs, the parts tend to stick together socially as well as musically, sometimes not even knowing the names of 'the others'.

Once upon a time, we used to live in domestic herds, partly because there were more children in the family and partly because three generations often lived under the one roof (the nuclear family household having become fashionable only since the early twentieth century). But as Western households have shrunk, the domestic herd has become a rarity. You can't have a herd of one, obviously, and two or three people don't constitute a herd either. Households of five or more people are now unusual in societies like Australia, where the average household contains just 2.5 people and we seem to be heading for an average of about 2.2. (The exception to the national trend is Sydney, where the rate of shrinkage has slowed and the number of single-person households actually fell between 2006 and 2011. There is new growth in larger households in Sydney – including multi-family and non-kin households – driven largely by the cost of real estate and the need to squeeze more people into the available space.)

So what happens to the herd instinct when the household no longer contains a domestic herd? At first glance, it might look like a paradox, but the shrinking household is actually one of the strongest factors driving the revival of local communities. If we are no longer to live in domestic herds, then we must look outside the home for other herds to join.

Most of us have always belonged to more than one herd (family, friendship group, workgroup, for example), but the shrinkage of our households has now reached the stage where our appetite for engagement with non-domestic, social-emotional herds has been sharpened.

If you want a friend in Washington, get a dog. Isn't that what US president Harry Truman said? Well, I'd say if you're new to Southwood like we were, and you want to make friends quickly, get a dog. Not because the dog will be your friend – although that's true too – but because there are some fabulous parks around here where dogs can be let off the leash, and the dog-owners are all so friendly with each other.

One of the fellows at the dog park in Southwood Fields always says, 'It's not only the dogs who are pack animals, it's their owners as well.' And he's right. My only problem is trying to remember which name belongs to the dog and which to its owner. So many people give their dogs human names these days – we've got Jeff and Mandy and Pete and Sal in our group – there's a real danger of greeting someone by the name of their dog. Don't laugh, I've done it. No one would mistake my dog's name for me – he's called Scratch, for obvious reasons. I'd be pretty offended if anyone called me that.

It's not really surprising – so many people use their dog as a child substitute, I suppose it's natural for them to use human-sounding names. There's one couple at the dog park who are quite open about it: 'We're trying ourselves out on a dog first,' they say. 'If we can cope with that, we might try for a baby.' I don't know why I find that so funny. Perhaps it's because we've got two kids under three, and a dog is a breeze by comparison, you can be sure of that.

I call it the dog park, but it's not just for dogs, of course. It's lovely, actually – there are kids kicking balls around and dads flying kites, or trying to, and people standing around in little groups chatting while their dogs frolic and fight. I always link up with the same group of women and we just walk round and round the perimeter of the park, keeping an eye on our dogs – always armed with a plastic bag, of course; people are very good about that, these days.

Those women have become close friends, yet we never socialise away from the park. We share all sorts of intimacies while we're walking, and we know more about each other's husbands than they might feel comfortable with. But it's real therapy, and we know we can trust each other. There's no idle gossip. Oh, a bit of gossip, maybe, but never malicious. 9

Southwood Glee meets weekly, under the direction of Julian Frisk, who is also the head of music at Southwood High. Most weeks, he wonders whether he can crank up the energy, yet again, to face his enthusiastic band of mainly middle-aged choristers, yet every week he leaves the rehearsal feeling reinvigorated and affirmed. As do the members of the choir – the primitive act of making music together lifts their spirits while also helping to satisfy their herd instinct.

The choir was once known as Old Southwood Glee Club and the membership, being by invitation only, was unofficially confined to people who lived in the old part of Southwood. But when Julian was invited to take over after the death of the choir's founder, he insisted on the change of name and a widening of the membership base. He began by inviting the parents of some of his students to join. The influx of new members from all over Southwood and the new name – judged 'trendy' by some of the choir's stalwarts (by whom no harsher judgement could be made) – drove some older voices away, and Julian was not displeased by that outcome.

Let's drop in on a rehearsal, taking place in a painted weatherboard building on Hereford Street that was once the Sunday-school hall of the Presbyterian Church. When the Sunday school was disbanded for lack of interest, the hall was used sporadically for church-related social events. Then the Presbyterian Church was absorbed into the Uniting Church in 1977, the hall was offered to the council for a peppercorn rent, and the church building itself was sold. It became a briefly fashionable restaurant, then an antique shop and finally a Persian rug store, perpetually closing down. The hall is maintained by the council and administered by the Southwood Community Association. It is used for a wide assortment of meetings, functions, rehearsals and productions by the Southwood Players, and is affectionately known to the locals as the Opera House.

~

'Time to start, everyone. Please? Sopranos, can you save whatever it is you're doing until the end? Harriet, could you put that knitting away, please. You look like Madame Defarge. Let's see . . . we seem to be two tenors short. I haven't had any apologies. Do please let me know if you're going to be away. Could someone call Luca and Adam later and check they're still alive? Roland, would you do that?

'Some warm-ups, then. Everybody standing, please. Arms loosely by your sides. By your sides, Eddie. You can't produce a beautiful sound if you're folding your hands in front of your crotch in that defensive way. Pam, are you eating? Please spit it into a tissue. Here.' Julian passes a box of tissues along the row to Pam, as if he had brought it specifically for this purpose.

'Actually, I'm thinking of instituting a detention system. Nothing too onerous.'

There's an audible intake of breath as, just for a moment, some members of the choir think Julian might actually be serious. 'Only joking,' he says, unleashing one of his winning smiles and raising his hands to begin work. A couple of the altos giggle involuntarily, perhaps with relief.

Julian decided long ago that he would treat his Glee group exactly as he treats his high school pupils. Although they occasion-ally mutter about it, the choristers respond well to his rather acerbic leadership. They respect the fact that he obviously knows his stuff and they are proud of the results they achieve under his leadership. (Half the women are also secretly in love with him, though most of them are at least twenty years his senior.) His professional reputation as a musician and teacher is formidable: he has become famous for taking classes of rather reluctant high school music students and gradually turning them into keen young musicians who not only play and sing like angels, but write their own music.

Towards the end of the rehearsal, Julian announces that there is to be a Southwood centenary festival and the choir has been invited to come up with some suggestions about how they might participate. 'Something suitable, I was told, though I haven't yet discovered what "suitable" might entail,' he says. 'If anyone has any ideas, put them to me by all means. I'm hoping there might be a serious choral concert including us and the Southwood High madrigal group, and maybe some of the primary schools. That would be festive, don't you think? But I fear we may be asked to stand on the back of a truck, singing our way down the main street as part of a procession while praying for rain to save us from further humiliation.'

'Who's responsible for organising this?' asks one of the tenors.

'The Community Association has appointed an executive committee. Judith MacGregor seems to be a prime mover, as you might expect.'

Significant looks are exchanged between several of the women. Judith was once a member of Southwood Glee, but she missed so many rehearsals Julian asked her to consider her position and so she did. On balance, she decided her talents could be more productively deployed elsewhere in the community.

'Anyway, I'd quite like to pre-empt whatever they might be dreaming up, so people should let me know if they have any thoughts.' Julian looks at his watch. 'Okay, not much time left. I want to make a start on a new piece written by one of my students – "Dancing in Heaven". Don't be put off by the title.'

'I thought all the dancing went on in hell,' murmurs a tenor as copies of the new music are passed along the rows of choristers.

'Quite,' says his companion. 'That reminds me of an old Baptist joke my Dad told me about a hundred and eighty-six times. Why does God disapprove of premarital sex?'

'I'll bite.'

'He thinks it might lead to dancing.'

Julian glares at the two tenors, and they smile apologetically. He raises his hands and leads the choir in their first run-through of the new piece, everyone relying heavily on the piano accompaniment for clues as to where they should be. None of them has seen the music before, and the pianist is almost as much at sea as the singers, but she struggles through. (She, too, is secretly in love with Julian and is mortified whenever she falls short of his high musical standards. She is old enough to be his mother.)

'A question, Julian,' says one of the talkative tenors. 'Is it going to be *darn*cing with a Southwood Rise long "a" or *dan*cing with a Southwood Fields short "a"?'

Julian opts for the short 'a'.

Everyone enjoys this little exchange. No members of Glee come from Southwood Rise.

The rehearsal ends and there's a clatter of chairs being stacked and a babble of cheerful voices. People seem reluctant to leave:

when the hall is locked up, a small group remains talking on the footpath.

~

Without setting foot outside Southwood, you can sign up for adult education classes on practically anything you like – Stress Management, Anger Management, Time Management and Pet Management, just for starters. Beginning with the letter 'a', you can do abseiling, accounting, acrobatics, aerobics, anatomy, animal welfare, ant farming, anthropology, art, archery, Asian cultures, astrology, astronomy, astral travel . . . the list goes on.

Most courses are well attended: it seems almost to be a case of 'put it on and the people will come'. The people who do come, in droves, are no doubt interested in the subjects on offer, but there's a definite herding aspect to the growing enthusiasm for all these classes, particularly among those who keep attending program after program, regardless of the topic. Some courses are run under the banner of the University of the Third Age (U3A), some are organised by the education officer at the library, and some are run by the tireless Jim Glasson at Southwood East Community Church. TAFE has a modest presence here, too, and the tech. ed. teachers at Southwood High run occasional workshops. Although many participants are drawn from the ranks of the retired, plenty of younger people also attend – notably the 'The Prospect of Parenthood' program put on by Jim, that often leads young couples to postpone, sometimes indefinitely, the decision about whether to have children or not.

Southwood's birthrate, at 1.6 babies per woman, sits a little below the national average, and Jim, for reasons he can't explain (since he has long been an advocate for zero population growth for the planet), feels he should do his bit to edge it up a little. All the signs are that the rising generation of young adults – the potential parents of Southwood – are going to keep their options open for at least as long as the cohort ahead of them did. But there's a great deal of interest in Jim's program: many young adults are genuinely perplexed about the prospect of becoming parents, and simply can't imagine how they would cope. 'Too much to give up' is a popular response, once they've seen what's involved, laid out for them by Jim's very comprehensive course. (Before his wife left him, she used to say that the course should be called 'The Appalling Prospect of Parenthood'. She often accused Jim of letting his natural pessimism infect everything he did.) There is some anecdotal evidence to suggest that the birthrate among participants in 'The Prospect of Parenthood' is somewhat lower than for the general population, so perhaps Jim is inadvertently doing his bit for ZPG, after all.

Jim is a great believer in the power of the small group. He won't enrol more than eight people – usually four couples – in each parenthood course, or in any of the other courses he runs at the church. He is convinced that the intimacy of a small group encourages real engagement, and he respects the ancient tradition of teachers being in constant, lively exchange with their students.

Jim understands that the dynamics of a herd-sized group can be even more powerful than the pull of a crowd. Most of us need to belong to both herds and tribes to generate a complete sense of our identity: we need to know we are part of an extended family *and* a nuclear family; we need the muscle of the organisation and the intimacy of our own group within it; the umbrella of the profession and the close connection with a few colleagues; the political party and the local branch; the global religion and a local congregation; the suburb and the street. The tribe, on its own, is never enough because herds do something that tribes can never do: they reassure us that we are being taken seriously as individuals. In that way, herds simultaneously help to clarify our personal *and* social identity: we are most sure of who we are when we know where we belong.

For women with babies and preschoolers, mothers'groups thrive in various parts of Southwood. Some spring up spontaneously, as mothers in a particular street or area come to identify others in the same boat, but mostly it's the result of an initiative taken by a paediatric nurse employed by Southwood Council. Her job is to look out for new mothers coming to the council's maternal and child health clinic, and to encourage them either to link up with an existing group in their area or to help form a new group. The council nurse attends the first couple of meetings, to introduce the women to each other and guide the initial discussion. Some women drop out after a few meetings, but most people stay and the groups become effective social units, offering new mothers a supportive environment for sharing stories about their baby's development. Though most members of these groups don't become close personal friends, the groups often persist for two or three years, and the level of mutual support is strong.

Jasmine Sharma responded to an approach from the council nurse and decided to attend a meeting of a new mothers' group in her part of Old Southwood:

It's worked out brilliantly for me. I went to the first meeting with some reluctance, even a bit of trepidation, because I was new to Southwood as well as being new to motherhood. But the nurse was just lovely – she put us all at our ease, and before long we found ourselves swapping horror stories about being sleep-deprived, and the challenge of trying to make sure we were out of our pyjamas by the time our husbands got home at night. We exchange tips on everything from breastfeeding to the best places to shop for baby clothes. And it's been really interesting to see how our babies develop at different rates . . . I thought mine was never going to walk, but they all get there in the end!

A couple of the girls meet outside the group. They are both single parents – one had a marriage break-up while she was pregnant, and the other one didn't have a partner but decided she wanted a baby before it was too late, so she used a sperm bank. Neither of them has any family nearby, and I think they find motherhood quite a struggle. It's wonderful to see how they've been supporting each other – they've become a sort of surrogate family.

The rest of us mainly see each other at the meetings of the group – we meet once a month now – and of course we had a party for each baby's first birthday. Sometimes, it's quite emotional, but mostly it's just really, really practical support – and some very welcome adult company, too, in those early months when life seemed to be about nothing but feeding and changing nappies. We all swapped phone numbers right at the start, and it's always been really reassuring to know that we can ring each other if we need a bit of help in a crisis, or just someone to talk things over with.

Now I'm pregnant with my second, and so are three other women in the group. So we'll be seeing each other for a while yet. 9

One of Southwood's favourite forms of herding is the book club. There were about thirty book clubs in Southwood at last tally – though any attempt to count them probably overlooks some of the informal meetings that use book-reading as an excuse for getting together. Judith MacGregor had once proposed that there be a book club coordinator and nominated herself for the post, but no one else could see the point of formalising it to that extent: if people didn't like the way their club was operating, they were free to move to another or even to start one of their own.

Some retired people belong to more than one book club as a form of discipline, to encourage themselves to keep up with their reading. Most working people belong to one group only, and meet at night. The membership is overwhelmingly female, but there are a number of men's clubs forming and three or four mixed clubs – they are regarded as the most serious of the groups, mainly concentrating on non-fiction ('I can't see the point of novels' is an oft-repeated and much-mocked quote from a male member of one of these groups). They tend to favour current affairs, history and biography. They are also regarded as more serious because it is said of them, in some awe, that they actually stick to the set topic.

The standing joke among less serious book-club members is that at some point in the session, someone always feels it necessary to say, 'Don't you think we should say something about the book?'

●I heard about our book club from Elvira, a woman I sit next to on the train to work every morning. We both work in the city, and we've struck up quite a friendship. She and her partner live in the Ponds and we live in the Fields, so we're not that far away from each other. We haven't started socialising with our partners, but she asked me to join her book club and I was intrigued. I'd never done anything like that before.

I wondered if it would be a bit too intellectual for me. I'm not a graduate or anything, but I think of myself as a reasonably intelligent woman. Elvira assured me it was a lot of fun, and I really liked the idea of having a set book to read each month. I've always been a reader but lately I find it's very easy to flop in front of the TV after dinner, so I thought this would be quite good for me.

Anyway, I gave it a go, and it's been awesome. The other girls are so friendly, and we move around from house to house, so it will soon be my turn. I've noticed some of the girls rather overdo the catering – like some of them try to organise food and drink that ties in with the book somehow, which can be fun but it can also be a bit forced. We had that book about the last woman in Iceland to be executed, and the host tried to give us smoked lamb and fermented eggs. No, thanks. I won't be trying anything like that at my place.

There are theoretically eight of us, although there's often one or two missing. So it's really easy and comfortable. We always start with a drink and a chat, and that sometimes goes on a bit, but it's up to the host to keep us on the straight and narrow. She acts as the sort of chairperson.

The main thing I've found is that it has put me in touch with a lovely group of women I might not have met otherwise. My partner and I are pretty new to Southwood, and the people in our street have been a bit slow to make us welcome, although the woman next door – an older lady – did bake us cake when we moved in, which I thought was sweet. So this book club has been like a group of instant friends. I no longer feel new and strange. I've even run into a couple of them at the supermarket, and it's just so nice to see a familiar face.

I really look forward to it now. I think my partner is quite jealous. I tell him he should join a book club too, but he's not really a reader – not much of a talker, either.

I wasn't sure we would stay here in Southwood, long term, once we started a family, but now I think we might.

There are four garden clubs in Southwood. One specialises in roses, one in azaleas and camellias, one in geraniums and pelargoniums, and one is for people interested in garden design. Some people belong to all four. Not all the members are serious gardeners, but they share a serious love of gardens and an appreciation of flowers. Lola has been a member of the garden design club for three years, ever since she retired from full-time work. She and her husband, also retired, live in the Ponds.

I'm much better at ordering my husband around in the garden than I am at doing it myself. But the garden club meeting is the highlight of my month. I have plenty of friends in Southwood but there's a special bond between gardeners, I always think. Or garden lovers, anyway. Close to the soil or something – I don't know what it is. It's sort of manual work and yet it's also sort of creative work. I find gardening unique in that respect. My own garden is nothing to write home about, but that's not the point. We don't show off our gardens to each other – although some people try to – we're there more for the companionship and our common love of flowers. And Nature, if that doesn't sound too pompous.

I wouldn't mind if we met a bit more often, in fact. We usually have a speaker, which is terrific, but I think sometimes we could have a bit more social time together, and just have people sharing their own experiences. That's the thing about gardeners – they're always happy to tell you what they've learnt, or how they've solved problems with pests and things like that. We swap cuttings, and advice.

There is one funny thing I should tell you: gardeners can be fiercely political, too. I don't mean party politics – oh, no, I mean our own club politics. I don't get involved, but I watch from the sidelines, and it amazes me how intense it can become. People fight for positions on the committee as if they're running for parliament – I mean, *gardeners*? Judith MacGregor is our president – she isn't very well liked, I'd have to say, but I think she's doing an okay sort of job. She plotted and campaigned so hard to get elected, I think a lot of people voted for her just to shut her up.

Anyway, Judith was up on her hind legs at our last meeting, going on about this centenary festival that is apparently being planned. 'What does a festival make you think of?' she asked us. Someone said 'feasting', but that was the wrong answer, of course. 'Come on,' said Judith – she can be quite bossy, you know – 'what would you expect to see at a Southwood Centenary Festival?'

Marlene, who is not one of Judith's greatest fans, although they are practically neighbours in Old Southwood, piped up and said, 'Well, since you're asking the garden club, I'm guessing you're thinking gardens. A floral display? A garden ramble? Something like that?'

'Precisely,' said Judith. 'I think I can say I have the ear of the planning committee – Dom Fin is the key man – and I'm sure I can convince them that gardens should be one of the features of the festival. In fact, I've already floated the idea. I mean, we think of Southwood as a garden suburb, don't we? That was the very phrase used by the developer who first promoted the place. So put your thinking caps on, and give me any ideas. Think big!'

That's the way Judith talks.

There's a garden-based herd of a quite different kind that works a small patch of land behind Southwood High where the deputy principal, Marcus Li, has established a community garden – open to anyone, but designed with refugees in mind.

There are several refugee households in Southwood East, managed by volunteers with financial support from the community and some generous backing from the council. Marcus's idea was that a community garden would be a way of integrating these refugees into the community, while also allowing them to save money by growing their own vegetables. The local Lions Club has organised a roster of drivers to ferry the refugees to and from the garden. It's been a huge success and already other groups are looking for vacant land where similar community gardens could be established. The produce is fresh, household budgets are eased, and new herds are established.

❧

With all this vigorous herding going on, some of the traditional volunteer organisations – service clubs like Rotary and Lions, the hospital auxiliary, and the parent associations at the various schools – are complaining of dwindling numbers and falling support. In particular, they complain of a lack of interest among younger people.

Perhaps they haven't understood the changing social dynamics of twenty-first-century Southwood. There's no shortage of people to sign up for short-term projects (whether educational seminars or local clean-up campaigns), but there's a growing reluctance to make a long-term commitment to formally 'join' an organisation that might demand attendance at weekly or monthly meetings stretching into eternity. People are busier than ever – particularly those who are juggling full-time work with the business of raising a family and running a household – but that's not the whole story and, in any case, even busy people need to make connections with the neighbourhood to build their sense of security and belonging.

There's also a cultural factor operating here, particularly involving the rising generation of adults under forty who have been shaped by a society undergoing rapid and accelerating change. They have grown up with the idea of impermanence; change is the air they breathe. As a result, they have learnt to keep their options open and to be constantly asking themselves: 'What else is there?' That helps to explain why they are postponing marriage, parenthood, mortgages and a commitment to straight-line careers. Their world is not like that.

Yet, for that very reason, they are the greatest herders of all time. Being the offspring of a highly-divorced generation of parents, they have had to cope with the experience of disrupted and fragmented families in greater numbers than any previous generation, but they are the 'children of the revolution' (economic, social, cultural, technological) in other ways. In response, they have decided that their most precious resource for coping with life in an unstable and unpredictable world is *each other.* Their tribal connections are powerful – online and off – and their herds have enriched the meaning of 'peer group'. *Friends are the new family* says contemporary folklore, and it's true.

Offer them a group to belong to for a while – long enough to get the job done, but not so long as to seem interminable or (*gasp!*) permanent – and they'll respond. Ask them to do something on the basis that 'we'll see what happens' and they'll get on board – particularly if it's something they can do with their friends. They like to hunt in packs.

They are as community-minded as anyone else; they'll be as willing to volunteer as anyone else; but their terms will be different. Think of them as herd animals constantly seeking fresh pastures.

Up on Liesl Crescent, Petra Ritchie is standing on her back deck, looking over the Fields at dusk. Her husband, Bill, is staring out the front window, brooding.

The view from the deck pleases Petra. It is early autumn, and there are wisps of smoke rising from the chimneys of houses in the Fields. Though most homes rely on electricity or gas for heating, some diehards continue to burn wood, generally judged to be less efficient but more romantic than the alternatives. Away to the south, the setting sun is imparting a soft pink hue to the surface of the Ponds, and pinpricks of light are appearing in houses all over Southwood. From this height and at this time, Petra can almost imagine she is looking across a peaceful rural valley. There's an autumnal dampness in the air and she can catch the smell of rotting leaves from the Koutsoukases' garden next door. The floodlights are on at the sports oval and, even from this distance, she can make out the tiny figures scurrying across the field after a ball that's invisible to her. There is a silent stream of headlights moving down Hereford Street and the lights of a train gliding into Southwood station. A faint hum reaches her from the traffic on the highway behind her, invisible from where she is standing. The scene below her is beautiful enough in the fading light for Petra to remember why they came to Southwood in the first place.

She loved the slightly rural aspect of the Fields and she was grateful that their combined salaries had made possible the purchase of a home on Southwood Rise, though the street had never felt much like her natural habitat.

Petra always wanted children, but since being married to Bill, she has gone cold on the idea. As she has remarked to close friends, it would be like having two kids to look after – the baby and Bill – so she contents herself with the children in her care at school. Petra knows the birthrate is way below replacement level and she sometimes speculates about the number of women who might be in precisely her situation – keen on the idea but not able to face it in practice (or, at least, not able to face it with this particular partner). In some of her darkest moments, she wonders whether Women's Lib has not only offered women the power to make such choices for themselves, but has also encouraged some men to embrace so heartily the life they lead with a working wife – a stimulating companion, well groomed, earning an independent income – that they resist the idea of children who might complicate things.

At times like this, when Petra is in a reflective mood, she realises just how dreadful her life with Bill is becoming, how tired she is of his moroseness, how much, by contrast, she enjoys her job as a teacher and her relationships with her colleagues . . . and how deeply she resents the starkness of that contrast. She is devoted to Bill; sorry for him; perhaps she still loves him. But she feels he has moved beyond her reach.

In that moment, she decides she will have to start acting more independently. If Bill doesn't want to do the things she wants to do, or go to the places she wants to go, then so be it. She must go alone. She must find other people to spend her time with. Her social life can't be confined to lunch in the staffroom at school.

No one has a more urgent need of herding than Petra, except possibly Michael Koutsoukas. Though he is crazy about Angie, still desires her, and is proud to have such a beautiful woman as his wife, he is increasingly frustrated by her unwillingness to enter into any kind of life with him, beyond letting him accompany her to the glamorous theatrical and musical events she loves to attend (and be seen at). Once or twice, yearning for greater closeness between him and Angie, Michael has mentioned the possibility of having children, but Angie, committed to maintaining both her current lifestyle and her sleek figure, refuses even to entertain the idea. As for socialising with the locals, she had been reluctant enough before, but since being innocently caught up in her firm's involvement in the Southwood Central Mall scam, she has been too embarrassed to show her face around Southwood.

Like Petra, Michael is beginning to think it's time he did a few things by himself . . .

At the lecture on Syria organised by the library as part of its 'World in Focus' series, Petra sits near the front and is enthralled. This is just the kind of stimulation she's been craving and – what luck! – a really pleasant woman from the Fields is sitting beside her, and is willing to chat during the coffee break. Her name is Fran and she and Petra agree to sit together again at the following week's lecture.

As they are leaving the building to head for the carpark, Petra realises the man in front of them is Michael Koutsoukas, walking alone. She calls to him and introduces him to Fran who, it turns out, already knows him. The company she works for is a client of Michael's law firm and Michael had been a regular visitor to their office during some protracted contract negotiations.

'We should have car-pooled,' Michael says to Petra, and they arrange for him to drive her to the following week's lecture.

As the weeks go by, Petra finds herself part of a small group of people who begin meeting for a meal in the library cafe each Thursday evening before attending the lecture.

Our little 'World in Focus' gang has grown to five – two guys and three women, including a lovely lady who's a bit older than the rest of us. She must be in her fifties, Grace. She attached herself to Fran and me during one of the coffee breaks and we sort of chummed up. We started meeting for a quick meal before the lecture each week and then, when the series ended, we decided to keep on meeting at the same time. We've all signed up for the next series – 'The Industrial Revolution: Are we there yet?' – so we're becoming quite a fixture at the little cafe in the library. There are art-history classes about to start at the new gallery, so we might even sign up for them. There's so much we'd all like to do!

The second male member of our group is Marcus Li, a chalkie like me. He's deputy head at Southwood High. I'm not sure how he got involved – I think Grace has a nephew at the high school. Marcus is also on the executive committee for the centenary festival thing we're apparently going to have in the spring. He has some hilarious tales of the goings-on at their meetings. I'm sure the schools will be roped into the festival, one way or another, so they'd better hurry up and tell us what's happening. I have a class of littlies who are up for anything, but we'll need plenty of time to prepare if they're going to be performing in public. You only need one or two mothers to wave at them and they're all at sea.

By the way, I sense a bit of a frisson between Michael and Fran. There might even be some history there. They certainly greeted each other very warmly when I thought I was introducing them on that first night. Good luck to them, anyway. I gather Fran's been on her own for a few years now, and Michael – well, from the few remarks he's let slip during our trips to and fro in his car, I gather Angie is rather high maintenance. I must say she always dresses beautifully and she's a striking-looking woman. But I don't think there's a lot of fun in that marriage.

God, who am I to talk?

The strange thing is, Bill has cheered up quite a bit in these past few weeks. He really encouraged me to go to these lectures and seemed perfectly happy with the idea of me having dinner with the gang beforehand. He even seems a bit more pleased to see me when I get home.

Perhaps we do need a bit of time apart, doing our own thing – people say that can be good for a relationship. Anyway, I wouldn't give up our little gang for the world now, especially our meals together. It's given me a whole new perspective on living in Southwood.

Herds play such a powerful part in developing and nurturing our sense of identity and emotional security, it's easy to overlook their potential power to diminish us, as well. Conformity is not always good for us. In our desire to be accepted by a herd we wish to belong to, we can sometimes find we are giving up too much. Rather than our membership of a herd helping to harmonise our personal and social identities, we may find that our desire to belong is so powerful that we allow our personal identity (including our personal values and aspirations) to be swamped by the demands of social acceptance.

Rick Swanson, principal of Southwood High School, has been worried that the school's enviable reputation for being a warm, caring, friendly community might actually be inhibiting the academic performance of the some of the abler pupils. 'I've noticed this in a couple of other schools I've worked in,' says Rick. 'Some of the brighter kids just don't push themselves too hard for fear of being singled out as a nerd or a swot. Being accepted by the group is everything to some of these kids, and I can understand the pressure that puts on them to hang back a bit.'

Rick's solution has been to create a series of 'Hot-shot' coaching clinics, run by visiting academics and limited to eight pupils per session. He presents them as the academic equivalent of coaching clinics for the top sporting teams and makes entrance highly selective, depending on recent academic performance: 'We're not ashamed of being a bit elitist about sport – I'm just trying to engender the same kind of attitude towards our academic high achievers.'

His theory is that the positive dynamics generated within a small group of potential high achievers will reduce the sense among those pupils that they are 'different': rather than having to stand out as individuals who may feel isolated from the school community, they can identify with the group.

The pressure of the herd is not always so explicit as to cause students to consciously under-perform in their quest for social acceptance; sometimes, it's simply a case of so much time being spent socialising with the group that schoolwork is neglected. In both cases, it can seem to a young person that the rewards of herd membership outweigh the rewards of 'doing well'.

Herds can 'dumb us down' in other ways. Group pressure can exert a reinforcing influence on many forms of unhealthy behaviour – from harmful eating and drinking habits to drug-taking; from vandalism to self-harm. Because we are social creatures, it's hard for us to resist the pressure – whether positive or negative – of any group that has welcomed us as a member: 'hanging out with the gang' creates a dynamic in which each member tends to conform to the standards of the gang, and the standards tend to drop to the least demanding level: 'Everyone has a Coke and chips after school – of course you're going to join in. Why wouldn't you?' The pressure can work equally effectively in the opposite direction, of course – *Everyone goes for a run at lunchtime and I don't want to be the odd one out* – but the common experience of herds as hotbeds of gossip or whingeing, for instance, is a reminder that while conformity is natural, it can also diminish us or tarnish our personal integrity.

The phenomenon at work here is what US psychologist Robert Cialdini (*Influence*, 1983) dubs 'social proof': if it looks as if 'everyone else is doing it', this creates strong pressure on individuals to assume that this is either the right thing to do or, at least, an acceptable thing to do.

For good or ill, we need our herds, and that's why the herd remains the social unit in most human societies. One of the easiest ways to connect with the human herd is to 'graze with the herd', so it's no accident that the incidence of public, communal eating has increased dramatically in shrinking-household societies like Australia and the US, where most households are too small to qualify as 'domestic herds'. The proliferation of coffee shops and cafes and the establishment of so-called 'food courts' provide more opportunities than ever for people who like to eat out – particularly if they would otherwise have to eat alone.

Which brings us to the communal power of food . . .

4

Breaking bread

At lunchtime on any weekday, the food court at Southwood Central Mall is packed. Some customers grab their food and take it back to work to be eaten at their desks. Some take it outside for an ambulatory lunch. Most stay and eat at one of the dozens of tables, large and small, that fill the open space between the many food outlets.

Will Pickering is one of the regulars. A teller in the Southwood branch of a major bank, Will is twenty-six, unattached, and rents a studio apartment in Southwood Central. He doesn't own a car, walks to work, and runs to Dysart Park and back twice a week. He's joined the Lions Club and, encouraged by a community-minded manager at work, he and two of his colleagues volunteer at the Ostara Foundation one Sunday a month. His great passion is film, and he's a regular at the Lewis cinema, often going there with the same two workmates.

When he first started work in the bank, Will was posted to a big city branch where the staff tended to congregate in the lunch room to socialise. As a raw recruit, he valued that time as a way of getting to know his colleagues and soaking up the culture of the bank. Then he was transferred to a small country branch where the manager went home for lunch, and the only other employee, a woman in her thirties, usually lunched with a friend. So Will developed the habit of having a sandwich and coffee at a cafe right next door to the bank, where the owner took a maternal interest in him and would often sit with him and chat.

At Southwood, he soon discovered the food court. Sometimes he goes with one or two colleagues from work; sometimes he eats alone. He doesn't enjoy cooking just for himself, and usually tries to make lunch his main meal of the day. He loves the variety on offer and finds that even when he's there on his own, he never feels alone. He likes the buzz of the place, and has taken to sitting at a particular table where a small group of regulars congregate most days.

Will has always felt that eating alone is as strange – if not quite as dangerous – as drinking alone.

'Grazing with the herd' is a universal practice in human societies. Though eating can be done alone and in private, our most natural inclination is to share the experience with others. Our cultural heritage teaches us that eating is an occasion for social as well as bodily nourishment. So even if it's not an explicitly social event, the idea of eating *with* others is generally appealing. When eating alone but in public, you don't have to strike up a conversation or even exchange pleasantries if you don't feel like it; even being in the same 'paddock' can create a sense of connection with the herd.

Communal eating is one of the most basic of all the symbols of human companionship and connection, so is it any wonder that, when times are tough, eating together becomes an even more important source of solace and solidarity? When there's an economic downturn and retailers are gnashing their teeth, the restaurant business tends to remain afloat, testament to the fact that even when money is tight, communal eating is one of the last things we want to give up. At its best, a cafe, even visited alone, is a place of interaction; a place of human presence; a place of reassurance and the comfort of ritual.

In *Eating Heaven* (2013), the Australian chef, social researcher and minister of religion Simon Carey Holt also reminds us that to eat together is to be equal:

> To sit at the same table, eye-to-eye and fork-to-fork – or chopstick-to-chopstick – is to meet on common ground. The civil rights movement of the 1950s in the southern United States began as a dispute over the right of 'negroes' to eat at the same lunch counters as the whites. More than that, it was the right to sit there *with* the whites. To share food at the same table is a covenantal act. It always has been. In the Ancient Near East, the incubator of food culture, the sharing of food carried lifelong bonds of obligation for host and guest . . . The Bantu people of southern Africa call it 'the clanship of porridge'. When we sit at a table together, we engage in an act of relational intimacy. We are forever connected in a particular way.

Within a family or among friends, preparing food for someone else is one of our most eloquent ways of expressing love, care, friendship, welcome, forgiveness or even reconciliation. Sitting down to a meal together elevates an encounter beyond a mere meeting, and that can apply even in the workplace. Here's how *Monocle* magazine (December 2013/January 2014) describes the role of communal eating for workers in an Italian fashion house:

> Lunchtime at Brunello Cucinelli's factory in Umbria is an hour and a half long. In the canteen, a former farmhouse, the staff sit down at a long wooden table to a subsidised meal of regional produce. Cucinelli believes that a proper lunch is a sacred ritual – *il pranzo e'sacro* – and one that ups the creativity of his workers and fosters a familial cohesion in the office and on the factory floor.

The act of communal eating has symbolic significance, and some-times seems to carry almost mystical connotations.

'Mystical connotations? You obviously haven't had breakfast at our place!' you might well object, and it would be silly to suggest that *every* meal feels like a magic moment of communion, let alone Brunello Cucinelli's 'sacred ritual'. Many parents and carers will tell you that the relentlessness of meal preparation is one of the most gruelling aspects of their role: *What on earth will I cook tonight?* Some parents complain that when they suggest ordering a takeaway pizza or going out for a hamburger, everyone cheers, which only makes them feel worse: *No one cheers my grilled chops.*

In Southwood Fields, mealtimes in the Coghlan household – Catherine, Gareth and their two teenage sons – are often chaotic. Catherine sometimes despairs of ever getting the family to sit down together for long enough to sustain a conversation about anything except family administration.

Breakfast is a lost cause. I don't call eating on the run, one eye on the clock, 'sharing a meal', and neither is simply pouring your breakfast cereal from the same packet at roughly the same time as everyone else in the household. Two people standing in the middle of the kitchen, mug of coffee in hand, running through the arrangements for the day and trying to figure out who will be home first and who will cook tonight hardly qualifies as a social interaction, let alone a mystical experience. But still . . . we have our moments. When it's just Gareth and me, we sometimes light a candle and do it properly. Of course, if the kids were ever to burst in on one of those moments, they'd puke at the sight of us.

At least I've trained the boys – and Gareth needed a bit of training, too – to accept that eating together is an important ritual and about the only opportunity we ever get to sit and talk to each other. It doesn't have to be heavy. But I do draw the line at anyone bringing mobile phones or iPads to the table, and I flatly refuse to have the TV on while we're eating. And to be fair, the boys are sometimes lovely at dinner. We have some very animated conversations and I sometimes wish I could freeze the moment.❜

Most fantasies about an ideal family occasion or a meeting of friends involve food. The picture of a lively group of friends or family members sharing a meal is inherently appealing at the most primitive, visceral level. That's why most of us are appalled by the idea of members of a family squandering time that might have been spent interacting with each other by sitting in front of the TV while eating a meal on their lap (though most of us do it occasionally).

Does it matter? In a less busy, less tightly scheduled era, it mightn't have mattered so much (though in a less frenetic era, family time – or couple time – was not so hard to carve out of the day). But in many households, the main meal of the day is one of the very few times when everyone is present, when there's a stretch of time available to spend together and when the act of sharing a meal works, even if unconsciously, as a symbolic bond.

For families with young children, the value of eating together is not confined to the pleasures of social interaction. A fifteen-year study by Dr Catherine Snow of Harvard's Graduate School of Education showed that family mealtime conversations played a bigger role in children's language acquisition than having stories read to them. Studies from the University of Illinois and Columbia University's National Center on Addiction and Substance Abuse show a strong positive correlation between shared family mealtimes and performance at school. Many studies show that children's sense of belonging to a family is enhanced when they participate in regular family mealtimes, and this can yield benefits ranging from the development of conversational and other social skills to lower drug use in adolescence. A study of five hundred teenagers coordinated by Dr Blake Bowden of Cincinnati Children's Hospital found that 'kids who ate dinner with their families at least five times per week were the least likely to take drugs, feel depressed or get into trouble'. No wonder Purdue University's Center for Families urges families to 'make mealtimes a priority'!

~

Given that our nature is essentially *social*, the table – whether at home, in a cafe, at a picnic, in a club, in a staff canteen or even in a church – is the place where our need of each other is often most poignantly expressed. 'Let's meet for coffee' usually means 'Let's meet'. 'Why don't we have dinner together?' usually means 'I'd like to get to know you better' or 'I want to acknowledge our relationship in a more significant way'. 'Come and have a meal with us' is an overture to deeper connection – a declaration of friendly intent.

The absence of an offer of food can be as eloquent as any sign of resentment at having to cook. If you visit someone's home and they fail to offer you food or drink, it doesn't feel quite right. Am I not really welcome? Are they impatient for me to leave? Do they not understand the conventions of hospitality? It never feels like a warm occasion. Similarly, if you meet someone in their office and there's not even a glass of water on offer, you know this is strictly business and no time will be wasted on pleasantries.

If you think food is just fuel, there are plenty of fast-food outlets to fill you up when you're hungry. And eating obviously does entail refuelling: we must eat to live. But if that's all it was about, we could eat pretty much the same thing, day in, day out. In fact, the diversity of our diet is about much more than ensuring we regularly eat from all the right food groups: it's a by-product of all the different ways we *use* food, and all the different factors that contribute to an eating occasion. We welcome and farewell each other with food. We mark birthdays and other special occasions with food. We reassure and comfort ourselves and each other with food.

A favourite meal might be prepared for a partner as a declaration of rock-solid loyalty. Above all, we show our interdependence through the sharing of food.

Sometimes, food is a celebration; sometimes it's a punctuation mark in the day – an excuse or a reason to pause. It may be laden with the weight of emotional expectation when it is used romantically or as a symbol of apology, contrition or bridge-building. Even a routine family meal can turn out to be the ideal time to air grievances, resolve differences and restore a sense of unity and harmony to the group. It may also signify a parent's continuing faithfulness and devotion to the family.

In Hereford Street, some unpleasantness occurred when a couple of students, skylarking in the early hours of the morning, broke a window of their neighbours' house with a cricket ball. The neighbours were Rob and Jan Laccy, a middle-aged couple who run the takeaway food store in Southwood East. They were already running out of patience with the students because of recurring noise problems, and the broken window was the last straw.

An ugly confrontation ensued. Angry words were exchanged. The students agreed to pay for the repair to the window readily enough, but were outraged by some of the wild accusations about their behaviour made in the heat of the moment by Rob.

When the window was repaired, Rob slid the glazier's bill under the students' door without knocking. They paid promptly.

Several weeks passed without further incident. Then, one evening, two of the students were drinking on the front porch of their cottage when Rob walked by on his way home from work.

On an impulse, one of the students called to him: 'Hey, Mr Lacey, come and have a drink with us.'

Startled, Rob was unsure how to respond. He hesitated, looking like a man who wanted to be anywhere but there, but recognising how ungracious it would seem to ignore such an invitation.

'Thank you,' he said at last. 'I'll just whip inside and get a bottle of something.'

'No, don't do that,' said the student. 'We've got plenty of drinks here. This one's on us. We've even got something to eat.' He looked at his mate quizzically. 'At least, I think we have.'

Rob Lacey walked up the path, accepted the offered bottle of beer and waited while one of the students went inside to prepare a plate of crackers and cheese.

'See?' said the student. 'We're not entirely uncivilised. And we are very sorry about what happened.'

'Cheers,' said Rob, raising his bottle and managing a smile.

An hour later, Rob said he must be going. They shook hands. 'I'll just fetch your cricket ball,' said Rob.

Cooking and serving food is a blend of the creative and performance arts. Like all other artforms, it makes most sense when there's an audience. It's true that some poets and novelists scribble away for years without ever letting another eye fall on their work. Some composers create music for their own ears only. Many people play the piano, sing or dance for their own private pleasure and would be embarrassed if they were to be seen or heard. And, for all I know, some people might go to great lengths to cook an elaborate meal just for themselves.

But most serious attempts to be creative only come to final fruition when they are shared. In fact, it's tempting to say that keeping a creative act to yourself is selfish to the point of weird. We create to express ourselves, that's true; we also create to communicate, and that can't happen in an empty room. We need someone to share, to respond, to admire, to appreciate . . . to take in through their senses what we have created. By 'consuming' it, they bring our creation, or our performance, to its natural conclusion. And a meal is a creation uniquely capable of being consumed and appreciated by all five of our senses.

Signs of hope (or clutching at straws?): TV cooks, recipe books, new appliances

'Let's get sex off TV ... and back on the streets where it belongs,' said a 1960s headline in *Mad* magazine. The same might now be said of cooking (and dancing, for that matter). We still cook, of course, but cooking is increasingly becoming a spectator sport – or a form of entertainment, as Ray Newell, one of Australia's most astute marketing strategists, predicted more than thirty years ago.

Do we watch cooking programs to be inspired to rise to greater culinary heights in our own kitchens? To be better equipped to place exotic orders in restaurants? To marvel at the outer limits of the human imagination? To let ourselves off the hook, rather as golfers do when they see a champion in action on their TV screens (either because the gulf between champions and the rest of us seems unbridgeable, or because even the professionals sometimes mess up)? Or to get some technical tips that will allow us to take more shortcuts, or find ways to present our own humble offerings in more sophisticated guises: cloaked in a sauce, topped with a sprig of something pretty, or set out on the plate as if it's a work of art?

Or is it pure entertainment?

Here's the view of David Dale, Australian author and commentator, who writes the popular culture column 'The Tribal Mind' for Fairfax media:

> The most-watched program on Australian television in 2009 was the grand final of *MasterChef*, which pulled more than five million

viewers nationally. It did even better in 2010, with 5.5 million viewers, but faded a little in 2011, being only the fourth most-watched program, with 3.5 million viewers. In 2012 it was replaced in public esteem by a similar show called *My Kitchen Rules* which went on to become the most-watched show of 2013, with five million viewers.

Does this mean Australia is going through a cooking craze? No, I don't think the appeal of *MasterChef* and *My Kitchen Rules* is primarily about the food (although many Australians do use the recipes).

These programs function as soap operas. The producers have turned what looks like a talent quest into a melodrama. They use an exhaustive audition process to choose a cast of characters who will go through a classic 'journey' — heroes, villains, jesters, mentors, neurotics, tricksters, motherly types, sexy types, mystery men. By editing and cutting hundreds of hours of film, the producers become storytellers. They create what seems to be a narrative with a series of cliffhangers that keep the audience thrilled and engaged. The drama is intensified by the music soundtrack, which signals how the viewer is supposed to feel.

MasterChef and *My Kitchen Rules* differ from earlier 'reality' soaps such as *Big Brother* in allowing viewers to feel they are involved in something worthwhile — cooking and nurturing the family. The characters in *Big Brother* were mostly contemptible attention-seekers, so many viewers felt embarrassed about watching them. The characters in *MasterChef* are admirable, and we let ourselves become addicted because the cooking element suggests we are learning to be better people. But it's really about the drama.

We don't only watch food being cooked on television in our millions; we are insatiable readers of books about cooking, too. Take a look at the bestseller lists any Christmas — and most other times of the year. There will always be some cookbooks on the list, and food-related books sometimes occupy the top few spots.

(Who doesn't have Jamie Oliver, Donna Hay or Stephanie Alexander on their kitchen shelf?) Celebrity cooks, regional recipes, seasonal recipes, quick meals, slow meals, secrets of the great chefs, food scandals, lifting the lid on hotel kitchens, monsoon wedding feasts, Arctic funeral food, vegetarian cooking, the inner life of sauerkraut, the fondue revival, buffalo-milk pancake recipes, cooking for kids, cooking for dunces, festive fare in the royal courts of Europe, the erotic art of grape-peeling, the gastronomic delights of practically anywhere on earth . . .

What do we do with all those cookbooks we buy? In most cases, they sit on a shelf, waiting to be culled when we round up our offerings for a school fete or some other local fundraiser. We might have extracted one or two really good recipes from each of them, and we will have enjoyed the photography, since food photography has become a highly sophisticated visual artform. When they've been given away, or stored in a box in the attic, they will be replaced by the next and next . . . endless waves of tantalising possibilities, purchased as a reminder that we *know* how important cooking is; we *know* what a wonderfully symbolic thing it is; we *intend* to lift our game in this area; we *yearn* for the day when even our own children will actually notice what we've put on their plates and might even pause in the inhalation of their food, turn their grateful faces towards us and thank us.

That's perhaps hoping for too much, but the *idea* of being known as a 'good cook' is inherently appealing, because it taps into one of our richest and deepest cultural archetypes: the cook as nurturer and sustainer. We know it can't be all that hard: people have been applying heat to food for centuries, after all, and the recipes make it all sound so straightforward. But the gap between the dream (or the photograph of the dream in a cookbook) and the meal on the plate yawns at us reproachfully.

Which is where the appliance market comes in. If the recipes can't turn me into a gourmet cook — or even into a cook who can be relied on not to poison my family and guests – surely one of these new appliances will do the trick for me. And they keep appearing at almost the same rate as cookbooks: beaters, mixers, blenders, slicers, juicers, toasters, bread-makers, so-called sandwich-makers (that don't actually make sandwiches, by the way). Their names roll off the tongue: Mixmaster, Magimix, Bamix, Thermomix, Kitchen Aid, Kitchen Whizz, Kitchen Magician . . .

Cheryl, a science teacher at Southwood High, swears by her Thermomix – an appliance that claims to combine ten appliances in one. Cheryl has never regarded herself as much of a cook, but she claims that her Thermomix, with its thermometer, scales and assorted components for cutting, blending, mixing and, yes, even cooking, is more like 'doing science' than cooking.

The TV shows, the glossy books, the latest appliance . . . we find all these things irresistible because they keep reminding us of the centrality of food to our culture, its importance in our social lives, and the weight of responsibility on us when we prepare a meal. Meat and three veg? Nice try.

The gender question

'Most cooks are women; most great chefs are men.'

Historically true, but unhelpful.

If you were a male supremacist, you'd want to argue that the reason most creative artists through history – painters, composers, poets, novelists, sculptors and chefs – have been male is because men are simply more creative than women. (Yes, there have been men who say that. There are men who *still* say that.)

If you were a feminist (or even a reasonably balanced human being), you'd want to argue that, through history, men did most of the hunting and gathering – or the symbolic equivalent of those 'breadwinning' things – while women were assigned nurturing roles as housekeepers and mothers. So to say that 'most creative artists have been men' is the same thing as saying 'most garbage collectors have been men' or 'most scientists have been men', as have most accountants, theologians, grocers and bus drivers. It's a proposition that ignores the swirling tides of social change.

Women are now moving into every imaginable area of work, partly because they are better educated than ever before, partly because they are more explicitly encouraged to push the boundaries than ever before, and partly because the whole point of the women's liberation movement was that women are entitled to the same freedom of choice as men. (That includes choices about partnering and parenting as well as employment. Most households with two adults in them, with or without children, are destined to be two-income households, and that's not only about financial pressure; it's also a sign of a cultural revolution.)

Male supremacists are still about, though. They pop up in all kinds of places – politics, boardrooms, backyard barbecues with tongs in hand . . . but rarely in the kitchen. That barbecue thing is interesting: even in these enlightened and liberated times, as soon as the cooking moves outside, the men tend to take over while the women stay inside preparing salads and other accompaniments to soften the impact of the meat being charred on the barbecue. Even today, it is more unusual to see a woman cooking at an outdoor barbecue than it is to see a man cooking in a kitchen.

Margie Isherwood, recently returned to the city from her life on a rural property, has been trying for years to explain that to her own satisfaction:

> Ken has always had an interest in cooking. Even when the children were young, he would do all the cooking on weekends. During the week, it wasn't really practical, because he was out on a tractor until dark, or doing something else around the place, so I just got on with preparing the dinner.

The thing about Ken in the kitchen is this: almost regardless of what he cooks, he seems to use every pot and pan in the place and to leave the kitchen in an unholy mess. Then he trots out the old thing about 'the one who cooks doesn't have to clean up' and I've been silly enough to fall for it. No, that's not fair – he usually cleans up after I've cooked dinner in the evening.

But the barbecue is the one area where he feels as though traditional gender roles should be preserved. It's no affront to his masculinity to cook a meal in the kitchen, although he does always insist on doing 'something special' – he's no short-order cook, Ken – but he seems to think it would be an affront to his masculinity if I cooked something on the barbecue. It's very definitely *his* barbecue. It's not about skill, by the way – he burns as many sausages as the next bloke – it's something that goes deep into the male psyche. Maybe it's the old hunter-gatherer thing? Although even that doesn't work, because the hunters surely brought the kill home for the women to deal with. But there is something primitive going on, I'm sure of it.

Look, it's probably as simple as this – he loves being outside, he doesn't mind a bit of smoke in his hair, he loves having a drink with his mates while he's cooking . . . there are lots of factors. I'd never call Ken a male chauvinist, but I'd certainly call him a barbecue Nazi.

Many women, particularly those juggling child-rearing with paid employment, come to resent the expectation that they will automatically be the one in the family to shoulder the burden of daily meal preparation. Many men now take meal preparation in their stride, and younger couples are increasingly inclined to share the cooking, so any hint of expectation that 'women *should* do the cooking', based on residual gender stereotyping, can create deep and understandable resentment.

In this respect, at least, some women experience separation and divorce as a very particular kind of liberation. When Leonie Mills left her husband and bought an apartment in Southwood Central, her first declaration, made to anyone who would listen, was this: 'That's the end of cooking. I'm never going to cook another meal.' And she has stuck to it, too. She occasionally prepares a bowl of pasta or poaches an egg, but she makes heavy use of frozen meals, eats out a lot, and strenuously resists any temptation to invite anyone home for a meal – even her own adult son and daughter, who rarely visit and have resigned themselves to this arrangement. They've talked about it to each other, and have come to the conclusion that their mother never really enjoyed cooking, never experienced it as a loving act, never felt she was doing something creative and emotionally nurturing for the family. They recall that it had always seemed a chore to her and that, even when she was married to their father, she tended to invite friends to go out with them rather than cook something at home.

Whenever they have reflected on the implications of all this, they have felt some sadness – for their mother, certainly, because of what they assume she missed out on by refusing to let meal preparation mean anything more to her than the organisation of a refuelling depot; for their father, who always envied friends with larger families who tended to have noisier and more exuberant meals together; and for themselves, because, looking back, they realise they had always sensed their mother's resentment at being expected to prepare every meal (though she never worked outside the home, and they assumed this was an arrangement settled between their parents). They have sometimes wondered whether it was motherhood she really resented – with all the demands that family life entailed – and suspect her resistance to cooking may have merely been a symptom of that.

Leonie's case might be extreme, her negative attitude to cooking (and perhaps even to motherhood) exacerbated by a miserable marriage; but many women, ground down by the daily demands of meal preparation, could relate to the relief Leonie felt when she was no longer *required* to cook. Cooking was once unequivocally regarded as 'women's work' – the sign of a good housekeeper, a good wife, a good mother, a good entertainer. Today, in Western societies, any such assumption would be regarded as dangerous and patronising. On the other hand, the arrival of large numbers of men in the kitchen has created a fresh source of gender tension: being new to the role, many men still expect praise for their efforts, as though their culinary achievements are extraordinary – or, at least, a sign that they are at the cutting edge of cultural change. By contrast, in some households, women's efforts are regarded as more routine and less remarkable since (in a disturbing echo of old-style male chauvinism) 'cooking comes more naturally to women'.

Baking bread

Of all the symbols of food's cultural significance, perhaps none is quite as potent as bread you have baked yourself. It's primitive; it's earthy; it's basic; it seems simple (though that's an illusion). Bread, after all, is 'the staff of life'. And it has acquired heavy religious significance. In the Christian tradition, Jesus is quoted as saying 'I am the bread of life' and, at the Last Supper, describing the bread he was eating with his disciples as 'my body' – a symbol of the corporate nature of the meal. The New Testament story about the feeding of four or five thousand people with five loaves of bread and two fish is presumably supposed to represent the sustaining power of love: keep giving it, and it keeps multiplying; keep it to yourself and your stocks will soon be depleted. In other words, it's a story about sharing, and bread is the chosen symbol. In the Jewish tradition, unleavened bread is used as a reminder of the Jews' exodus from Egypt, when, in their hasty preparation of bread for the journey, there wasn't time for the dough to rise. Again, bread is chosen as the symbol of an entire cultural narrative – a symbol that has retained its potency over millennia.

'This is a bread-and-butter issue,' says Mary Kippax at a Southwood council meeting, wanting to emphasise how basic an issue it is. 'He took the bread out my mouth,' says someone whose livelihood has been diminished by another's greed. And we all know 'which side our bread is buttered on'.

All this cultural freight carried by one simple item of food! In a way, bread has become, for Westerners, the symbol of food itself. And, as the easiest of all foods to 'break', it was bound to be put into service as the ultimate symbol of sharing.

You might take pride in your beef bourguignon. Your salads might be famous in the extended family: *Get Caroline to bring one of her rice salads.* Your soufflé might have earned you a reputation as a serious cook. Your way with fish might be legendary. Ah, but can you bake a decent loaf of bread?

∾

Over dinner before the lecture, Petra Ritchie often regales her 'World in Focus' companions with tales of her early days as a young teacher working in various country schools:

When I got my first posting to the country, I lived in a cute little cottage on a rural property that I was sharing with three other teachers. We did everything together and had a whale of a time. I was determined to throw myself into the country life. I didn't have enough money to buy a four-wheel drive, but I think I would have if I could have. I certainly bought a pair of moleskins and an Akubra hat. The photos are embarrassing.

I became fanatical about the idea of baking my own bread. I thought it was such a *rustic* thing to do. The other three thought I was mad – 'What's wrong with the bread in the supermarket?'

they wanted to know. Frankly, the bread in the supermarket was pretty awful back then. It's got a lot better recently – in fact, we're spoiled for choice.

There was this great fad at the time for a beer-based recipe for bread, so I thought – yep, that's easy enough. No drama, no yeast, just pour in a can of beer. The first time I tried it, it looked very promising but it actually tasted like a scone. So I tried and tried – all I got was scone after scone. The thing was, the other girls loved it. They got so attached to 'Petra's giant scone', they refused to let me try any more elaborate or ambitious bread recipes and so that's as far as I ever got. But every time I made it, I did feel as if I was the earth mother of the group. I even wore an apron. I probably still have that apron somewhere.

Writing in the *New Yorker* ('Bread and Women', 4 November 2013), Adam Gopnik describes his own experiences with the baking of bread, including a weekend he spent with his mother, learning her bread-baking secrets.

Like many men who cook a lot, I'm good at doing several things that look hard but aren't – béarnaise sauce, tuna au poivre – and not very good at doing some things that are harder than they look. I can't make a decent vinaigrette, anything involving a 'salt crust' baffles me, and, until quite recently, I had never baked a loaf of bread.

Gopnik had told himself that, living in New York, he didn't need to bake his own bread for the same reason he didn't need to drive a car: the bakeries and supermarkets – and subways – of the city made such skills redundant.

Then he came across a recipe for 'Martha's Bread', beautifully hand-lettered and framed, written for his wife, Martha, by her mother. It turned out his wife had been a keen baker of oat-and-honey bread in her late teens – a time when she also sewed all her own clothes. (Culturally, you can see how the two things might go together.) Failing to persuade his wife to drop everything and make some of this bread – 'My bread's not that easy,' she had said rather loftily – he became obsessed with the idea of baking his own bread. Rather like Petra, he found a 'No Knead Bread' recipe ('bread that sort of makes itself') and set about the task of producing his very own loaf. It came out of the oven recognisable as bread, but not as *good* bread, and he became determined to master the skill, spending a weekend at his parents' house for some maternal tuition. (Who better than one's mother to be the authority on something as elemental as bread?)

Eventually, Martha baked a loaf of her bread for him: 'When it was baked, sixty minutes in a slow oven, her loaf looked beautiful, braided like the blond hair of a Swedish child . . . Women, I thought, remember everything. Bread forgives us all.'

That's how we talk about bread. That's how writers write about it.

Food *can* be a cultural bridge

Nothing makes a stranger in our midst feel more welcome than the offer of a meal. And nothing shows our willingness to enter into the cultural experience of a person from a different ethnic background more obviously than our acceptance of an invitation to share their food.

That point has become controversial. In immigrant societies like Australia and the US, it was once taken for granted that as each new wave of immigrants arrived, at least some aspects of their distinct ethnic heritage would enrich the host culture – and none more so than food. We thought this was a thing to celebrate, because we regarded the appreciation and appropriation of new tastes in food as signs of a larger integration. Food was widely regarded as a bridge between ethnic communities.

At some point, the narrative changed. We began to be told that this concept of food as a cultural bridge was offensive to immigrants. People from different ethnic backgrounds wanted to be welcomed and accepted for themselves, not for their food. In *Eating Between the Lines* (2008), Australian social researcher Rebecca Huntley described a televised discussion of multiculturalism, with references to the demands it makes on our tolerance of difference and the challenges it poses to our sense of community. Towards the end of the discussion, the journalist David Marr made a lighthearted reference to Lebanese recipes for lamb: 'In our hearts,' he said, 'we know that the best people for cooking lamb in the world are Lebs ... It's just a joke to think that my grandmother's leg of lamb beats the kind of recipes you get from the Middle East.'

Huntley reported that this provoked 'hearty chuckles of agreement from the Anglo members of the audience' but that the camera cut to 'a somewhat strained smile on the face of a young Muslim man'. She acknowledged that Marr would not overtly argue that 'the best contribution migrants have to offer Australia is better recipes for meat' but wondered whether his comment might inadvertently reinforce that prejudice. 'We should not suppose too close or too simple a link,' Huntley writes, 'between the availability of ethnic food and the acceptance of ethnic diversity' and she is right to point out that, in the past, Greeks who established popular restaurants in Australia were not shielded from racist taunts. (Nor, much earlier, were Chinese.)

Nevertheless, it is an appealing idea that we first eat the food of another culture and then, bit by bit, come to accept other aspects of that culture. Food is a symbol of openness to otherness – ask any tourist. Of course immigrants want to be accepted for *who* they are, but the symbols of acceptance are important too, and eating each other's food as a sign of cross-cultural communion has always been a powerful gesture.

A friend tells of attending a feast in an Egyptian household where, as a special treat, she was served the eye of a sheep. To decline it would have been offensive, yet the very idea of eating it was repugnant to her. She ate it. Another friend tells a similar story of being treated to a banquet in Vietnam where the centrepiece turned out to be the killing of a cobra for eating. (My friend claims he had misheard, and thought he was being taken out for a 'snack'.) As the guest of honour, he was offered the still-beating cobra's heart in a beaker of clear rice wine. He swallowed it, with a chaser of wine, snake's blood and bile. Eating the cooked flesh of the snake later was the easy part.

It's a long way from such explicit symbolism to the purchase of Pad Thai from a takeaway in Southwood Central. Even so, 'eating my food' is one of the signs we look for, all over the world, when we judge whether or not we are being accepted. We can't easily learn the language of foreigners. We can't always appreciate, at first exposure, their music, or understand the significance of their cultural festivals or religious practices. Whether we are visiting them in their homeland or welcoming them to ours, sharing food is an eloquent way of saying: I would like to get to know you.

It goes without saying that eating the food of a particular ethnic group does not guarantee that you will feel more accepting towards that group. Eating in a different ethnic restaurant every night of the week doesn't guarantee that you will befriend the people represented by that food, or even that you will embrace the concept of multiculturalism. But food is certainly one way of introducing us to the idea of cultural diversity as an integral part of our way of life. The important point, obviously, is that there's no inherent magic in the food itself: it's the *sharing* of the food that builds the bridge.

～

Jim Glasson occasionally runs a 'World Food Night' at his church in Southwood East, and is usually swamped by enthusiastic locals, keen to try whatever is on offer. Jim always invites representatives of a particular ethnic group to give a short description of the food, and to explain something of their own cultural heritage.

He has been heavily criticised for these events. Dom Fin, the deputy mayor, regards the whole idea as potentially offensive to the ethnic groups concerned: 'You're just emphasising our differences, Jim,' he has said. 'Plus, you're making it look as if the only reason these people are welcome is because they have brought some exotic food with them.'

'Quite the reverse, Dom,' says Jim. 'We want to show that we're interested in the culture they come from, and isn't food the easiest way into that? The main thing is to make them feel that we're interested in them, that we take them seriously, that we want to understand what they've left behind. There's no point in denying that they are who they are.'

'They're Australians, now,' Dom replies. 'Look, my parents came out here from Italy, but I don't want you going around calling me an Italian, or even an Italian-Australian. Let's get integrated! I know assimilation is a dirty word at the moment, but I'm all for it.'

Jim responds as gently as he can: 'It is a dirty word, Dom, because it makes it sound as if we're trying to smother the things that people have brought here. Why not accept that there are differences? Why not celebrate them, especially for some of these people who've had a really rugged time getting here? I'm not against integration, Dom. It's inevitable, over time, but I don't think we should rush it. I've just found that, in the first few years, the new arrivals like us to show some genuine interest not just in who they are, but also in where they came from and what they've brought with them. Mightn't it be a bit arrogant to ignore that? We all came from somewhere, Dom. Anyway, come to our next World Food Night – we've got that new Sudanese family cooking for us. Have you met them yet? Give it a go.'

~

One thing the immigrants from southern Europe have certainly done for Australian food culture is to put coffee on the map. Australians now drink more coffee than tea, a situation unthinkable in the 1940s or 50s, or even in the 70s. The revolution might have been slow to gain momentum, but it has finally transformed us into a coffee culture.

Ken Isherwood had long declared that one of the things he was most looking forward to when he and Margie returned to the city was access to decent espresso coffee. Even so, he was astonished when he discovered the range and quality of coffee on offer in Southwood. A trip to the local cafe became a daily ritual and Ken freely admitted his addiction to the bean.

For his sixtieth birthday, Margie bought him an espresso machine – a sleek and gleaming object imported from Italy. On the morning of his birthday, after opening this lavish and spectacular gift, Ken insisted that they go to their usual haunt for their morning coffee. Margie had assumed he would want to brew his first cup at home, right then on the morning of his birthday, but that was not to be.

The machine stood on the kitchen bench for a full week, unused. Various friends dropped in, and Ken proudly showed them his new toy. 'Have you tried it?' they all asked. 'I'm waiting for the right moment,' was the guarded reply.

Puzzled by Ken's reluctance, Margie eventually offered to take the machine on its maiden voyage herself. It was a miserable flop – the coffee was grey; the flavour was insipid; the froth on her cappuccino collapsed before her very eyes. The less said about Ken's short black the better.

Off they went to the cafe, where Margie saw clearly what she had not seen before: that this ritual was about much more than coffee, and Ken's enjoyment of the coffee was a function of the ambience, their time out together, the buzz of the cafe and the skill of a barista for whom this was as much about art as coffee. She knew at once that no matter how thoroughly they mastered the art of making good coffee at home, part of the joy of coffee, for Ken, was about not being at home.

Simon Carey Holt captures the point in *Eating Heaven*, likening coffee in a cafe to the experience of listening to jazz in 'the dark and moody ambience of a venue dedicated to its performance and appreciation'. According to Holt, 'The cafe is about more than flat whites and long blacks, perfectly drawn. Coffee is about relationship, connection, theatre and community.'

Relationship, connection, theatre and community? If that's true for coffee, it's equally true for food, more generally. The sharing of food is perhaps our most ancient ritual for expressing the need to nurture the relationships, the families, the communities that sustain us. 'Breaking bread' together symbolises our need for social and emotional as well as physical sustenance. Without having to put it into words, the kind of meal we offer someone, and the way we present it to them, can convey messages as diverse as welcome, acceptance, friendship, collegiality, sympathy, rapprochement, apology, forgiveness, and love.

5

The hubs

Any community is a dynamic, evolving, delicate organism, full of contradictions and tensions. It's a place where people's personal dreams sometimes harmonise and sometimes collide. Because a local neighbourhood is where we are most obviously called on to share our common living spaces, facilities and infrastructure – our roads, footpaths, parks, shops, cafes, schools, libraries, churches, public transport, water and electricity supplies, medical and other services – this is the place where we are also most likely to experience the universal human struggle between our independence and our interdependence. Local neighbourhoods are where we bump into each other unintentionally, incidentally, and where, if we've understood our destiny as social beings, we do our best to get along with each other.

The thing that builds communities is engagement and the crucial ingredient in engagement is time. Far from being a time-wasting activity, 'hanging out' with the people in the neighbourhood – or the office, the club, or any other place where people congregate – is how we build social capital; how we nurture our relationship with a community; how we establish our connections with each other; how we master the art of belonging and create the feeling of trustful safety we always hope a community will give us in return.

As social beings, our lifeblood is communication, and that doesn't always have to be deep and meaningful. A chat about the weather with someone you meet at the bus stop makes a tangible contribution to the life of any community, by reinforcing our awareness that we share this space and are pleased to acknowledge each other's existence. Such apparently inconsequential encounters – *g'day/how are you?/we need rain/this bus often runs late* – signify that we take each other seriously enough to devote a little time to the ordinary courtesies of everyday life. And the converse is true: when we ignore people we pass in the street, or fail to respond to a smile or a greeting, however fleeting, we are denying our community the chance for a little nurturing.

From a rational point of view, a remark like *We need rain* is pointless – if we need rain, everyone knows it, and there's not a thing anyone can do about it. But *We need rain* is a reliable, non-controversial opening gambit that establishes our willingness to enter into an encounter: it's a remark more about *us* than the weather, rather like a conversational handshake. Similarly, *How are you?* may seem an odd thing to enquire of someone you barely know: the last thing you would want is a full account of their recent medical history. But, again, it's a declaration with precisely the same social significance as *Good morning*. We are acknowledging each other; we are observing the small social niceties; we are demonstrating that we want to maintain the personal civility fundamental to a civil society.

Every community needs its hubs – places that facilitate and encourage these incidental encounters; places that heighten our awareness that we are part of a larger whole. One cause of social problems in new housing estates is the lack of hubs – no 'village centre'; no places where the life of the community can be fostered.

If we all live in our own little boxes, come and go by car, and do all our socialising, shopping, public eating and talking elsewhere, the area we inhabit will feel not only like a mere dormitory, but also like a wasteland. Smart planners and developers have begun to understand that, from the very beginning, a new suburb needs places that will evolve into natural hubs: a cafe, a supermarket, a hairdresser, a library branch, a meeting hall, parks ... places that encourage those incidental encounters so vital to the early development of a neighbourhood's soul.

In the semi-rural village where I live, the local store promotes itself as 'the heart of the village', and so it is. That's where we meet each other without having arranged to do so; where a trip to collect the mail can turn into a pleasant catch-up with neighbours; where people who thought they were going to have a cup of coffee alone will rarely be alone for long. It's our hub.

Southwood has many hubs. Here are some of them ...

The library

Of all the institutions, establishments and facilities that might qualify as community hubs, the one most likely to evolve into a modern, urbanised version of the village green, the one most likely to cater for people at every stage of the lifecycle, and the one most likely to be entering a golden age of creativity, relevance and community service is ... the local library.

The local library? But surely all the dire predictions of the death of the book and the inroads made into our browsing, reading and communication habits by the internet will make the library redundant – or at least reduce it to a rump of its former self.

Not so.

Although books are far from finished (and, for the foreseeable future, not all books found in a library will be accessible online, even if you might prefer to read them on a screen), the future of libraries actually has very little to do with the future of books, whether in printed or electronic form.

If you were to think of a library purely as a place where books are kept, where the literary canon is preserved, and where people can go for a good read in a quiet and comfortable place, then you might be inclined to expect a decline in its relevance to a modern, wired community. But if you think of a library as a source of information and ideas in the broadest sense, and as a place where ideas can be exchanged and debated – in other words, if you were to add a *community* dimension to your understanding of the role and function of a library – you would see it all very differently. And that applies whether the community in question is a local neighbourhood, a school, a university, a club or a retirement village.

The modern librarian is a kind of entrepreneur, creating and managing an array of services that have dramatically enhanced the role of libraries and, in the process, enriched the life of the communities they serve. Reflecting the shift, libraries are no longer exclusively staffed by people trained as professional librarians: many libraries now employ events managers and people with skills that were developed in areas as diverse as marketing and teaching.

Libraries are far more vibrant places than they used to be – and noisier, too. There's often a low buzz of conversation, or some spillage of sound from a children's storytelling session being conducted in one corner, or a lecture being delivered in another. If you *want* silence, though, there are designated quiet rooms where you can go to read a newspaper or magazine (including one in your own language if you're not yet comfortable with English), browse through a book you might be thinking of borrowing, do your homework or surf the internet.

If you doubt it, go to your local library and take a look. If your municipal council is enlightened, the first thing you'll notice is that the place is well resourced; in many cases, you'll be looking at a new building or an old one that's been extensively remodelled to reflect the changing role and function of a library; the changing meanings of the very word 'library' itself. Staff will smile at you and probably ask you if you need any help. There won't be an intimidating face in sight, because this is a place for members of the community to gather and interact; it's a marketplace for ideas, and marketplaces are neither quiet nor sleepy.

In Southwood, the recently renovated and extended library building is now called the 'Library and Cultural Centre', a name insisted on by a council intensely proud of the new development, but resisted by the general manager of the library – a dynamic woman called Roslyn Kennedy – who felt that 'cultural' was rather a case of gilding the lily. But given the councillors' enthusiasm for the project, Roslyn acquiesced.

Its offerings are impressive. There is of course the book collection itself, most of which is available for borrowing. The collection includes many works in languages other than English, reflecting the growing ethnic diversity of Southwood. There is a home library service that, drawing on the work of volunteers, takes books to the housebound. Ten of Southwood's thirty-odd book clubs meet at the library, in one of its several meeting rooms. Those rooms are also used for small-group coaching classes for high school students, particularly those struggling with English. There are 'baby book clubs' designed to introduce young mothers to starter books they might not otherwise be aware of, storytelling groups for preschoolers and school-holiday activities designed to encourage curiosity and creativity. There's a library of toys and games, including video games. There are banks of computers, and facilities for people to bring in their own computers to take advantage of the library's free wi-fi connection.

The library has recently employed an adult-education specialist who is developing programs such as those attended by Petra Ritchie and her friends – current affairs, history, philosophy and psychology are the most popular offerings so far. The local history group is based in the library, and often arranges talks and displays of historical material. Author talks are regularly arranged and usually booked out. The new art gallery annexe offers courses in art appreciation and art history, with help from the head of art at Southwood High.

Although Roslyn is a familiar figure around the library, few people know her by name. She is a great delegator, and the various specialist staff members are responsible for organising and promoting their own activities, and for dealing directly with the library's customers. As we are about to discover, Roslyn is excited by the new world opening up for libraries and she is determined that Southwood will be in the forefront.

⟨I was a real bookworm when I was a kid which is, of course, the worst possible reason for deciding to become a librarian – all those books and no time to read any of them! But even when I was training, which wasn't all that long ago, I had no idea what would happen to library services. I remember going to a conference soon after I graduated where this chap was talking about the future for libraries and I was thinking, 'In your dreams . . . if only!' Yet here we are and it's happening even more quickly than he predicted. The whole internet revolution has moved way beyond anything he was talking about fifteen years ago – for instance, we've only had Facebook for the past ten years, and Twitter for even less, so goodness knows what's around the corner.

But the thing I find is that the more high-tech we're becoming, the more there's a real hunger for personal interaction. It's as if people know they can get whatever information they want by simply Googling it, so now they want somewhere to go where they can discuss it and interpret it, and listen to other people's opinions – sometimes expert opinions, such as in our current affairs and history programs. We all know that information – data – is a very different thing from wisdom and understanding, so I guess it was inevitable that as information became more plentiful and easier to access, there'd be a corresponding demand for someone to help us make sense of it all.

So I think of our library as having several layers of activity. We supply the information, sure, but we also provide access to people who can explain and interpret it, and we're a forum for people to explore and discuss their own reactions to it. And that starts with the preschoolers – we have some terrific casual staff we can bring in to read to the littlies, but also to encourage them to think about the story, and maybe extend it or make up a sequel of their own. So they're already exploring what they're hearing, playing with it a bit, trying it out for themselves.

I find all that pretty exciting – it's a far cry, I can tell you, from cataloguing books and lending them out and demanding fines if people brought them back late! We've abolished fines, by the way. The library isn't the rather daunting place of old. I just love seeing the place full of activity – littlies in the morning, then the pensioners and retired people coming through in the middle of the day. We get lots of primary school kids from three o'clock on and the teenagers a bit later. Then we get another wave of people coming through on their way home from work to return and borrow books to read on the train, or to attend one of our Lifelong Learning programs.

We couldn't survive without our volunteers, especially for our home-delivery service. Or the Friends of the Library; their fundraising gives a nice boost to our acquisitions budget and also funds our kids' programs. The goodwill is tremendous – I think people are really waking up to what we're doing here, and its value to the community. The council has been superb – the mayor and deputy really get it. We had a minor contretemps over them wanting to add 'cultural' to the name of the centre. I thought it was a bit pretentious, but that's a small price to pay for their support. It all sounds a bit too good to be true, doesn't it? I think it's just that we've really caught a wave. I sometimes think we're filling the gap left by the old parish church. You know — a sort of hub for the community, with lots of different things on, even if you weren't a mad keen churchgoer. I'm not knocking the churches, by the way, but I do think they've lost that role and we seem to have picked it up. And to take the analogy one step further, you don't have to be a believer in books — a bookworm like I used to be — to be a fully engaged customer of the library these days. There's so much more to it than reading. Don't think books — think information and ideas. ⁹

The railway station

Southwood station is a busy place. Architecturally, it's a pleasing blend of the old and new. Built in the early 1920s, its rather Edwardian appearance has been well maintained, including a spacious alcove, not quite a formal waiting room, for protection from inclement weather. But all the new technology is here, too: electronic timetable displays, recorded announcements giving information about train arrivals, automated ticketing, food- and drink-dispensing machines.

Harry Goodman has been the stationmaster for the past twelve years and hopes to remain here until he retires. He grew up in rural England, where he would hang over the railing at his local station watching the trains, the signals, the stationmaster with his flag and whistle. He used to gather up discarded tickets to add to his collection. He never wanted to do anything but work on the railways. His parents migrated to Australia when Harry was eleven, and his attachment to trains remained as strong as ever. He never aspired to be a driver; it was the life of the station that intrigued him. After postings all over the system, city and country, his appointment as stationmaster at Southwood was the fulfilment of a long ambition. He had two brief appointments at busy inner-city stations where he deplored the fact that there was no time for what he calls 'railway culture'. At such stations, life was all about moving masses of people as efficiently as possible: there was no possibility of getting to know any of the customers and little time to develop some esprit de corps among the staff. Everywhere he's worked, Harry has been conscientious about the appearance of the station – not just basic cleanliness, but attention to paintwork, maintenance of equipment, establishment and care of floral displays in pots or, where feasible, in garden beds. The absence of gardens was one of the many things Harry disliked about inner-city stations. At Southwood, he's been in his element: there's a large garden bed at either end of the single platform and all the buildings were renovated and repainted within six months of his arrival.

There are three tracks – the up and down lines to and from the city, plus a rarely-used siding. A pedestrian bridge connecting Heywood Place to Railway Parade has a single broad flight of steps running down to the platform. This makes access to Southwood station virtually impossible for people with mobility difficulties, and Harry is constantly raising this with his superiors. Many stations of no greater importance than Southwood already have lifts installed, and Harry has been promised one in the near future.

Like all suburban stations, Southwood's rail users come in great pulsing waves that build and disperse and build again, according to the time of day and the day of the week: commuters, city shoppers, school children and students, people attending sporting and cultural events as well as the gentler tides of visitors coming here for social reasons. Children are a less common sight than they used to be, Harry has observed, since so many parents now prefer to ferry their offspring about, whether to school, sport, concerts, the movies or elsewhere.

Harry is almost as interested in social analysis as he is in train movements. He has always regarded the railway station as the natural hub of any community and has enjoyed monitoring the changes in the behaviour of his passengers over the years.

We only have them with us when they're actually waiting to catch a train. If they're alighting, you don't see them for dust. Up the stairs and off. Stations aren't places where people hang around by choice, although I imagine that could change one day. A fellow I talk to in the early morning – he's always on the 6.27 to the city, regular as clockwork, the man and the train – gave me an article he'd torn out of a fancy magazine that was all about the future for European railway stations – going a bit in the direction of mini-airports with shops, child-care centres, gyms, cafes and bars.

It's already happened at the big city stations, to some extent, but I'd really like to see it at suburban stations like ours. There's plenty of room to go up, so you can imagine really making something of a place like this. Why not? People could meet here for coffee before they catch their train, or have a snack before they go to a show in town. A more contemporary version of the old Railway Refreshment Rooms – remember those? Young mums could leave their kids in child-care while they have a few hours shopping in the city. Makes sense to me. We'd need better parking, of course, but the council is working on that one. Kentwell has the big commuter carpark, so that pulls a lot of people away from Southwood – the station *and* the shops.

Train travel will come back into fashion. You watch. It's already starting to happen. The 'station of the future' thing could be a big factor. At present, the two big gaps in our customer profile are senior executive and professional types, and mothers of young kids. We don't see many of them here, but we see everyone else.

And when you look at the lines of traffic into the city, you wonder why anyone would go by car.

In the mornings, most of the kids we see are travelling to private schools out of Southwood. They hang about in ones and twos – even kids from the same school seem to ignore each other – and often look as if they're still half asleep. But once they get on board, it's a different matter entirely. They get into their little huddles, all intimate and intense. It's a rich social life they have on the train. Up to a certain age, they stick to their separate groups of boys and girls, but then the groups start to mingle.

The mobile phone has revolutionised the railway station. You used to hear a low murmur of conversation here and there, mainly inside the waiting alcoves, but it was mostly silence among the adults. Now, there are always people talking into their mobiles – there's a kind of muted shout they use. You can hear their side of the conversation quite clearly and you can often imagine what's going on at the other end. Now, if they're quiet, it's probably because they're checking or sending text messages or emails or tweeting, or whatever. I suppose it's quite good that they're all so connected, but I sometimes wish they'd talk to the person standing next to them – particularly if they've been standing in that same spot at the same time, year after year.

The guards say that most passengers on the train keep to themselves – just reading their paper or a book, or doing things with their mobile phones and iPads. Lots of people use those little earbuds. But everything changes when there's some big event on, like a major sporting carnival or a cultural event of some kind. Even big news items, like 9/11 or floods or bushfires. There's a real buzz. Everyone talks to each other for a day or two, and then – wham! It's back to silence and hiding behind their newspapers or staring at their screens.

I'll tell you something else I've noticed. People – especially the young adults – seem more edgy. Very few people seem to just stand or sit quietly, using the time to think or relax. They're all so overstimulated – all plugged in to some device or other. Do you think we're losing the art of patience? You should see the way they carry on if their train is running late. It's beyond my control, but some of them talk to me as if I've personally gone out of my way to ruin their arrangements.

There's a lot more eating on the station than there used to be. And those wretched bottles of water. Until a few years ago, we had drinking fountains on every station – all gone. Go and buy a bottle if you're thirsty. The big companies evidently leant on the state government to get the drinking fountains taken away. It's criminal, really. We used to encourage people to hydrate – now we discourage them by making them pay.

The other thing I find is people are less embarrassed about doing personal stuff in public than they used to be. Some young women wait until they get to the station to start doing their make-up. I've got a couple of blokes who regularly whip their electric shavers out of their backpacks or briefcases and stand there shaving. Quite a bit of public kissing goes on, too – that never used to happen.

You know what I love most of all about this job? Yes, the trains are getting sleeker and quieter, more comfortable and more reliable, and our information systems are world-class. But here's the thing – in spite of all that, you still have to wave the flag and blow the whistle. They haven't found a way to improve on that.

The cafe/bookshop

Three minutes' walk from the railway station, just around the corner from Heywood Place, is Eine Kleine Caffeine, where Marco Lestrange (Italian mother omnipresent; French father long gone) presides over the closest thing Southwood has to a literary and

philosophical hub in the tradition of the European cafe. The name
looked clever and catchy in print when Marco devised it twenty
years ago – and still looks impressive on the shop's awning – but
as no one could quite work out how to say it, the place quickly
became known as 'E.K.'.

It started as a modest coffee shop; evolved into a cafe serving
cakes, pastries and light lunches, plus all-day breakfasts on
weekends; added a wall of second-hand books that many
customers took to leafing through as they sipped their coffee
(a practice intellectually endorsed but commercially frowned on
by Marco); eventually acquired a liquor licence and became a wine
bar as well. When the small bookshop next door was about to
close down, Marco took over its lease, negotiated for an opening
to be cut in the wall between the two shops, and E.K. became a
fully-fledged bookshop. Here in Southwood Central, Marco has
seized the chance to make a lifelong dream come true: to create
an environment where people will want to sit and talk, argue and
explore serious topics while they drink superb coffee and eat
cake. (Marco himself is a peerless barista.) When things are not
busy behind the counter, Marco occasionally takes a seat at a table
where he judges the conversation is becoming interesting: having
Marco join you is regarded as a compliment by his regulars.

As they hit their mid-teens, some of the more intellectually
curious and adventurous pupils from Southwood High discover
E.K., almost as a rite of passage. They revel in the raffish ambience
Marco fosters, and feel as if they have permission to say whatever
they think and read whatever they like. The somewhat eccentric
stock of second-hand books appeals to them, and many have had
their first brush with Baldwin, Sartre, Camus, Joyce, Kerouac,
Nabokov or Jung under Marco's benign gaze. (If you're in school
uniform, he makes no objection to your taking a second-hand
book off the shelf and reading it in instalments, visit after visit.)
The one thing Marco expects is seriousness: Eine Kleine Caffeine

is not a place for teen romance – there's a milk bar down the road for that kind of frivolity.

Children are not encouraged: there are no high chairs or special menu items for children and the atmosphere makes it clear to parents that this is at the opposite end of the spectrum from McDonald's. Marco has three kids of his own, but has never aspired to run a 'family' establishment: 'This is a place for minds, not kids, to wander,' he says. 'Wandering kids are a distraction.' A distraction from serious conversation, he means.

Early on, Marco used to have small tables at which lone patrons could sit and read and drink in solitude. Then he found that, consistent with the spirit of the enterprise, people would push tables together so they could join in conversation with other patrons, including total strangers. So the small tables went, to be replaced by a couple of refectory-style tables that could accommodate up to eight people – the 'club tables' Marco calls them – and a patron perched alone at one end of a long table is now an unusual sight. Conversation is definitely on the menu at E.K. In fact, Marco has erected a sign behind the counter that says: *No, we don't have wi-fi. We'd rather you talked to each other.*

Even people who rarely patronise it appreciate the presence of E.K. in Southwood. Its very existence makes people feel good about living here and good about themselves. 'Authentic', 'old-world', 'anti-glitz', 'counter-cultural', 'Bohemian' . . . these are some of the ways the locals describe their positive feelings about E.K.

Two book clubs use E.K. as their meeting place. Committees of several organisations use it for informal discussion before and after their more formal meetings. Candidates for local council elections negotiate their voting tickets here. Key players in the local political party branches meet here to wheel and deal. Officers of council come here to thrash out their differences with each other or with disgruntled ratepayers; people from local businesses meet their accountants and solicitors here; doctors from the twenty-four-hour medical practice sometimes huddle together in a corner, their low voices discreetly debating the diagnosis of a difficult patient . . . If asked why they come here, they would all say, 'Where else would you go?' E.K. is an institution.

There was a time when the Southwood Inn served some of these purposes, but the character of the pub has been forever changed by the introduction of serried ranks of poker machines and other gambling devices, and by the continuous running of horse races – some of them computer simulations – on a huge monitor in the bar. The poker machine invasion, in particular, has transformed the character of the pub from a place for social drinking and eating to a place increasingly devoted to solitary gambling. Serious conversation is no longer possible, though the pub's role as a social hub is somewhat restored on Friday and Saturday nights during the football season, when a large crowd gathers to watch a game on the giant screen. Trivia nights run on behalf of local charities are also popular at the pub, though Marco occasionally runs those as well. If it's an E.K. event, Marco insists on the questions being set by an academic who frequents the establishment – 'trivia', in those cases, being something of a misnomer.

E.K. is also the scene of regular performances by local musicians, and Marco has instituted a monthly poetry night, when people are encouraged to read their favourite poems and local poets can strut their stuff to a receptive audience.

Marco's greatest thrill, though, is when groups of students drop in on their way home from university, particularly on Thursday nights, and the place rings with debate, much of it heated, about issues that apparently arise more naturally here than in the rather sterile coffee shops provided on the Kentwell campus or in the tutorials that the students tell Marco are too big and too formal to permit robust exchanges. This is when Marco feels his dream really is coming true: when he sees earnest young people locked in argument over wine or coffee, voices raised, fists sometimes coming down on his tables and other patrons pausing to hear what the rising generation's take might be on the meaning of life.

The schools

School communities are rather like tribes. The much-vaunted 'school spirit' has a powerfully bonding effect on the members of those communities – teachers, pupils, parents (though it's often the teachers who are most restrained in these matters and the parents least so). Inevitably, the tribal spirit sometimes generates feelings of hostility towards the tribes of other schools. Religion plays its part here, too: faith-based schools have a kind of double-barrelled identity which creates a double target for inter-school hostility – or, in its more civilised manifestation, friendly inter-school rivalry.

School-based tribalism is at its most naked on the sporting field, where even the youngest teams are decked out like mini-professionals, with parents lining the field, making video recordings and shouting encouragement or criticism as if their personal reputations were at stake. Referees of school games occasionally have to banish a parent from the sidelines in an attempt to lower the temperature and restore some civility to the proceedings.

Rivalries naturally extend to academic performance as well: parents get to know where the 'gun' teachers are, and which schools are doing best in preparing primary children for the secondary school of their parents' choice.

Among younger children, the pupils of other schools simply appear alien, rather like children from another suburb: different, rather than threatening. The full tribal power of 'school spirit' is not typically felt until the upper-primary and secondary school years: puberty, in this way as in so many others, tends to bring out our most primitive urges, and none is more primitive than the tribal urge.

The role of schools as local community hubs can be seen in the swarming of parents around the school gates when children are being dropped off and collected; in the crowds that attend fundraising activities; in the willingness of parents and grandparents to volunteer to coach slow readers, mentor students who are struggling academically or socially, paint classrooms, run barbecues at sports carnivals, serve in the school canteen, offer clerical assistance in the school office or library, or help with supervision on school excursions and camps. It can be seen in the intense interest shown in the appointment of new school or preschool principals, and in any school-based gossip. It's not only a matter of schools and preschools being places where our children are being educated, nurtured and influenced by strangers (so we want to know as much as possible about those strangers); it's also that a local school is a highly visible symbol of the health and wellbeing of a community.

That's a two-way street. A strong local community is likely to show a strong – and generally benign – interest in the performance of its local public schools, and a school that appears to be function-ing well is a source of pride for its local community. 'Functioning well' is, of course, a highly subjective term, but parents and other adults in the community are generally impressed by a combination of academic and sporting performance, though outstanding art and music (particularly in kindergarten and lower-primary classes) also attract strong approval. The behaviour of children in the community beyond the school is an enduring focus of attention: politeness and courtesy towards each other and towards adults they encounter in the street or on public transport are widely regarded as indicators of a 'good' school.

The strength of the link between local communities and their schools varies greatly, mainly under the influence of the personal style of the school principal: when it comes to being integrated with the local community, some principals are keener and more creative than others. Generally speaking, the heads of state schools seem more attuned to the concept than is typical of private schools. With some admirable exceptions, the neighbourhood that surrounds a private school is unlikely to feel any particular connection with the school at all, unless it impinges in a negative way on the lives of the locals – by creating traffic congestion, for instance, or unacceptable noise levels, or through the antisocial behaviour of its pupils. Private schools often function like 'islands' in their neighbourhoods, and sometimes attract local hostility as a result. Being a good neighbour is rarely articulated as one of the criteria of a 'good' school, and when buildings and other infrastructure are under contemplation or construction, a school's neighbours may feel as if they have no real link to the process – perhaps not feeling as if they were seriously consulted about its impact on their lives. When private schools (themselves generously funded by government grants) fail to share such facilities as playing fields, auditoriums and libraries with less well-resourced government schools in the area, or with the community at large, this only widens the perceived chasm between the school and its local neighbourhood.

Universities have sometimes been criticised on the same grounds. Addressing the 2013 conference of the Association of Commonwealth Universities, the (now retired) vice-chancellor of the University of Western Sydney, Professor Janice Reid, acknowledged that there have been periods 'when universities, at least in public perception, have been more isolated and inward-looking than they have been engaged or embedded in the lives of those who through their taxes help to fund them, or those who experience their presence, not always welcome, in their neighbourhoods'. Reid quotes examples of several universities that, having previously remained aloof from their local communities, had found ways of connecting and engaging. The most dramatic case was the University of Pennsylvania, where 'the murder of a faculty member, the shooting of a student and a rash of armed robberies near the campus, were the initial spur to a multifaceted program of outreach, city partnerships, student volunteering, information exchange and joining of hands with local residents and organisations in university-led urban renewal'. In *The University and Urban Revival* (2007), the president of the University of Pennsylvania, Judith Rodin, wrote: 'If Penn could make discoveries that contributed to saving lives and driving the global economy, then surely we could demonstrate both the capacity and moral obligation to use our intellectual might to make things right at our doorstep.'

Most private schools see themselves as self-contained 'villages'; school families that have no particular link with their neighbourhood and no desire to forge one. If they perceive their own 'school family' as part of a larger 'extended family', that will typically be the pool of schools that compete against each other in sport. School spirit and the more obvious signs of tribalism (uniforms, argot, accent, attitudes) are perhaps most strongly associated with private schools, and that reinforces the reluctance of the members of private-school communities to forge connections with the neighbourhood that surrounds the school.

Australian parents, unusually among Western societies, are showing an increasing preference for private (non-government) schools for their children's secondary education. Perhaps this is inevitable in a society that has lost its appetite for egalitarianism, but it tends to promote social divisions, heighten and institutionalise a sense of 'class', and foster feelings of entitlement, exclusivity and superiority among the children who attend such schools. There are many wonderful exceptions, of course: some private schools actively promote the sharing of their facilities with less well-endowed government schools or with the community-at-large; some invite their neighbours to attend school events; some tour their musical groups to deprived or remote areas, rather than following the fashion for lavish overseas tours.

Southwood has seven primary schools (five public, two Roman Catholic) and one secondary school, Southwood High. The citizens feel some communal pride whenever the *Gazette* features academic, sporting, creative or other achievements by pupils from the local schools. Stories about the exploits of Southwood children who attend private schools in other suburbs evoke a more ambiguous response: there's a strong public-education lobby group in Southwood that regards families who send their children 'away' to private schools as traitors to the cause. A serious push by nearby Lewis Grammar School to establish a feeder primary school in Southwood Fields was strongly resisted: the pupils of Lewis Grammar have acquired a reputation for arrogance that does not endear them to the Southwood community. The only other private school close to Southwood, Kentwell College, has such a formidable reputation for sporting prowess that its pupils are generally stereotyped as mere 'jocks' – thereby attracting a complex blend of awe and derision from other school-based tribes and, indeed, from the Southwood community more generally.

The contest for places at Southwood's twenty-five preschools and day-care centres is ferocious. The demand is driven by a combination of a well-established acceptance of the value of preschool education and the desire for a place where children below school age will be both safe and stimulated while their parents are at work all day. The concept of the two-income family is now so deeply entrenched – and so powerfully linked to the image of the modern, well-educated, liberated woman – that the very idea of either father or mother staying home with the children seems bizarre, 'backward', financially impractical or, for many affluent couples, simply unthinkable.

Finland is often cited as the world's best school education system, and some people are puzzled when they hear that Finnish children only begin primary school at the age of seven. While that's true, it's also true that most of them begin preschool at the age of three, so they typically have four years of play-based learning before being exposed to the more formal demands of the classroom.

Helga, the director of the Southwood Fields preschool, is in no doubt about the value of preschool education for her children.

I recently attended a conference where a British academic was extolling the virtues of preschool education and my colleagues and I were all nodding and smiling enthusiastically. We see all the wonderful effects of socialisation, and the responsiveness of children to having stories read to them, and the joy of learning to sing and dance and paint. Some of them come from pretty sad circumstances, and we know that what we're doing can help make up for some of the deficiencies in homes where no one reads stories or sings, or even plays music to them.

Anyway, this chap put a chart on the screen showing some quantitative measures of the long-term benefits of preschool education. A couple of the items were okay – like kids with a preschool education were less likely to become criminals. Good, I thought; you'd certainly hope so. But then he proudly showed the indicators of the benefits in later life and do you know what they were? Higher incomes. More expensive homes. More expensive cars. I couldn't believe it. I wanted to call out: What about kindness? What about learning tolerance and respect for other people? What about getting that wonderful sense of belonging to a community outside the family at such an early age? What about being accepted and valued, and learning to accept and value others?

I'd like to think that these are the *real* benefits, but I guess they're hard to quantify. And when I was chatting to my colleagues over the morning tea break at that conference, you know what? They thought the parents would be pretty pleased with the idea that we were setting their kids on the road to higher incomes and bigger houses. Maybe they're right. But I see the benefits of belonging to our little preschool community for the parents as well as the children. We have social events – and not just for fundraising – like barbecues and film nights, and I do little seminars for the parents on aspects of child development.

So, okay, maybe they want their little darlings to end up with big houses and flash cars, and maybe there are material benefits, long-term, from the preschool experience, but I'd like to think we're giving the children and their families something much richer than that along the way – even if they don't realise they're getting it. I like to think of these children as precious little people, not potential merchant bankers. '

In the staffroom at Southwood Fields primary school, Petra Ritchie is immersed in a conversation that has turned, as it often does, to the vexed questions of teacher quality, school funding, and the tensions that arise between teachers and overanxious parents with inflated impressions of their children's abilities and/or unrealistic expectations about what the school should do for them. The teachers often say that, these days, the parents are more trouble than the kids. Let's listen to staffroom conversation . . .

'I suppose it sounds funny coming from a teacher, but not everything can be perfect, even in the best-run school. People talk about "education" as if it's the be-all and end-all, and of course

I agree up to a point, but it depends what you mean by education. After all, kids learn from bad experiences as well as good ones, don't you think?'

'Absolutely!' says Petra. 'Some of those appalling old-school teachers who seemed so cold and robotic ... I mean, they'd devoted their lives to teaching and they were doing their best –'

'And they gave us a rich source of anecdote, of course. They were the ones we talked about most. I once had a teacher – this was in a supposedly-classy private school – and if anyone put their hand up to ask a question, he'd say, "Put that thing down – we've gotta breathe this air." It wasn't exactly ideal pedagogy, but I suppose we muddled through, and now I'm a teacher!'

'Yes, I've often wondered about that, too. I sometimes think the very injustice of it taught us about injustice – and also taught us about the value of interaction between teachers and pupils because we were so often denied it.'

'It seems crazy, doesn't it, but it's not only schools – it's institutions in general where authority is vested in people regardless of their incompetence, pomposity, insensitivity or insecurity. Maybe kids have to learn that when they're at school – respect the teacher for being the teacher, even if she isn't the greatest teacher in the world. You're going to come across a lot of people whose position you'll have to respect, even if they don't strike you as being too brilliant. Does this make sense? I mean, school is the place where most of us learnt about the abuse of power. God, I certainly knew all about unfairness before I'd left primary school.'

'That's pretty true, but I wouldn't say so to any of my parents. "Yeah, I guess I fucked up, but don't worry, your child has to learn that teachers aren't perfect." Imagine the reaction!'

'Well, that's the truth. We aren't perfect. And we aren't perfect as sporting referees or officials, either. Remember that mother who rushed up to me after the sports carnival last year claiming to have video evidence of the fact that her son had come third in his race, not fourth? That's what we're up against.'

'I wouldn't say this outside this room but, you know, I sometimes wonder if all the fuss about facilities is justified. Sure, we want decent facilities, but I quite like the fact that this place isn't exactly state-of-the-art.'

'You can say that again.'

'But do you see what I mean? My husband works in the corporate world and he says it's an axiom of corporate life that once the perfect office premises have been constructed, the rot sets in: complacency, arrogance, triumphalism . . . he reckons the United Nations started losing its punch after it moved into its grand headquarters in New York – they were better off when they were muddling along in less than ideal circumstances.'

'That raises the whole question of school funding, of course. We keep being told that money for schools has doubled in the past ten years and yet, by the measure of Naplan and other tests of literacy and numeracy, we've been going steadily backwards. So whoever thought the answer was to throw more money at the schools? Teacher training – that's where the money should be going. If you really want better schools and better outcomes, up the quality of the teaching, don't spend more money on buildings and equipment.'

'Try telling that to Kentwell College! Have you seen the new grandstand at their sportsground? I mean, it's like a mini-Olympic stadium over there. And they solved their space problem – so-called – by building their new gymnasium underground. Where did the money come from for that?'

'Oh, they had a building appeal, of course, but we all know where most of the money came from – us! The taxpayers! Those parents want to opt out of the public education system but they still expect public money to help them do it. I honestly don't get it.'

'Anyway, you know what I'm saying? They can have their grand buildings and their sports psychologists ... and their peptide program, for all I know. Sure, we complain about some of our facilities being substandard, but we make do, and I think it's quite good for the kids not to have it all laid on for them.'

'You know what? The fact that we have to get parents to help out with jobs around the school, and a bit of volunteering in the office and even in the classroom, I think that does wonders for their involvement with the school. They get a real insight into the way the place works. They get to know the boss in a less formal way. And they see us all doing our best – I mean, who's more conscientious than a bunch of primary school teachers? We're on stage all day. We can't just duck out for coffee with a mate. I think it's good for parents to see what we do, up close.'

'Good point. If it's all fully resourced and everything's beautiful – well, they'll think *everything* has to be perfect. And it won't be, of course. This is not an argument for shoddy equipment – we desperately need a new scanner – but I'm just saying that too much glitz creates the wrong atmosphere for the parents as well as the kids.'

In the staffroom at Southwood High, the teachers are up in arms about a different issue: they've heard the government is devising a test to assess the suitability – perhaps even the level of passion and commitment – of students wanting to become teachers.

'We'll be next,' warns the head of science, darkly. 'Once they've devised the test, why stop at students? Why not hunt down the passionless teachers and weed them out?'

The PE teacher nods sagely. 'I could see this coming. Haven't I always said these seismic rumbles about performance pay are just the tip of the iceberg?'

The head of English mentally stores this up for her next departmental meeting. The PE teacher is a reliable source of mixed metaphors and has found his way, anonymously, into several exam questions.

The mention of performance pay sets the head of science off again. 'Ah, yes. Performance pay. Wonderful concept. I think we all agree, don't we, that performance pay for teachers should be the very next thing the government does after it introduces performance pay for ministers, all the way up to prime ministers? Brilliant!'

'Enough politics,' says Marcus Li, the deputy principal. 'Did you realise Southwood is soon to celebrate its centenary and there's to be a festival?'

Groans all around the room.

'Hang on. Give us a moment. Everyone is supposed to be thinking of things they can do to contribute. People will expect the school to come up with something. Will you give it some thought? I'm sure the music department will get involved – Julian? What about history? What about drama? What about science and technology? Anyway, I'll raise it again at next week's meeting. Meanwhile, has anyone had any creative ideas for solving the parking problem? The volunteers are complaining there's nowhere for them to park, and I think they have a point. They are doing us a favour, after all. Can we all take another look at car-pooling, please?'

All Southwood's schools are supported by active parents' associations. For some parents, the school attended by their children becomes the focal point of their community involvement, and the schools tap into this engagement by offering a variety of volunteering opportunities for parents to become involved in the life of the school. Some schools also run educational programs for parents on aspects of child psychology, on the principles of modern education and the content of the curriculum. The more adventurous principals – including Rick Swanson at Southwood High – have also instituted courses on parenting, with the dual purpose of shifting some of the responsibility for child-rearing back from the school to the family, and encouraging parents to adopt a more realistic set of expectations about the role of the school in their children's lives. Rick is fond of saying that the two things parents most often expect of a school – values and discipline – are really the two most fundamental things a child should receive from its parents.

Two of the primary schools have a breakfast program for children whose parents are so rushed and harried in the mornings that they seem not to be able to find time to feed their children. Two others have devised community service programs for their year five and six pupils in which the children visit a local nursing home or retirement village, sometimes to sing for them and chat individually to the residents, and sometimes to do odd jobs around the grounds and garden. The children are carefully briefed on how to manage these various tasks and they invariably return to the school with a glow of satisfaction and a fund of stories about what the residents have said or done. Some parents also participate in these visits. The school principals say their purpose is not only to brighten the lives of the residents of these places, but to introduce children to the idea of volunteering and community engagement as a normal part of life.

At Southwood High, deputy principal Marcus Li's community garden project has been successfully functioning as a 'mini-hub', not only in engaging the refugees for whom he designed it, but also in bringing the school's own neighbours into the project and, in turn, into personal contact with refugees they might otherwise never have met.

As part of a council initiative, Southwood's schools have been encouraged to help cement their connections with their local neighbourhoods by opening their playgrounds after school hours, allowing children and their parents to use the school grounds as 'village greens'. Volunteer rangers were appointed and trained by the council to provide low-key supervision, and the council subsidised the extension of schools' existing public liability insurance to cover school grounds outside school hours.

School premises have also been opened to various adult education and musical groups, so the old criticism that public school premises were seriously under-utilised is gradually receding in the face of some creative 'dual occupancies'. The consequence is that some of the school premises are becoming social hubs even for people who don't have children attending them.

Looking back at their school years, most people unhesitatingly acknowledge the value of their primary education – literacy, numeracy, basic history and geography and science – but there's less consistency in their recollections of the secondary-school experience. Some individual teachers are warmly remembered and praised for having been inspirational; some are dismissed as pathetic; some are recalled as having behaved like adversaries; most are simply seen as the adults who populated the school community and were more or less colourful contributors to school life. The example of their behaviour *as adults* – ranging from the clothes they wore to the way they spoke or their level of respect for their pupils – often turned out to be more influential and memorable than the specific content of their lessons: *We had this really stylish French teacher – I think she taught us more about how to be a woman than how to speak French.*

Achievements in music, sport and art are sometimes recalled with incredulity: *Did I really do that?* The burden of homework seemed particularly and even pointlessly onerous; exams were often associated with stress and a sense of futility. But there's one point on which recent school-leavers themselves generally agree (and it's a point that older people, looking back, will generally acknowledge): the school experience was mainly about 'my friends' or 'the group'. Here's a nineteen-year-old ruminating on school life, soon after leaving Southwood High:

> When you're still there, you can't wait for it to be over *and*, at the same time, you're dreading leaving because you realise you won't be spending every day with your friends. Even if you all go to the same uni, which is unlikely, it won't be the same – you'll be in different faculties and stuff. And then, when you've left, you wish you were back, for that daily contact with your friends who were really like your family. You certainly don't want to go back for the exams, which were overrated anyway. The final exams were the worst – as if your whole life was being determined by a single mark. It was a real anticlimax when it actually happened – all that build-up and then … nothing. You asked yourself, 'What was that all about?' I don't suppose I'll actually *need* anything I learnt at high school, except as a prerequisite for something else. Some of the teachers were all right, but the main thing was your friends. That's what I miss. And the feeling of being part of that school community – sounds a bit random, but it was true. The school was good at making you feel as if you belonged, and that's what the good teachers did, too. It was a safe place.

Bad school experiences, by contrast, can have a devastatingly negative effect. When school feels to a pupil like a fundamentally unfriendly place, nothing can adequately compensate for that sense of alienation. Being socially excluded, feeling out of tune with the values and ethos of a school, feeling as if teachers are 'the enemy', being ridiculed or humiliated by a small number of fellow pupils or by even one teacher can all contribute to the sense that 'I don't belong here'. Here's one case:

❝I went to a perfectly good school – at least, that's what everyone said. But I couldn't wait to leave and I've never been back since. Kids who were good at sport were the heroes. If you didn't happen to be – and I didn't – you just didn't rate. There was this one maths teacher who took a total dislike to me – 'Wimpy Wal' he called me. He picked on me in every lesson and even mocked me when I did well – 'a great miscarriage of justice,' I remember him saying when I topped some test or other. It had a strange effect on the other kids in the class. They started acting as if there was something wrong with me, too. A couple of them were sympathetic, but almost as if I was a retarded kid. It really distanced me from them – and from the whole school, really. I used to dread those lessons, and so I began to dread going to the school. Looking back, I'd say I was permanently on the defensive, permanently anxious. Not a good frame of mind for learning, was it? Now, when I see how much my own kids love going to their school, and I hear the principal talking about 'the school family', I think how different it could all have been.❞

What is the purpose of education? Everyone has their own answer to that – ranging from learning 'the basics' or equipping yourself for the workforce or 'learning how to think' all the way up to discovering pathways to enlightenment. Whatever the academic or vocational purposes might be, every society with a formal school education system uses it to socialise and acculturate its young. So perhaps it's not surprising that, in retrospect, many people value that aspect of their school experience most highly. They are recalling a community where they were learning how to belong.

The churches

Local parish churches used to act as social as well as spiritual hubs for the neighbourhood. They were places where the community gathered – not just for church services, weddings, baptisms and funerals, but also for fetes and festivals, dances, concerts, Sunday school classes, and even sport: many churches once had a tennis court or organised social games at the local district courts, and church-based cricket and football teams in local competitions were not uncommon.

Church attendance has declined in many Western countries (in Australia, like the UK, only about 8 percent of the population attend church weekly, rising to about 25 percent at festivals such as Christmas and Easter, though more than 60 percent of the population still describe themselves as 'Christian' in the census). The role of local churches has therefore undergone a significant change. In Australia, there are still more churches than schools, though many church buildings stand idle except for a few hours per week and few of them have retained the status of genuine neighbourhood hubs. Yet, for the faithful, they remain unique meeting places where the members of the congregation can enjoy encounters with like-minded people who are not going to question their world-view, but reinforce it, and where they will be regularly reminded that they belong to a religious community, both local and global.

Today, churches that create something akin to a 'village within a church' (as opposed to the old 'church within a village') are experiencing a boom in attendance. Some of the so-called megachurches now attract congregations in their thousands, and the people who attend say they appreciate the strong sense of community they find there, generated not only by being part of a large and enthusiastic congregation – the well-documented bandwagon effect – but also by participation in the many other activities on offer, designed to engage and occupy them. These range from weekly discussion groups to children's activities, youth groups calibrated to particular ages, women's meetings, music ensembles, welfare and social justice agencies and annual conferences. The biggest of them boast professional marketing and catering operations as well as more conventional ministries.

Some of the larger city cathedrals and churches report steady attendance. For some people, it's a place to belong in an unfriendly and even hostile urban environment and, again, that sense of belonging is fostered through activities that range well beyond the formal weekly services to include meditation and study groups, adult education classes, retreats, conferences and social activities.

Such feelings of belonging may be even more intense for people who attend non-Christian places of worship, such as Jewish synagogues and Muslim mosques, in traditionally Christian societies. Their status as 'minorities' (sometimes even persecuted minorities) combines with the richness of their own unique rituals to reinforce both their religious and cultural identities.

Southwood has five churches. The Roman Catholic Church, with a Vietnamese priest, has the largest, most stable and most multi-ethnic congregation; the Anglican Church has been in sharp decline but maintains a faithful, though ageing, core of parishioners of mainly English descent. Because of the pleasing acoustics of the building, it has also developed a new role as a concert venue for musical events unrelated to the life of the church. The Uniting Church is struggling with dwindling numbers, though a new minister, Holly Greenwood, has attracted some young people to her 'Love In Action' program, aimed at offering practical help – gardening, cleaning, painting, shopping, reading – to elderly and disadvantaged members of the community. There's also a small but strong Greek Orthodox Church, providing a gathering place for a rather scattered congregation drawn from well beyond Southwood. And then there's Jim Glasson's Southwood East Community Church –

a place that Jim would say has tried to maintain the traditional role of the local parish church.

Jim was a Southwood boy, raised in the Fields, who, from the age of ten, aspired to enter the ministry of the Methodist Church. He went to Southwood High, then to university and then straight into theological college, in spite of the many people who told him he needed more 'life experience' first.

From the beginning, he loved his work. His passion was connecting people with each other: Jim was always a great networker with an aptitude for forging links between churches and their local neighbourhoods. By the time the Methodists threw in their lot with the Congregationalists and most of the Presbyterians to form the Uniting Church, Jim had become deeply disillusioned with the institution. He was a controversial figure who was regarded as 'difficult' by the church hierarchy, partly because of his emphasis on trying to meet the needs of the whole community rather than trying to increase the size of his own congregation, partly because of his outspoken opposition to Australia's involvement in the Vietnam war, and partly because of his vocal support for the decriminalisation of drugs: 'Prohibition has never worked anywhere,' he insisted, 'so why do they think it will work here?' When the Uniting Church merger was announced, Jim decided to accept an invitation to return to Southwood to lead a small independent congregation meeting in what had once been a Methodist Church, styling themselves 'Southwood East Community Church' and having a loose affiliation with three similarly non-denominational congregations in nearby suburbs.

The word 'community' sometimes causes them to be confused with the various manifestations of the Pentecostal movement – Christian City, Planetshakers, Hillsong, Metro, Christian Life, Assemblies of God – none of which has a presence in Southwood, but Jim's group is located at a quite different point on the theological spectrum and has never attracted the vast numbers drawn to the Pentecostalists' megachurches. Jim and his ilk are determinedly non-charismatic (no 'speaking in tongues', clapping or swooning, for instance) and are strongly committed to a liberal theology linked to a strong social conscience.

Let's hear Jim's approach from the man himself:

I'm under no illusions about the reasons people come to my church, or any church. One of my closest friends is a Jewish rabbi and he's fond of quoting his grandfather: 'Jews go to the synagogue to sit next to other Jews.' There's more to it than that, of course, but the social drivers are very, very powerful. Religious practice has always been communal, tribal, from the most ancient and primitive times. Take one of the distinctively Christian rituals – the communion – that's a symbol of the fact that we belong to each other. 'We are the body of Christ', we say. Corporate, see? You can't get away from the social dimension. That's why the Muslims pray *together.*

I'm certainly not in the business of setting up hurdles for people to jump over before they can feel welcome here. If they come for the social context, what's wrong with that? Some people go to cathedrals for the music or the robes and rituals, or the incense. Okay by me. If people come here in search of a community that makes them feel as if they belong, somewhere safe, then I'm delighted. What they choose to believe is their business. I recommend the Christian faith to them, naturally, but I don't push it and I certainly don't demand it. This is a hybrid community, and any healthy community thrives on diversity and difference more than the stifling conformity you see in some churches. I think that's why so many people eventually feel as if they have to escape – the demands are too rigid, too formulaic.

Most of my parishioners do have some form of religious faith and, as I see it, that's a source of dignity and comfort for them, not oppression. If their faith consoles them, that's wonderful. I don't want to be peddling a religion based on fear and guilt – there are plenty of other places they can go if guilt's what they're after. Some people come here when they've become disillusioned with other churches – they often use the word 'relief' to describe how they feel about this place. I can't see that as anything but good.

We have our share of agnostics, and why not? Faith is a great leap of the imagination and even people who take the leap often find they are plagued by doubt. I'd even say they go hand in hand, faith and doubt. I do feel that if there's any room for doubt, there's room for some kind of faith – or at least for the possibility of faith.

I'm often criticised for being too tolerant. 'Look at the churches that are growing,' people say to me. 'They are more hardline, more prescriptive about what they expect people to believe – that's what their people want.' Well, okay, that's what *some* people want and they know where they can get it. I'm a bit unfashionable, I guess. Still, we have a grand time here. Lots of robust debate and dissent. Some of our Friday night meetings become a bit rowdy and some pretty heretical things get said. There are no holds barred. We call them our Gold Panner sessions – we pick up plenty of gravel and mud as well as getting the occasional speck of gold. When it comes to the crunch, I'm always prepared to put what I see as the Christian position.

I admit I concentrate more on reaching out to the community than simply feeding my flock, if I can put it like that. Depends how you define 'flock', of course. I love to get out and meet the people. There are always new people arriving, needing a bit of a welcome, or a few introductions to neighbours, things like that. And I'm quite shameless about putting things on for the community that have no obvious connection with the life of the church, as such. I simply want people to feel welcome here, comfortable here, in case there's ever a crisis and they need someone to talk to or somewhere to go for help. If they've been here a bit, they won't feel so awkward about approaching us – for food, advice, a bit of cash, a sympathetic ear, whatever it might be.

Everybody needs to feel they belong somewhere, but not everybody has the knack of making it happen. Some are too shy, some are too wounded, some are too sad. Some are too proud, of course. A lot of people become socially isolated, even in a place like Southwood, and that can be very bad for them. There's a bit of an art to fitting in – finding your place.

The hairdresser

Field of Dreams is the only hairdressing salon in Southwood Fields. There are six other salons dotted through Southwood and competition is particularly strong in Central, but Judy Lyell is proud to say that Field of Dreams draws clients from all over Southwood. The salon has expanded steadily in the ten years she has owned it: there are now six full-time stylists, two colourists and a beauty therapist.

Judy grew up in Southwood East, worked in a large city salon as an apprentice and went to college one day a week. Once she was qualified she moved to London and worked there for five years, before returning to Southwood with an English husband – an advertising copywriter – to buy a salon with money she had inherited from her parents. Now forty, she has no children and is devoted both to the salon and to Southwood. Here's her story:

I always said that once I shook the dust of Southwood off my feet, I'd never come back. But the place sort of tugs at you, you know? All my best friends live here, and I had a fantastic childhood, really. I wasn't keen on Southwood High, but that was my fault, not theirs. I sometimes see one of my old science teachers around the place and I almost feel like going up and apologising to him for having been such a twat. I said *almost*. We just smile at each other – no hard feelings either way, I guess.

So, anyway, I came back and here I am. Love it. Wouldn't want to live anywhere else in the entire world. Really. Whenever my husband talks vaguely about going back to the UK, I tell him: 'You'd be on your own, Buster.' That quietens him down. Anyway, we go back to see his mum and dad every January when things are less busy at the salon and at his agency.

I can't tell you what it is about Southwood – there is a kind of pride in the place. You can feel it. Some people might find it boring, but there's plenty going on to keep us both interested and occupied. It's what you make of it, isn't it? Anyway, I'm six days a week in the salon.

I've never regretted taking up hairdressing – it was my dad's idea, strangely enough. I was never what you'd call academic and he felt this might be a good option; I always had a bit of an artistic streak and I love people, of course, which is practically the main thing in this business. My only regret is that I can't spend more time being a hands-on stylist – running the business takes up more of my time than I'd like.

The thing about hairdressing is that you get really, really close to a lot of your clients. They come right out and say it – it's like therapy for them. People might say beauty is skin deep, but the effects of beauty therapy are not as superficial as you might think. It's not just about making your hair look gorgeous, or getting a bit of a makeover, although those things are therapeutic in themselves – people usually walk out of here feeling terrific as well as looking terrific and if they didn't, I'd want to know why.

For a lot of my customers, it's about being touched – almost like being caressed, really. A head massage is a wonderfully therapeutic thing; people even respond to having their head held in your hands while you're sizing up what you're going to do. The beauty therapists say the same thing: their clients love the result, but they love the process, the attention, even more.

And then there's the talking. While customers are having their hair or their nails done, a lot of talking goes on, I can tell you, and a lot of listening on our part. A *lot* of listening. I always say to my staff, this is like the confessional – if I ever heard anyone repeating what a client had told them in confidence, they'd be out. These people trust us to be discreet. Nothing is off-limits – marriages, affairs, divorces, kids, mother-in-law issues, you name it. I could tell you stuff that would make your hair stand on end – no pun intended – but of course I never would. That's the whole point. This is a safe place for people – they know they can trust us with their secrets.

I'll tell you something, though. It would warm your heart to hear a lot of what we hear. People really do look out for each other around here. Some of our older ladies get driven here by neighbours, and people can be wonderfully kind if anyone is in trouble. That's another thing about older clients, too – a lot of them don't get touched as much as they did when they were younger, so that's an important thing we offer them. We try to make them look lovely, but we want them to feel lovely too. To feel . . . well, loved, I guess. Pampered, anyway. Taken seriously.

The playing fields

Here they come, descending on Dysart Park in droves. It's eight o'clock on a Saturday morning, and the place is already abuzz. They've arrived on foot, on bikes and scooters, and in advancing columns of SUVs. The under-eight football games – mixed boy and girl teams – are about to get started, their young teenage referees bustling with importance. The tennis coaches have their pint-sized charges lined up at the net for a pep talk. At the other end of the park, basketballs are being bounced and flung by young players eager to get started and irritated by bleary-eyed referees arriving late. After the first swarm of juvenile athletes has departed, there will be an ever-changing rotation of players and spectators – some district teams, some school teams – until mid-afternoon, when the really serious stuff gets under way and the young adults, hormones surging, strut their stuff on pitch and court. All day, there'll be whacking, thumping, grunting and groaning all over this vast parkland, accompanied by shouts of encouragement (and some abuse) from parents, the incessant ringing of mobile phones, the sizzle of sausages on hotplates manned by sweaty fathers, and the murmur of earnest conversation about a thousand topics that engross the dutiful mother-and-father spectators and threaten to distract them at that one crucial moment when a son or daughter most needs them to be paying attention.

'Did you see my goal?'

'It was wonderful.'

'Wonderful? It was awesome! You didn't see it, did you?'

Coaches come and go, and the appointment of a new one always provokes comment. Is he or she as good as the last one? Will there be more or less favouritism than before? Will my son/ daughter get a fair go? Though all the coaches and referees are volunteers (except in the case of tennis, where fees are willingly paid, perhaps in anticipation of a lucrative life on the professional circuit), the parents criticise them as if they are professionals and the games are a matter of life and death. For some parents, the games *are* a matter of life and death to their personal reputations. The sullen silence in some of the cars conveying members of a losing team back home is not only because of disappointed kids; it's sometimes because of absurdly, shamefully disappointed fathers.

'Why didn't you pass the ball when I told you to?'

'You can't hear anything out there, Dad. Anyway, you do better.'

On and on, the recycling of those ancient stories of hunt and battle, those ancient rivalries, those ancient tensions between the old, whose glories are long past, and the young, who have yet to prove their capacity – or even their desire – for glory.

'Competition is good for them,' the parents say to each other, trying to believe it, too often forgetting that cooperation is an even more important lesson to be learnt from team sport.

Covering five hectares, Dysart Park is a reclaimed swamp, located at the end of Hereford Street, between Southwood Ponds and Southwood East. The reclamation caused uproar in the community when it was first mooted: some people wanted the swamp preserved because of the rich bird life it encouraged; others couldn't wait to eliminate its rich insect life – particularly the outsized mosquitoes known to the locals as Southwood Greys, for which the area had become notorious.

The champion of the idea was Wally Dysart, a much-loved former footballer and long-serving Southwood councillor. His arguments prevailed and the grateful residents proposed the new playing fields, soon to become the pride of the district, should be named after him.

The park is like a magnet. All weekend, formal games take place, and there's much training activity during the week – after school and at night, under lights. Between times, the local kids throw balls and frisbees, fly their kites, chase their dogs and hatch their plans. The cricket and football clubs have a roster of retired men and women who patrol the area in the afternoons wearing fluoro jackets, supposedly to make sure no one is damaging the various playing surfaces, but also to keep a discreet eye on proceedings.

A car was once driven onto the middle of Dysart Park in the dead of night, and the signs of high-speed 'doughnuts' and skids that had carved up the surface disgusted and angered the children who found them next morning. An appeal for funds to fence the entire area was launched and the residents responded with alacrity. They know what an asset they have. They know – and their children will come to discover – that some of their most pleasant memories of life in Southwood are made right here; some of their loveliest and least demanding acquaintanceships begin here; some of their most tranquil and restorative moments are spent simply walking around the perimeter of the park, whether games are in progress or not.

Wally Dysart himself can still be seen most weekends, cruising the parkland in a motorised wheelchair and waving indiscriminately.

～

Southwood Central Mall feels like a hub to some people – though others find it too impersonal and 'artificial', and worry about its negative impact on the social role of local neighbourhood shops – a worry soon to be heightened by the construction of the Old Southwood Village development on Hereford Street.

The gym, Pilates and yoga studios feel to their patrons like mini-hubs where social connections may occur as a sideshow to the main event.

Southwood has its service clubs, a beef and burgundy club, a golf club, the Glee, the Players and other clubs and associations that feel like social hubs for the people who join them, but their selective membership makes them more like tribal stamping grounds than true hubs. The key feature of a hub is that people can be drawn to it from all over the community and you might theoretically run into anyone at all – people you like, strangers, people unlike you. It's those unplanned, unexpected, accidental encounters that teach us some of the most important lessons about the art of belonging.

6

Singletons

Demographers sometimes use strange terms to describe the categories they analyse. 'Singletons' is a classic case. It refers to people who live alone. (The same word is used in maternity wards to describe single births, as opposed to twins or triplets.)

Whatever label you use, the main thing to be said about people in this category is that it is hardly a category at all: they are an extraordinarily diverse collection of individuals who, either by choice or circumstance, happen to live by themselves.

The growth in the number of single-person households is the big story of modern Western societies. Solo households are like the 'global warming' of population statistics: a phenomenon we knew was coming but failed to appreciate the rate of its acceleration; a radical change resulting from complex causes and leading to a wide range of consequences, some yet unknown. While some demographers and economists have warned of an approaching tsunami of elderly people making increasing demands on medical and social services while no longer contributing to the economy, others have insisted that the really big demographic revolution would be the shrinking household. And so it has turned out to be: the rising incidence of one- and two-person households and the dramatic increase in the number of childless households is changing the character and culture of many neighbourhoods.

To give you an idea of how prevalent solo households are becoming: in Australia, this is the single biggest category, accounting for more than 25 percent of all households. It's also the fastest growing category, predicted to exceed 30 percent of all households by 2030. (Caution: these are *household* statistics. This doesn't mean that 30 percent of *people* will be living alone, since more people obviously live in larger households than smaller. It means that 30 percent of all households will contain just one person, which is still a huge change.) Australia is not alone in this. Western Europe and North America are on the same track – over one-third of all new households being created in the US are single-person households, and many European countries have topped the 30 percent mark – including Norway, Denmark, Germany and Belgium.

Two-person households are also more common than ever: the combination of one- and two-person households now accounts for well over 50 percent of households in most Western societies, which is why the average household size in Australia is down to about 2.5 persons, and falling.

Generalisations are pointless and insensitive to the many varieties of 'singleton'. Households have shrunk because of delayed marriage among the young, lower fertility rates, the high incidence of divorce and increased longevity – which explains why lone householders are to be found at all stages of the lifecycle. Some singletons are committed soloists who have actively sought the freedom, tranquillity and privacy of the solo household. Others are determined not to settle into this state because they didn't choose it, don't enjoy it, and are actively resisting acceptance of it: they are refusing to unpack their removal boxes, hang pictures on the wall or put plants in the pots on the balcony of their rented apartment. Some are drinking heavily to mask their loneliness; others are raising a cheerful glass to celebrate their liberation from whatever situation they had wanted to flee.

Every third household in Southwood contains just one person. Let's hear some of their stories:

I certainly never expected to be living alone, and I can't say I like it much. When my marriage ended, I really had no choice. The kids stayed with my ex-wife and I wanted to live somewhere reasonably close by, so I found this flat in Southwood Fields – it's really a granny flat at the back of someone's house. It's small enough to look after easily, but big enough for the boys to camp here on weekends and occasional weeknights, and we're allowed to use the backyard.

There are advantages, of course. You don't have to please anyone else – although maybe that isn't good for anyone, long term. A bit of give and take, a bit of compromise, keeps our feet on the ground, I always think. Anyway, for a while it felt quite liberating, going to bed whenever I felt like it, getting up when I pleased, eating whatever I liked – mostly takeaways in those first few months, I must admit. Same as television – I watched far too much television in the beginning.

Lonely? Yeah, sometimes. The weekends when I don't have the boys are the worst. It's like a big hole you have to try to fill. I have friends I can see, but they're all married and they have busy weekends. So I wait to be invited, and I'm usually not. That's natural. People don't include you so much when you become single again.

Some nights I used to lie awake and wonder how it got to this – forty years of age, alone in a tiny rented flat, no wife, no kids with me . . . but then you realise you're just feeling sorry for yourself. Lots of people – especially old people or poor people – are far worse off than I am.

It all changed for me when a mate at work suggested I should offer my services to the Ostara Foundation. It's a great organisation, set up right here in Southwood by a group of people who had a bit of spare cash and a lot of vision. They look after homeless and poor people – give them a feed each day and help find them a bed. They also offer English classes to new arrivals, mostly refugees. So I do that on alternate weekends, and it really opens your eyes. People don't realise there's a need for that kind of thing around here – it's fairly well hidden, but it's there all right.

The volunteers are a great group, too. It's like a little family in itself. They really welcome you in and make you feel part of the place. I wouldn't mind doing a bit more of it; I really look forward to those Saturdays. I've met someone there, too – a woman in a similar situation to mine. It might go somewhere; it might not. But I don't imagine myself living alone forever.

Some are pitchforked into solo living; some seek it out as a respite from the demands of group living. Many young people opt for periods of solo living as a way of asserting their independence. Their motives are quite specific and their experience is partly shaped by those motives. Yet, as we shall hear from a twenty-eight-year-old single woman living in an apartment near Southwood railway station, some themes are common to all singletons.

I shared with other girls for a few years after I moved out of home. It was great, but eventually you get sick of cleaning up after the messy ones, or making polite conversation over breakfast with some guy you've never seen before, or hassles about who owes money for the rent. So I found this gorgeous little place in Southwood Central. It's in a new block of flats, right near the station, and right in the heart of everything.

I mostly eat out – I usually grab a coffee and muffin downstairs on my way to the station in the morning.

I'd have to say I feel really, really liberated. My parents don't nag me to tidy up, and I don't have to take anyone else into consideration. I suppose it makes me a bit selfish, but it's not bad for a while. I don't think I'll still be on my own in five years, but who knows? A guy would have to be pretty good to compete with my life as it is right now.

Sometimes I eat baked beans out of a can. Sometimes I stay in my PJs all weekend. Someone said I should get a cat. *A cat?* I don't want to be responsible for anyone or anything else just now – not at this stage of my life.

Still, I'm sometimes gripped by this crazy panic about being alone. What if I get sick in the night? What if I fall over and break my leg? And sometimes, if I can't sleep, I feel really, really scared of the dark. Isn't that silly? I notice other silly things, too. I sometimes expect there to be someone in the kitchen when I come out in the morning. Or I wait for someone to come and sing 'Happy Birthday' to me while I'm still in bed. Silly things like that. It's not exactly loneliness – I'm enjoying myself too much for that. But, just for that moment, you go, *Maybe I'm not meant to be alone.*

The two people we have heard from are living alone for entirely different reasons – one involuntary and reluctant, one voluntary and enthusiastic. Yet both of them see this as a phase of their lives rather than a permanent way of living. They are classic 'episodic soloists' – people who move in and out of solo households at various stages of their lives. So we need to acknowledge that the singleton statistics are not describing an emerging breed of Westerners who have decided to become hermits for life. What the statistics are telling us is that more people than ever before will spend *some part of their lives* in solo households, often returning to a two-or-more-person household at a later stage. A snapshot of household composition, taken at any one moment, tells us that about 10 percent of Australians are living alone, but says nothing about how long this situation will remain for these particular people. Many of them will be replaced by the next wave of soloists, so the number of people who will live alone at some stage of their lives is probably closer to 20 percent of the population.

The ageing of the population means that bereaved, elderly people will generate a constant supply of new singletons. Some of them will struggle, particularly if they have never previously lived alone.

❛We had been together for over fifty years, so you can imagine. I had never lived by myself in my entire life. I went from my parents' home to the little flat we rented when we got married. That was normal in those days. So there I was, at seventy-five years old, on my own for the very first time. Five years later, I still can't bear people using that word: 'widow'.

The worst thing is getting up in the morning. The house is so quiet, and no one is offering to make me a cup of tea. I leave the radio on all day for company. Coming home at night is pretty bad, too. I've learnt to leave plenty of lights on when I go out – even if it's still daylight – and I always turn the TV on before I go out, just so the house won't seem so empty when I come back.

My son died of cancer in his forties, which was hard enough at the time, but I really miss him now. My daughter lives overseas with her husband, and I rarely see them. No grandchildren, unfortunately.

I don't know what I'd do without the neighbours. The people on both sides are kind and thoughtful. I know they'd help me out if I got into any sort of difficulty. Sometimes when I lie awake at night, I hear them coming and going and I find that quite reassuring. The young couple on one side are expecting a baby, and I'm looking forward to that.

You can feel very strange going out on your own. I try to get a friend to come with me if I want to go to the pictures, or a concert. I don't like eating in a cafe by myself, either. And I don't go to church if I know my friend isn't going to be there.

Everything would change if I got sick, of course, so I try not to think about that.

At any age, the experience of living through a spouse's illness and death creates many challenges, but the one that's hardest to anticipate is the adjustment to living alone. Families and friends tend to assume you'll just carry on as before, minus the spouse, but many people in that situation report that they never get over the loss. They simply try to find ways of minimising the ache.

In Railway Parade, Reg Blakey is coming to terms with the premature death of his wife.

Your life goes through stages, doesn't it? I used to live in a big, noisy house with my wife and five children. You never had time to think much; you certainly never had time to feel sorry for yourself. Then the kids started moving out – although one of our sons has moved back in three times – and we started talking about downsizing. We were never attracted to a retirement village, although now I must say I think it might have been a good idea. Towards the end, it was very hard to look after my wife on my own, even with the neighbours popping in regularly and offering to do bits of shopping and so on.

Anyway, now it's just me. The place is too big and I'm starting to think about moving into an apartment or a townhouse or something. I'll stay in Southwood, though.

When my wife was diagnosed, I decided to retire from work. Now I miss it, and I probably packed it in sooner than I should have. But what can you do? She needed constant care, and that meant me. But I'm not as lonely as I was when I was looking after her towards the end. Nothing cuts you off like that. I could scarcely go out without having someone here to keep an eye on her. You start to think there's nothing much going on beyond the walls of your own house. It's a strange feeling of isolation, I suppose. I sometimes used to think, 'I'll watch the news on TV – that will put me in touch.' But of course all you get is everyone else's bad news. You don't get any idea of what's happening round the corner or down the street.

These days, I'm on Facebook, and that's quite good fun, especially with the grandchildren, who are scattered all over the place, none of them close enough to visit regularly. But it's the neighbours you rely on most. Not many of the old crowd are still here, but some of the new ones are quite friendly. You don't get to know them so well – everyone's so busy, aren't they? I don't even know the surnames of some of the people in my own street.

But it still feels like 'my' street, and I love that feeling. It's my home, this street, this place – not just this house. I'm sort of locked in, what with Probus and the book club . . . and my history here, I guess. I was reading where some psychologists found that social contact and social cohesion in your neighbourhood improves wellbeing later in life. Well, I could have told them that.

I'll tell you something strange that happened at the post office, though. The woman in front of me in the queue was handing in a letter that had been wrongly delivered to her. The postmaster looked at the address and said to her, 'But this is next door to your place.' The woman said, 'I realise that, but we don't know them.' The postmaster just shook his head, and so did I. I thought it was a sign of something, but I'm not sure what. People seem to be feeling more cut off from each other. I have to try and make sure that doesn't happen to me. Which reminds me, I must go and introduce myself to the young family who've moved into number 12. I won't be baking the traditional cake, but at least I can say hello and see if they need any advice – like where's the best butcher.'

Loneliness can be a particular problem for people who have been transferred away from their home base as part of the job: many of them take immediate steps to connect with an established group that might help them find a place to belong within a new and strange community – frequenting a popular pub, joining a service or sporting club or an adult education class, attending a church, volunteering.

Even some younger people who have chosen to live alone and seem generally happy with their lot can be surprised by loneliness, like a virus lying dormant that sometimes strikes unexpectedly.

'Lonely? Sometimes it clutches at my heart. I never know when it's going to happen, but I feel very bad when it does. Sometimes I just go out – even to the supermarket – just to feel as if I'm connected to the passing parade.

I really don't understand it. I'm a reasonably intelligent, well-educated woman and I think I have my life pretty well sorted. Good job. Good friends. Supportive parents. A sister who includes me in a lot of her family stuff – I'm really enjoying being an aunt.

Then, out of the blue, *wham*! I feel like bursting into tears. It's not depression. It's not anxiety, although I admit I do get anxious sometimes, along the lines of 'what will become of me?' But, no, it's a really basic, really visceral sense that I am alone, and most people aren't. I don't even feel sorry for myself – it's not that. It's like a sickness that descends on me like some existential thing.'

Loneliness is not confined to those who live alone. Writing in the *Sydney Morning Herald*'s *Good Weekend* magazine ('All the Lonely People', 31 August 2013), Stephanie Wood described a Facebook exchange with a friend who was married with kids, had plenty of friends and gave the impression of leading a full and satisfying life. In spite of all that, this man revealed that loneliness had been his lifelong companion.

Feeling lonely in a crowd is not an uncommon experience. Even being in the midst of a friendly, noisy group can be an isolating experience if this does not feel like a place where you belong; if there is no sense of connection or acceptance at a level deeper than superficial sociability.

Though it can strike anyone, at odd times and in unexpected places, loneliness is a more obvious hazard for singletons than for people in multiple-person households. If the antidote to loneliness is the comfort of companionship, then being isolated in a single-person household creates the obvious difficulty that such companionship might not always be available on demand. Wood also quoted journalist Sam de Brito, who is separated from his partner and experiences his most acute loneliness when he is left alone after visiting his young daughter: 'It sits in my stomach; it's like a cold ball of intense negativity.' That's a common experience among parents who have been reduced to 'visiting rights' after a separation or divorce. The aching sense of absence, and even of exclusion, is one of the most distressing demonstrations of the need to belong.

All of which raises some big questions. You won't find me arguing for people to stay together in relationships that have come to seem pointless, perhaps because they've lost their passion or even their comfortable sense of companionship and mutual support. Nor would I ever argue that a destructive or corrosive relationship should be persevered with beyond a reasonable attempt, perhaps with the aid of a counsellor, to establish whether it's worth salvaging. But our understanding of the power of belonging and the inherently social nature of our being does raise some interesting issues. How often have you heard people who have abandoned a relationship reflect wistfully, perhaps years later, that 'it wasn't so bad' or even that 'I think we could have maintained a good relationship and supported each other, even if it wasn't the marriage we had originally wanted or expected'? Such reassessments are most poignant where children are involved and where, on reflection, parents wonder if it was worth putting their children – even their adult offspring – through the trauma of a marriage break-up.

One factor contributing to such reflections is the awareness – often too late – that a marriage with children is a family, and a family is a community. A family is a place where not only the children but also the adults have a right to feel that they belong. The pain of loneliness described by Sam de Brito – and all the other parents (including me) who've been caught in that process – is as sharp as it is precisely because it feels like rejection; exclusion; the sense that, suddenly, there's nowhere you belong. There may be plenty of other networks and communities where we do, in fact, belong, but at a time of such intense, wrenching pain, that scarcely feels like compensation.

The decision to leave any relationship, particularly one that has produced children, is a classic case of the tension between a personal, individual desire for liberation (or whatever other personal goal is involved), and the demands of our social obligations to the small community we have created and nurtured. I repeat: this is not an argument for staying; it's an argument for taking *both* needs – the individual's and the family's – into account before deciding whether to stay or go.

When Leonie Mills left her marriage, she was absolutely deter-mined to go, even though she couldn't really explain why to her friends – and not even to her husband's satisfaction. After she'd settled in Southwood Central, she often found herself reflecting on how it had all happened.

⁶Some of my friends couldn't understand what was driving me when I left my marriage – some of them still can't. It was just a very clear sense that I was finished with that marriage and I had to get out. I had to find clear air, or something. So I bought this apartment in Southwood, close to the station, and I've been on my own ever since.

Early on, the freedom was heavenly. I could be alone when I wanted to be, with friends when I wanted to be. I could go out or stay home – it was entirely up to me. I was retired from work and my ex-husband was generous with the property settlement, so there was more flexibility in my life than I'd ever experienced.

The strange thing is, in spite of all I've said, I sometimes wish I'd never left. I sometimes wonder if we could have worked it out. What if I had simply told my husband I didn't want a sexual relationship any more? I wouldn't have minded him going off and having an affair, actually, if that was what he wanted. But I just wonder if we could have maintained a functioning family, a functioning household. Does that sound odd? People come to all kinds of arrangements – I realise that now – and I think the kids have never quite forgiven me for leaving.

Don't get me wrong – I love my apartment. The neighbours in this block are a bit stand-offish, but pleasant. I've linked up with a few women in the neighbourhood who are in a similar situation to mine, but I haven't found any soulmates. Two of them have discovered new partners – women, actually – and I find I quite envy them. Perhaps that's what was wrong with me all those years when I felt so uncomfortable in my marriage.

But when I'm at home sometimes – especially at night – I feel really conscious of the fact that there's no one else here. I suppose I'll eventually get to feel as if I belong in the local neighbourhood, but I haven't pushed that and, in any case, a single woman in her fifties is pretty invisible around here. It's all couples and young people. And my close friends aren't from Southwood – I usually meet them in the city. I'm not even sure why I moved to Southwood, frankly. The price was right, I liked the apartment . . . what else can I say? I was desperate to make a fresh start.

So, yes. I guess it's a form of loneliness. Yearning, really. What did I give up? Could we have kept it all together on some basis? Am I better off now than I was then? How did this happen, exactly? It's not how I expected to be living at this stage of my life – that's for sure.

Security looms as a major issue for many people living alone. Whether young or old, singletons are frequently gripped by the need to take extraordinary precautions to protect themselves and make their home feel safe. Some report becoming obsessive about locking doors and windows at night – including internal doors – and then worrying about how they would be rescued if there were some emergency. Some develop little rituals that reassure them all is well: turning on outside security lights before they retire, or checking and rechecking that power points are turned off, or locking doors and hiding the keys.

Some find themselves worrying into the night about their health, and how they would obtain help if they needed it. Some focus on the problem of financial security, worrying about the fact that 'it's all up to me'. Festivals like Christmas, strongly associated with families and communities, are a special challenge, as are sensational news items – extreme weather events, terrorist attacks – that remind them of the vulnerability of being all alone in a crisis.

Singletons typically seek no sympathy, especially if this is the state they have chosen for themselves. They don't wish to be regarded as unusual, let alone pitiable, because they know they are part of a growing proportion of the population, being increasingly catered for by housing developers, supermarkets, cafes and travel companies. In any case, for virtually all of them, aloneness has its pleasures and compensations.

And yet, the niggling doubt is always there: am I meant to be alone? Is this the best way for people to live? Is this all there is? The answer, of course, is that this is not all there is. Even the most contented singletons are still social creatures with social needs, including, most particularly, the need to belong. The solution is not necessarily to move into a larger household; the solution is to find communities – friendship circles, work groups, associations, groups of every kind – where you can feel both connected and sustained and where the great paradox of the human condition will be revealed: that we become whole by responding to the needs of others.

At the Southwood East Community Church, Pastor Jim Glasson had been looking for ways to increase the relevance of his 'faith community' to the life of the wider neighbourhood. Towards the end of the year, he became aware of the growing number of people who were planning to spend Christmas on their own. He mentioned this to his GP, Aubrey Jones, when he went in for a check-up and was surprised to hear that Aubrey was concerned about the very same thing among his patients.

The two of them teamed up and staged a Christmas dinner for singles in the church hall. They were swamped with responses and the event was such a success they resolved not only to make it an annual affair, but to start holding regular social events for singles throughout the year. Thus was born the Southwood East Singles, the name suggested by Aubrey. He thought 'SES' would catch on (forgetting, momentarily, the association of those initials with emergency services of a quite different kind). Everyone hated the name and it quickly became known among the regulars as 'J&A's dating agency' and then simply 'J&A's'. It boomed and, to Jim's delight, began attracting people who had no other connection with his church. He and Aubrey took it in turns to plan and run the monthly meetings, often in the form of outings to local restaurants or sometimes to the cinema. They also invited an assortment of visiting speakers – local historians, artists, authors – but there was a particularly strong response whenever either Jim or Aubrey themselves offered to speak about their own non-professional interests: Jim was a keen birdwatcher with an impressive collection of video footage shot locally, and Aubrey was an authority on the mating habits of primates – his talks, also lavishly illustrated, were received with bug-eyed eagerness, being the closest thing to pornography most of the members of the group had seen.

Two problems emerged as J&A's evolved. One was the number of singles in the group who had paired off during the course of the first year. While Jim welcomed this romantic development, he was unsure whether to suggest to the people concerned that, being couples, they might no longer be qualified to attend. On the other hand, several of these pairings proved to be short-lived, and the people concerned were soon welcomed back into the merry band of eligible singles. The return of recycled men to the common pool was especially welcome, since the group was heavily weighted in favour of females.

The other problem was that Jim, himself single since his wife had left him – scandalously, for an organist – was also inclined to go fishing from this rather convenient pier. Since his marriage ended, Jim had always been careful to avoid making overtures to the women in his own congregation, but the new group had brought in a steady supply of fresh talent from outside. None of his dates had led to anything serious, but word had got around and this had provoked some resentment among the women who had not been approached.

The matter was resolved when Jim was elected to the executive committee of the Southwood Community Association. With the centenary festival looming, and likely to take up more of his time, he decided to leave the running of the singles group to Aubrey. This led to a suggestion from some of the members that Aubrey might like to increase the frequency of his own talks.

At Lynwood Lodge, a small retirement village in Old Southwood, a scandal has erupted over an outbreak of unbridled passion between two of the residents, both women. Both had endured long and unhappy marriages, one child each, while denying the truth about their sexual identity and preference. Now widowed, they found love in each other's arms and have become inseparable.

The management is perplexed. The 'village' – essentially a large old house with modern extensions – was developed specifically for elderly singles (strictly one resident per room) and an archaic by-law specifies that residents may not entertain guests of the opposite sex in their rooms overnight – useful, according to Beth, one of the residents, as a defence against unwelcome advances from lonely old men who had lost their inhibitions.

'There's no objection to orgies in the afternoon, apparently,' Beth had told her daughter on one of her weekly visits. 'It's just overnight that's the problem, even though most of this lot are out cold by nine o'clock.'

The framers of the by-law had not foreseen, or could not imagine, the situation that had now arisen – though Beth assured her daughter, in a lowered voice, that there were plenty of other more discreet liaisons in progress; it's just that those two were being so openly exuberant about theirs. But the management was powerless to restrain same-sex lovers from sharing a bed, day and night, especially when they both owned rooms in the building. According to Beth, the residents are delighted by this rich source of fresh gossip. Daily rumours sweep the establishment, offering generally unreliable updates on the genteel tussle taking place between the management and the two women.

The offspring of the women have reacted in quite different ways. The daughter and son-in-law of one of them are supportive, enthusiastic and utterly unfazed. 'They knew she'd been unhappy for years,' Beth told her daughter, 'but they thought it was only because she was married to such a miserable old coot. Now they see her liberated from that and full of newfound joy. It's lovely to see the four of them together.'

'The other family not so keen?' asked her daughter.

'Oh! Very stitched up. Very sniffy. Visits have tapered off, and grandchildren are being discouraged from asking questions, in case Grandma proves too forthcoming for Mummy's liking.'

It's no wonder that 'village' has become almost universally accepted as the right word for a cluster of small dwellings occupied by singles and couples in retirement. The move from one's own home into a more communal setting is often traumatic, involving the shedding of many possessions and the adjustment to a more confined space and a new set of neighbours in closer proximity than before. The neighbours are also typically more homogenous, particularly across the age spectrum, than would be found in many suburban streets and many new arrivals have some trouble adjusting to that loss of diversity.

But the magical powers of a community soon weave their spell, and many people who live in retirement villages report that they love it, and wonder why they hadn't made the move years earlier. They may praise the convenience of a simpler life with fewer house-and-garden chores to be done, but the main benefit is the sense that they have been drawn into a fully-functioning community – generally more socially active and more closely bonded than is typical in a suburban street. 'A new lease of life' is how it is often described.

Enthusiasm for the idea of a community is not universal. There are hermits and isolates who enjoy nothing more than their own company – or 'peace and quiet' – and who rail against any attempts to create an all-singing, all-dancing neighbourhood spirit. Stewart Mercer is one of them. Stewart is a plumber who has recently returned to live in the small house in Old Southwood where he grew up as an only child. For many years he had lived alone in a rented apartment in the city, but when his parents died, he decided to move back into the family home.

> The only reason I live here is that I inherited the house and it was easier to move in rather than sell it and buy something else. It's alright. I have somewhere to park my van, which was always a hassle in the city. People mainly leave you alone around here, once they realise you're just a grumpy bastard. I don't try to hide the fact that I'm not one for all this 'community' crap. I don't mind everyone else getting involved in socialising and street parties and what have you – just leave me out of it. I work on my own as an emergency plumber and I live on my own, and that's the way I like it.
>
> There's a few of us around here who feel the same way. We usually have a drink together on Friday nights, and sometimes a meal at the pub. The conversation always gets around to the same

thing: why is everyone always so determined to be sociable? Okay, we get together, but we're a kind of anti-social social group, if you get what I mean. We're just a bunch of grouches. Misfits, I guess – at least that's what we like to call ourselves.

Unlike Stewart and his mates, there are genuine hermits for whom the word 'community' carries not just unattractive but vaguely frightening overtones. For them, Richard Eckersley's 'fuzzy cloud of relationships' (quoted in chapter 1) would feel like a blizzard of social expectations from which they would want to run a mile. Some of them seek physical isolation in remote locations – on a wild stretch of coastline somewhere, or in a largely uninhabited area of bushland – but most live and work in suburban settings, retreating to the privacy and security of their homes with gratitude and relief. For some of them, reading and watching TV are as close as they wish to get to 'society'; for others, the internet provides a safe way to tap into the wide world of cyberspace, without the strain of having to come face-to-face with any of the people they interact with.

Singletons may be as disparate as hermits and grieving widows. But hermits are the exception that proves the rule: most people who live alone feel the desire to belong as urgently as anyone else. The need for companionship never leaves a social creature and, as the number of single-person households grows, the challenge for any neighbourhood is to ensure that the singletons are not left out: aloneness can easily morph into loneliness, and loneliness into alienation. Addressing the problem of social exclusion is everyone's responsibility.

Writing in the *New Yorker* about the experience of living alone following the death of his wife, Roger Angell, at 93, still craves the intimacy of close companionship, and so do most of the people he knows:

Getting old is the second-biggest surprise of my life, but the first, by a mile, is our unceasing need for deep attachment and intimate love . . . I believe that everyone in the world wants to be with someone else tonight, together in the dark, with the sweet warmth of a hip or a foot or a bare expanse of shoulder within reach. Those of us who have lost that, whatever our age, never lose the longing: just look at our faces.

7

Online communities

The two Coghlan boys are away overnight at a school camp and Catherine and Gareth find themselves in the unusual situation of having a Saturday night entirely to themselves – no ferrying the boys to and from social events, no film showing at the Lewis cinema that they particularly want to see, no commitments with friends . . . a night alone together!

Gareth had suggested dining out, but Catherine decided she'd rather serve one of Gareth's favourite meals. She has set the table more formally than usual, and, with no boys around to embarrass, has lit a perfumed candle. Gareth is in an attentive and affectionate mood. They are looking forward to being in bed early, with no interruptions. Catherine has fished out a silk nightdress she hasn't worn for ages.

By ten o'clock, they are settled in bed, feeling the slightly guilty pleasure of off-duty parents devoting themselves to leisurely lovemaking.

At ten past ten, Catherine's smartphone rings. She invariably keeps it by the bed. Gareth assumes she will ignore it, and he continues stroking and kissing her. To his irritation, she turns her head away and says, 'It might be one of the boys.' She picks up the phone and answers it.

It is not one of the boys. It is Catherine's sister, calling from Nottingham. These calls occur with great frequency, and the conversations are never short. Gareth hears Catherine say, 'No, that's fine – we're just having an early night.' She turns on her bedside lamp (Catherine always maintains she can't talk on the phone in the dark), and Gareth rolls onto his back with his hands clasped behind his head.

After ten minutes, Gareth walks into the living room, grabs his iPad and returns to bed. He has a swag of emails he was planning to attend to on Sunday morning, but this now seems like a good moment to begin dealing with them.

A 2013 Galaxy survey found that 50 percent of Australians admitted to having interrupted sex to answer their mobile phone. The same number reported having had arguments with their partners over mobile-phone use. Perhaps it's not surprising that 50 percent also said they 'couldn't live without their mobile phone'.

Will Pickering, the twenty-six-year-old bank teller who frequents Southwood Central's food court, is as enthusiastic as any young mobile-phone user, but he draws the line at taking his phone on dates. His most recent date, with a fellow volunteer he met on a shift at the Ostara Foundation, took a turn for the worse when Will, irritated by the faint buzz of the girl's phone sitting on the restaurant table between them and shocked to see her hand edging towards it, said, 'You're not going to answer that, are you?'

The girl drew her hand back. The phone stopped ringing. She hesitated, staring at it, and said to Will, 'I'll just have to see who was calling.' She then proceeded to scroll through her messages while Will glanced around the restaurant, counting seven other heads bowed intently over various mobile devices.

As time went by and the girl seemed to have become utterly engrossed in what she was doing, Will said, 'Anything important?' His date gave a faint grunt of acknowledgement and kept staring at the screen, her thumbs occasionally springing into rapid action. After several more minutes had passed, Will slid out of his chair and stood beside the table. He coughed discreetly. The girl raised her eyebrows and very nearly succeeded in dragging her eyes away from the screen. Will waited another moment, then walked to the desk, paid the bill and left. As he closed the door of the restaurant behind him he looked back at the girl, still bent over her screen and oblivious to his departure.

Will took ten paces, hesitated, decided he was acting like a creep, turned and went back inside and resumed his seat at the table. The girl, presumably thinking he had been to the washroom, glanced up and half smiled, finished the message she was sending and placed the phone back on the table with a sigh of satisfaction.

They left soon after. The girl, hoping for coffee, was surprised to find Will had already paid and seemed anxious to leave. On the way to the carpark, Will said, 'Do you always have your phone with you?'

His date looked at him as if she didn't really understand the question. 'It's my lifeline,' she said.

Catherine and Gareth's romantic evening had suffered a major setback, but all was not lost. Catherine was on the phone to her sister for an hour, giving Gareth time to respond to the most pressing of his emails. He was surprised to receive two quick replies. 'What are they doing,' he said to himself, 'responding to emails at ten-thirty on a Saturday night – don't they have a life?' He acknowledged them both and closed his emails. Catherine was still in full cry, so he checked the local weather forecast for the next day, then for the next week, then for Nottingham, then, for no particular reason, Denmark. Drowsiness began to overwhelm him. He put the iPad on his bedside table, rolled onto his side, buried his face in Catherine's shoulder, slid his arm across her warm belly and, lulled by the sound of her voice, fell into a deep sleep. His last thought was: 'I must remember to complain about this in the morning.'

When Catherine finally finished talking to her sister, she turned off the light and settled down into the bed, knowing she had disappointed Gareth, but, having noted that he had been busy on his iPad, decided it had been a productive time for both of them. Her sister had been in good spirits and was full of news of the family: it was surprising how much had happened in the five days since they had last spoken.

When Catherine and Gareth woke up in the morning, they reached for each other, laughed at their failed attempt at a night of passion, and picked up where they had left off.

Over breakfast, Gareth said, 'Would you ever consider coming to bed without your phone?'

Catherine looked at him as if she didn't really understand the question. 'It's like my lifeline,' she said.

At the Meadowlarks child-care centre in Old Southwood, a three-year-old is gazing at the screen of a tablet, watching a video clip of a cat playing with a ball of wool. She is smiling and chirruping with obvious delight at the antics of the cat.

Suddenly, she is distracted by movement on the other side of the room. A cat has walked through the door to the playroom and is stretching on a mat. The girl screams, drops the tablet and runs in fright into the next room, pursued by a puzzled child-care worker.

Susan Greenfield, the British neuroscientist, wouldn't have been puzzled. She has long been concerned about the impact of computer technology on the development of children's brains and, in particular, about the distortion of reality for children who become so accustomed to images on a small two-dimensional screen that they may be surprised, shocked or frightened – as that Meadowlarks child was – by the full-sized, three-dimensional force of reality.

The Australian cartoonist Michael Leunig once drew a cartoon of a man sitting on the couch in his living room, gazing at the TV screen, on which the moon was rising. Through the window of the room, we could see the actual moon rising in the actual sky. Leunig's message was clear: we are at risk of settling too easily for mediated images rather than engaging with the real thing. We may watch all the nature documentaries we like, but unless we occasionally get out there, we are in danger of acquiring what some US psychologists have identified as Nature Deprivation Syndrome. (All those people watching *MasterChef* but never cooking are presumably in some similar category of risk.)

All over Southwood – all over the world – people have become accustomed to the idea of connectedness being a technology-based experience, at least as much as a face-to-face, social experience. We have accepted that many of our encounters and exchanges will be mediated – that is, transmitted and therefore filtered through the many varieties of media now at our disposal, from the telephone to social media like Facebook, Twitter, Instagram and the proliferating others that will have emerged between the writing and reading of this book.

We have even adapted to the idea of online *communities*, in which many users of social media claim the sense of belonging is every bit as sharp as it is for the members of offline communities (perhaps partly because the heaviest traffic on social media sites tends to be between people who already know each other offline). Where once we might have thought 'belonging' and even 'socialising' involved regular face-to-face contacts with a flesh-and-blood group of people, our enthusiastic adoption of the telephone in the twentieth century mounted the first serious challenge to that idea, by making us feel as if quite intimate contact is possible without actual human presence.

Ellen Lasso lives in Southwood Ponds and Gretel Hunt in Southwood Rise. They have been close friends since they were at university together, and it was a happy coincidence that they both ended up in Southwood. Their personal lives have followed parallel courses – marriage at about the same age; two children each; a return to part-time work when the younger child started school.

They used to meet about once a week for coffee and a sandwich, and occasionally arranged for the two families to do something together, though their husbands and children have never been close. As their lives became fuller, their meetings became less frequent and they resorted to long catch-ups on the telephone, often ringing each other two or three times a week.

Then they started exchanging emails, usually written late at night when the children were asleep and it was deemed too late to call. Occasionally, one would ring the other, but the flow of emails had become so constant, they each felt as if they knew what was going on in the other's life, and there seemed not much left to say when they spoke. The coffee meetings dropped off almost entirely.

Gretel went onto Facebook and asked Ellen to be her 'friend'. Realising that much of Gretel's news was now being shared with a wider circle, Ellen also went onto Facebook as a way of keeping in touch with Gretel, but made no postings of her own.

One morning, Ellen woke with a strange ache: she was thinking about Gretel and realised she was missing her. She examined that feeling and calculated that it had been a couple of months since the women had actually met face to face. She called Gretel and suggested an experiment: 'Let's try not emailing each other for two weeks. I won't even read your Facebook posts. Then let's meet for coffee and a proper catch-up.'

Gretel was initially taken aback, and was inclined to complain that she'd feel too out of touch, but she saw the point of Ellen's suggestion and decided to go along with it.

After two weeks, they met for coffee and a sandwich at E.K. They had a marvellous time, and agreed it had been too long since they had seen each other.

'The phone is supposed to be for keeping in touch with people you can't see,' said Ellen. 'I think we just got into the habit of picking up the phone because it's so easy. Then email. It's brilliant, of course, but it's a trap, too, don't you think? So convenient. You can be as cryptic or as discursive as you like — although I do find I'm not bothering with long emails these days. I've got into terrible trouble with Peter for not reading emails thoroughly. I think I just scan them, the way the kids do with their wretched texts.'

'Speaking of the kids,' Gretel said, 'I think an actual phone conversation is quite rare with them. Bec is fifteen now, and I'd say most of her contacts are via texts or Facebook. She sees her friends at school, of course, but they spend hours on their smartphones — though they never seem to do much actual talking. Oh, the exception is this boy who's obviously pursuing Bec. He likes to talk, but Bec tends to fob him off with text messages.'

'God! Remember the phone,' Ellen replied. 'It was an instrument of seduction in our day. Boys would say the most intimate things on the phone that they would never say to your face. I always thought the phone sped up the romance. Surely a boy's voice in your ear is a very different thing from a text message or a tweet.'

'Or maybe they really do emote in response to emoticons!' said Gretel.

Having re-established personal contact, Ellen and Gretel decided they really did need to keep seeing each other more. 'I miss your hugs,' Ellen said. She realised, but didn't say, that she also missed seeing some of Gretel's quirky facial expressions, and the peculiar way she shrugged one shoulder. They resumed their late-night emails, but kept them brief and often said 'more when I see you'.

Every media revolution changes us and, with each revolution, we are inclined to fear the worst. In Plato's *Phaedrus*, written early in the fourth century BCE, Socrates rails against the evils of the written word and, in particular, against the effects of writing on the art of memory. Every new medium – from the printing press to photography, the telephone, sound recording, the Nickelodeon, cinema, radio, television – has been attacked for its potential to corrupt us. The form of the feared corruption is usually the same: that we will be so captured by the new technology, we will allow ourselves to be distracted from each other, thus eroding the quality of our social interactions and perhaps even diminishing our humanity by encouraging the idea that human communication is possible without 'real' human presence.

In the case of the digital revolution, it's still too early to estimate the nature or extent of the changes to our way of life. The digital world is unfolding too quickly to see where it is taking us, even though strong hints are beginning to emerge about potentially positive effects on our level of tribal connectedness, and potentially negative effects on our brains, our social lives and our attention spans. One thing is certain: the new and emerging media will do the paradoxical thing that communication media have always done: while seeming to bring us together, they actually make it easier for us to stay apart.

In that way, every media revolution tends to seduce us away from engagement with our personal, 'offline' communities. Yet we are willing victims of this seduction, because every new medium is clever and appealing at some level: that's why all of them attract addicts – from the bookworm who prefers books to people, to the person who can't bear to turn off their smartphone, anytime, anywhere, to those who believe people's most telling revelations occur on Facebook or that a person's worth is measured by the number of followers they have on Twitter. It's easy to say that such people run some risk of losing touch with the communities that sustain them and nurture their social identity, but what if the meaning of 'social identity' is changing?

Carol Brunelli is a keen cyclist, and she often spends her Saturdays on long rides extending far beyond Southwood to the edge of the metropolitan area. Occasionally, she and some friends drive to a regional area for a full weekend of rural riding.

Although she prefers to ride alone, Carol has become part of an online community of cyclists who record their times over certain rides and post them on Strava for comparison with others' performance. Highly competitive by nature, Carol takes great pride in her place as 'queen of the segment' whenever she posts a better time than any of the other women sharing their performance data. But Carol has noticed that there's more going on than the obvious motivational effect of this online competition: a cooperative dimension to the online community has also emerged:

> Sometimes, if I fail to post a time, I'll get a message from one of the other riders saying 'You didn't put your ride on Strava this morning – did you not go out? Are you okay?' This from a total stranger! People let you know about good rides they've

discovered, and they share information about the weather and road surfaces – just the way a group of friends would, except we never actually meet. Even if you did happen to see someone riding who was a member of the online community, you wouldn't know they were.'

In fact, Carol had become so 'close' online to one rider who seemed to share many of her interests and to be at about the same performance level as Carol that they arranged to meet and now occasionally ride together. 'But we still post everything on Strava,' Carol says. 'You'd feel you weren't pulling your weight if you didn't stay in touch with the whole group.'

What happens to us when we go online?

Gareth Coghlan might be miffed when his wife is distracted from sex by a call on her smartphone, but by the time his teenage sons are into serious dating they might find themselves in competition with an ever-smarter generation of mobile technology. Tyler Cowan, an economics professor at Virginia's George Mason University and the author of *Average is Over* (2013), makes this playful prediction: 'During a date, a woman might consult a pocket device in the ladies room that tells her how much she really likes the guy. The machine could register her pulse, breathing, tone of voice, the level of detail in her narrative, or whichever biological features prove to have predictive power.' So much for intuition, the delicious sensation of falling in love, or the ability to trust one's judgement in matters of the heart (or the crucial learnings that arise from getting it wrong): now we could simply consult a machine that will sort out the most relevant bits of data and send us a red or green signal.

We might think that's going a bit far (and we might also baulk at Cowan's assertion that greater social inequality will become an inevitable feature of the technology-based 'hypermeritocracy' of the future), but we are already well down the path of assuming that because information technology is so clever and attractive – fast, efficient, stimulating – we should embrace it in every way we can. The sheer brilliance of the new media technologies may also tempt us into thinking that they are actually better 'communicators' than we are, leading us to blur the traditional distinction between communication and data transfer.

A father is chatting to his twenty-year-old daughter about the death of the father of one of her friends.

'Have you spoken to Harriet yet?'

'No, I'll send her a text.'

'For goodness' sake, don't send her a text. At least call her or, better still, go around and see her.'

'No, she'd want me to send her a text. That's cool.'

Later, the father reports this conversation to his wife. 'I couldn't believe she was just going to send Harriet a text.'

'Well,' says his wife, 'you've sent condolence cards to plenty of people in the past. Sometimes you can write things more easily than you can say them.'

'I accept that. But a *text* message? Isn't that a bit impersonal?'

'You might be surprised. They are pretty intimate with their texts, you know. It's a bit like a private language. We might think it's all so abbreviated, but I suspect they manage to fit a lot of subtlety in there somehow – maybe it's a bit like reading between the lines.'

'Maybe,' says her husband. 'But surely there's more to communication that that. At least my condolence cards are handwritten – there's more of a personal touch there, surely?'

This is a debate that will never end: which is the 'best' medium for conveying which type of message? While it's true that data transfer isn't the same thing as communication, but only a means to that end, we do appear to be becoming intent on conveying complexity and subtlety in ever simpler and more cryptic ways. The fact that many messages really can be conveyed in Twitter's maximum 140 characters, or in a text or an email, still raises an important question: what do we lose when we go for speed and efficiency over the more lumbering pace of face-to face contact?

In terms of the psychology of communication, the answer is: almost everything. Facial expressions, gestures, posture, the rate of speech, the tone of voice, the distance between us as we stand or sit together, the ambiance, the eloquence of a pat on the arm or the reassurance of a hug . . . all those nuanced 'messages' are lost when we go for a digital or even a handwritten message. A telephone call offers more – and at least has the advantage of continuous feedback – but still loses all the visual components that help us decode what's really meant by what is being said.

If anyone thinks the little coded abbreviations, emoticons and other bits of digital argot approach the complexity of a face-to-face encounter, they haven't been looking and listening closely enough. I have lost count of the number of misunderstandings that have occurred in my own experience – some of them serious – through emails that were not supported or illuminated by personal conversation. This is a problem being exacerbated by the speed and brevity of alternative modes of data transfer – Twitter in particular. Many users of email now scan their emails rather than reading them carefully, or else they might read only the first sentence or two to 'get the gist'.

This is not to denigrate or dismiss the value of online communication; nor is it to deny that some people feel a powerful emotional connection to their online networks. Of course the new social media have a role to play in our lives; that's why we have signed up to them in our millions. And of course many messages are so simple – *See you at 6, usual spot* – that nothing more subtle is needed, and greater subtlety might actually blur the clarity of the message. And we're all so *busy*, the sheer speed of online message transfers is inherently appealing: the idea of slowing it all down, even to the pace of a phone conversation, is increasingly unthinkable. Ever experienced relief when you've rung someone and encountered their voicemail service, where you can leave a simple message and not have to go to all the trouble of exchanging pleasantries? Then you already know how a revved-up life can actually begin to dehumanise us.

Relationships are not best founded on efficiency, nor are they best nurtured through the exchange (no matter how frequent) of inherently impersonal digital data. When you start feeling as if a text message or email is the best way to convey some important personal message, you've begun to lose your grip on what it means to be a social creature.

There's also a crucial difference between online and offline contact in the extent to which we make ourselves 'open', even vulnerable, to each other. As long as our contact is via a screen and keypad, we are able to maintain a certain distance. We have more control over the way we express ourselves and the amount of information we are prepared to reveal. That ability to control the dataflow may be welcome in many circumstances – including online flirtations or other relationships that are never intended to move offline – but it is a radically different experience of 'relationship' and 'community' from the complexity and unpredictability of a personal encounter.

This is not to suggest there's no role for speed and efficiency – or for the level of safety and control that goes with 'keeping our distance' – in the messages human beings exchange with each other. Online contacts have their own unique value, particularly as an augmentation of offline relationships. There is great efficacy in text messages, Facebook posts, tweets and all the endlessly proliferating ways of transferring data without actually talking to each other. They can be valuable as brief 'maintenance' messages – ways of staying in touch with someone you already know personally through your offline encounters. A Post-it note stuck on the fridge is an efficient way of telling your partner that you've taken the dog to the park; a text message is equally efficient. But texts, tweets and Post-it notes are no way to nurture relationships.

At Southwood's library and cultural centre, Roslyn Kennedy is a great believer in face-to-face contact, even though she has moved the library into the digital age to an extent that has made her the envy of many other library managers.

'We want our customers to have the most efficient and most sophisticated systems we can afford to give them. We want to make information access as easy as we possibly can,' she often says to her staff, 'but that means we have to be capable of providing very personal, very hands-on service when people need it. Some people get lost in the technology and some people are daunted by it. We want to give them the best possible experience of the library. And we must always remember – some people visit us because they're lonely.'

When it comes to contact with her own staff, Roslyn is constantly trying to find the right balance between online contact – email, mostly – and personal, face-to-face meetings. She is a great believer in meetings, not for their own sake, but as a way of clearing up misunderstandings that often seem to occur online, and also to maintain personal contact between her colleagues. Every Friday afternoon, she has a meeting to review the week, and that morphs into a period of less formal contact over drinks and nibbles.

Roslyn is fond of quoting Bill Gates, chairman of Microsoft and the high priest of the digital revolution, who once remarked that email is a great preparation for a meeting, and a great way of recording the outcome of a meeting, but it's no substitute for a meeting. Since Gates said that, email has become the way many people work and is, indeed, widely used as a substitute for meetings, but Roslyn insists that email always be regarded as a secondary medium in her dealings with staff members.

'Everything depends on trust,' she says, 'and trust depends on seeing the whites of their eyes.'

～

It's a simple calculation: the more time we spend online, the less time we have to devote to our personal relationships and the more we jeopardise their quality. (Ever been offended when you're with a friend or family member and their attention has strayed from what you're saying to a message coming in on their mobile device?) The richness of face-to-face communication feeds our relationships and deepens our intimacy. The loss of it reduces a relationship to an exchange of news bulletins or perfunctory declarations of friendship that imply we don't actually value each other highly enough to spend time together.

Forget 'quality time'. The only sure way to add quality to the time we spend together – whether in the family, among friends, between neighbours, at school or at work – is to extend it. When it comes to the time we devote to human encounters, quantity usually enriches the quality.

In a world where our appetite for digital data appears insatiable, it was inevitable that we would try to compensate for any loss of quality in our personal relationships by sharply increasing the quantity of our online connections. You have twenty followers on Twitter? A thousand? Ten thousand? Does that really make you feel as warm and wonderful as knowing there's a circle of flesh-and-blood friends or colleagues who have great affection and respect for you without feeling they have to 'follow' you? You have five hundred Facebook 'friends'? That simply means you've redefined 'friend' to make it mean something like 'a contact I exchange data with'. (No wonder we've had to invent BFF for our 'best friends forever', though we might hope they would know that without needing to be sent the acronym, and presumably they would also know that when we say 'forever', we mean 'for the time being'.)

None of this is an argument against online contacts or the development of 'online communities' that encourage a sense of belonging. It is simply an appeal to remember what we are losing whenever we are tempted to think that online data transfer is the same as – or even better than – face-to-face communication. Both are good, but if you had to choose where you would place your emphasis, why would you put a community in cyberspace ahead of people you can actually meet and interact with in the old-fashioned way? (It's a serious question.)

The functions of online communities can be valuable – for individuals and for organisations. Online communities are just as 'real', just as authentic, as offline communities. But the nature of the online experience is radically different from the experience of belonging to groups whose members meet in person. There are no incidental encounters online that correspond to those we have with colleagues we meet in the corridor, or neighbours we meet on the footpath or in the local shops. There is no easy way to sense, online, that someone is bit down and might need sensitive handling in the way that such things are obvious when we are face to face.

Above all, the online community offers us no opportunity to touch each other – lovingly, reassuringly, encouragingly. We can't shake hands; we can't hug; we can't pat someone on the shoulder, or touch them on the arm or kiss them on the cheek. In Western society, it is rare never to touch the people we see, and the lack of that ability, more than any other difference, highlights what we lose when we go online. (In some 'non-touching' cultures, online contact has correspondingly more appeal.)

Institutional use of online communities

Ever since he saw how engaged his own kids had become with Facebook, Mike Doherty has been looking for ways to harness this kind of engagement in the interests of better local government. As general manager of Southwood City Council, Mike is convinced that social media present local government with an opportunity to increase the level of community participation in the work of the council.

Mike came to Southwood from a similar position at a much smaller council in a rural shire. There, too, his emphasis had always been on trying to involve the local community in decisions that would shape the future of the region and affect their wellbeing. Social media had not yet arrived on the scene in a big way, and Mike had to rely on regular meetings in the towns and villages dotted around the shire. People were slow to respond at first, but Mike stuck to the plan and was rewarded by a gradual increase in the numbers who would turn up to his community meetings.

He tried the same thing in Southwood when he first arrived, but the council was lukewarm about the idea and there was little community support. 'Everyone's too busy' was a popular explanation; 'people think the council should get on with the job they were elected to do' was another.

The advent of social media opened up a new avenue for Mike to develop his ideas for encouraging greater community consultation. The council had long had a website, but it had been used almost exclusively as an electronic noticeboard, with no facility for people to interact. Mike changed all that, and also began sending mass emails to ratepayers, encouraging them to engage with the council via its Facebook page.

Already, the program has been bearing fruit. Mike has a small team responsible not only for maintaining the website and Facebook page, posting minutes of council meetings and reports of council activities, but also responding to enquiries and suggestions. Ideas and issues are regularly posted on Twitter, and the number of followers has been increasing dramatically. Mike is convinced that although much of the content is quite shallow, the long-term consequence will be a more engaged community.

Mike's next big project is to establish a participatory budget process. With the support of the mayor, Mary Kippax, he has begun recruiting panels of ratepayers who agree to take part in small group discussions about aspects of the council's budget, and the results of these deliberations are being incorporated into regular online surveys and open invitations to comment on specific items in the budget.

To Mike, the most pleasing outcome of this strategy, so far, has been the overwhelming response to his latest invitation to ratepayers to attend a public meeting to discuss the council's budget-planning process. The civic centre's auditorium was packed, the discussion spirited, the questions thoughtful and the mood of the occasion broadly positive.

'Oh, the cynics just stayed away,' said Dom Fin, deputy mayor, when he heard about the event. Dom and some of the other councillors are both sceptical and nervous about all this emphasis on transparency and participation, but Mike points out that the council is not abdicating its responsibilities, but merely increasing the quality of the community's input to the budgeting process.

~

Commercial and social research organisations are now forming online panels to encourage discussion of issues researchers would once have canvassed via face-to-face discussion in small groups (including so-called 'focus groups'). Such online networks are being used as an adjunct to more traditional methods of qualitative, exploratory research in situations where it is difficult, or too expensive, to assemble offline groups.

Similar online 'communities' are being created by marketing companies who wish to engage in direct exchanges with their consumers – new owners of a particular motor vehicle, for example, or users of a particular range of baby products. Retailers establish online links with customers, using email or social media to announce special deals and promotions in a way that seems more personally tailored to the individual customer than traditional mass marketing. Such micro-marketing is cheaper than the cost of mass-media advertising and can be effective in creating the impression of a personal relationship between company and customer. Even the promotional language used to recruit online contacts – *like us on Facebook, follow us on Twitter* – feeds the illusion that this is all somehow more chummy and less commercial than more traditional marketing channels.

Mass-media organisations are also harnessing the potential of social media to elicit reactions to particular programs (sometimes posting tweets on the TV screen during the program – thus distracting viewers from what is being said, since the eye usually beats the ear). 'Conversations', via Twitter, with media personalities and presenters are also being encouraged as a way of boosting our sense of engagement with media content. Some authors tweet incessantly, in the hope of stimulating sales of their books. Senior figures in many organisations have jumped on the social media bandwagon, using Facebook and Twitter as conduits for bulletins about the work of the organisation, to stimulate debate about social issues that concern the organisation – ranging from mental health to mining – or to strengthen our 'connection' with the organisation. ('Followers' and 'friends' feel like allies.) Many organisations have had to develop guidelines for the social media activities of their executives, now that Twitter has created the possibility of any employee posting their views, whether authorised or not.

The online communities generated by organisations are simply an attempt to exploit the social media for institutional or commercial purposes. Sometimes those purposes are noble; sometimes they are shamelessly propagandist. The 'communities' they create have about as much in common with offline communities as a tweet does with a face-to-face conversation. (And we need to remind ourselves that the social media themselves exist for commercial purposes: conceptually, they are no more a form of public service than any other commercial medium.)

Sometimes, a commercially-based online community will metamorphose into something more social. In Australia, for instance, owners of Land Rover vehicles have formed themselves into an informal online 'club' based on nothing more than common ownership of that make of vehicle. Members offer each other help and support ranging from vehicle trouble-shooting to advice about travel plans or house-swapping arrangements.

The joys and sorrows of online connectedness

Families scattered across the country or around the world love Facebook. Grandparents who can't see their grandchildren more than once or twice a year cherish their online contacts. Aunts, uncles, nieces, nephews and cousins who, in previous generations, might rarely have met each other are able to share family news and personal gossip in ways that heighten their sense of belonging to the extended family.

Friends who move interstate or overseas – especially the children of families who move – highly value the new ways of staying in touch created by social media, acknowledging that, in a bygone age, such continuing contact would have been difficult to maintain.

Ken and Margie Isherwood, the couple who felt socially excluded from Southwood Rise when we encountered them in chapter 2, moved to Southwood Ponds and soon came to feel at home there. But they continue to miss their friends from the rural district where they used to live, and no members of their extended family live nearby, so they have become assiduous users of social media.

I never thought I'd get Ken anywhere near a computer once he retired from the farm, but he's even keener than I am. One of the grandchildren is particularly attached to him online – she calls him her 'flat grandpa' because she mostly sees him on the screen, whereas her other grandpa lives nearby and she only ever sees him in three-dimensional reality.

One of our children used to live near where we had our property – our daughter is a teacher and her husband works for a transport company – but they've moved interstate with his work, and so we rarely see them or their children. But Facebook has been a lifesaver, really. And email too. I actually prefer email because it seems a bit more personal, a bit less public, somehow, although Ken says all our emails are monitored, so I don't know what 'private' means any more. I know when we see some of the grandchildren's stuff on Facebook, it's being shared with their friends. But I email my daughter every day. It saves a lot of time and money we would otherwise spend on the phone, and it seems less intrusive than a phone call, somehow – I know their lives are very busy.

Our son and his family are overseas, so it's even more vital with them. Until we got onto Facebook, we felt quite out of touch with our fifteen-year-old granddaughter. Now we really know everything that's going on – including some stuff we don't really need to know, but she doesn't seem to mind that we see it all. I know more about make-up than I've ever known before, and I think I know more about her menstrual problems than I knew with my own daughter, who was much more secretive than this little one. She's just starting to have boyfriends, so we get all that, plus the usual schoolyard tiffs. I have the feeling it's all more intense than it used to be. Or maybe it's just that they are furiously swapping all these stories online and they have to dress them up to sound more dramatic.'

It's not just families who value the channels of connection now available via web-based platforms. The quality of 'distance education' offered to students living in remote regional locations has been immeasurably improved through quicker and more convenient connections between teacher and pupil, and through the ability of students to connect online with other similarly isolated students.

Medical practitioners working in rural and regional locations are now able to access colleagues and supervisors in a 'virtual community of practice' that improves knowledge sharing and helps to overcome professional isolation via online forums, 'webinars', shared resources – including the invaluable resource of online 'chat'.

In such cases as those, online communities are created to compensate for the lack of access to offline communities. But universities around the world are now creating so-called Massive Open Online Courses (MOOCs) in which the purpose is not only to compensate for a lack of access to live lectures, but to offer those lectures as an alternative to – and perhaps even a replacement for – the traditional theatre-based lecture. This development has generated heated controversy within academic communities. On the one hand, it is acknowledged that MOOC presentations can be 'model lectures' delivered by the best available teachers – with a status rather like that of an audio-visual textbook. On the other hand, the idea of a student undertaking a degree without ever setting foot on a campus, meeting academics and fellow students in face-to-face encounters, drinking coffee in the cafeteria, hanging around 'the quad', staying up late to crack the meaning of life, or joining student political societies or drama groups calls for a fundamental rethink of what a university education is supposed to offer. In some universities, the MOOC phenomenon is reviving enthusiasm for the traditional small-group tutorial model, where the impersonal MOOC lectures (again, just like textbooks) may come to be regarded as mere input to more intense, more lively interaction between students and tutors.

When it comes to working out whether online connectedness is 'good for us' and, in particular, good for our children, take your pick: the research evidence is pouring in, and any conclusion we draw today might be contradicted by new evidence tomorrow. While some researchers insist it's mainly good news – a 'safe' way for young people to explore their identity, stimulate their imagination and hone their networking skills – others worry about the long-term impact of the trade-off between face-to-face time and screen time. There is also the continuing debate among neuroscientists about brain effects, pointing not only to the obvious risks – addiction to digital stimulation, and shortening of the attention span – but also to the possibility that increasing computer use might have unpredictable microcellular effects on the brain's structure.

Meanwhile, argument rages over the effects on young people of their growing use of social media sites like Facebook. A 2011 paper by University of Sydney researchers Bridianne O'Dea and

Andrew Campbell ('Online Social Networking Amongst Teens: Friend or Foe?' in *Annual Review of Cybertherapy and Telemedicine*) reported on a study of four hundred secondary school students aged thirteen to sixteen years in which it turned out that 'spending large amounts of time online for social purposes may increase psychological distress and have a negative impact on self-esteem'.

That finding chimes with an emerging body of research suggesting that for all the positive benefits of social media use, there's a distinct downside. University of Michigan psychologist Ethan Kross has found that Facebook use often makes people feel sad and lonely. Robert Kraut of Carnegie Mellon University was reporting in 1998 (pre-Facebook) that the more people used the internet, the lonelier and more depressed they felt. His research led him to conclude that users' feelings of wellbeing and social connectedness decreased as a function of how often they used the internet.

It's not only the internet: similar findings emerged in a 2013 Kent State University study of mobile phone use among five hundred undergraduates. The researchers – Andrew Lepp, Jacob Barkley and Aryn Karpinski – reported that heavy mobile phone users were more likely to have lower average marks, higher levels of anxiety and lower levels of life satisfaction than less heavy users. It's always important to acknowledge that such correlations don't necessarily point to direct causation ('If you use your phone too much, your anxiety level will rise'), but the pattern of these results is significant: at the very least, it suggests that heavy phone use is a symptom (and quite possibly a cause) of poorer academic performance and a reduced sense of wellbeing. Why? Perhaps it's a case of time management – too much time spent on the phone at the expense of study time, or too much phone contact (via text or voice messages) at the expense of the richness of face-to-face contact.

Obvious question: why spend so much time online – or on the phone – if the effects are potentially so negative? One obvious answer: the fear of missing out (FOMO). I need to know what's going on, so I keep trawling through my texts, or my friends' social media postings, even if I end up feeling envious of the good time everyone else seems to be having, and disturbed by the sense that so many people seem generally more wonderful than I am. (There's an echo here of the effects on many of us of reading our friends' circular Christmas letters: learning that someone's five-year-old has just composed her third string quartet to wild acclaim and their ten-year-old is on the brink of finding a cure for the common cold is pretty depressing, to say nothing of the discovery that everyone else's travel experiences seem to have been positive – no lost bags, no airport delays, no stomach bugs, no family feuds.)

But the emerging picture is not clear-cut. Summarising current research for the *New Yorker* online, Maria Konnikova, author of *Mastermind: How to think like Sherlock Holmes* (2012), quotes a recent study from Carnegie Mellon which found that when people were *actively* engaged with social media sites – posting, messaging or 'liking' – their feelings of social bonding increased and their loneliness decreased. No surprises there: as in offline communities, our sense of belonging is directly related to our level of engagement. The more passively we trawl (online) or observe (offline), the more disconnected, lonely and bored we will feel; the more we participate, the better we will feel.

Social connections online may be profoundly different from face-to-face interaction, yet their effects can be positive and even therapeutic, as long as we are actively engaging and transacting with others. In *Social: Why our brains are wired to connect* (2013), Matthew Lieberman argues that online social networks offer us extremely convenient and accessible ways to share information with each other, and that the very act of sharing – even via social media – promotes our psychological health.

Even so, there's an inherent risk for us in becoming over-reliant on digital platforms: we may find it hard to break away from them; we may become addicted to them as a source of continuous stimulation ('something is always happening') and then, as Maria Konnikova concludes, we may find we are 'forgetting the path to proper, fulfilling engagement'.

The school counsellor at Southwood High, Jocelyn Hart, is particularly worried about the level of addiction to online games among some of the younger students at the school and the effects of this addiction on their social development.

I know it's easy to panic about these things, and to feel threatened by them because we don't really understand them yet, but I must say the video game thing worries me. I've had parents coming to me saying they have been having trouble disconnecting their kids from some of these games and when they do, the kids seem to exhibit withdrawal symptoms – mood swings, a tendency to violent behaviour. It's very disturbing for the parents.

I know Marcus is worried about the impact of online games on some of the boys, especially. He feels as if they are just putting in the minimum effort to get by at school, and they're devoting every available minute to games. They link up with other players – could be anywhere in the world – and they become fiercely competitive.

I read about a counselling service in the UK that deals with kids who sometimes spend twenty hours a day online. I've never seen anything as extreme as that – when would they have time to go to school? – but I do worry about the lack of social development in some of these kids. It's almost as if there's a new breed of nerd: just as socially inept on the outside, but seething with violence inside.

The British architect Frank Duffy is a passionate believer in the idea that we must create working spaces that counteract the isolating effects of online activity by encouraging incidental contacts. In 'The Death and Life of the Urban Office' (a chapter in *The Endless City*, edited by Ricky Burdett, 2007), Duffy argues that real places – as opposed to anywhere in cyberspace – offer 'a level of meaning and vitality built into streets and squares, rooms and anterooms, that the virtual world cannot rival'.

Roslyn Kennedy at the Southwood library agrees strongly – hence her emphasis on regular face-to-face meetings. So does Mike Doherty at the council: he is a great fan of open-plan offices, provided there are plenty of private spaces people can also use when they need to – for a confidential phone call or a conversation with a colleague that might distract others. But Mike is convinced that the open layout encourages the very kind of incidental encounter Duffy refers to when he writes of 'encounters between people and groups that occur in more or less accidental but nevertheless semi-planned ways'. Duffy also refers to the role of physical space in generating the kind of creative tension and spontaneity – stimulation and cross-fertilisation – that simply can't arise online. 'Place supports discourse,' he writes, 'because it is harder for people to hide, making both contradiction and agreement more likely.'

Another strong supporter of the Duffy argument is Rick Swanson, principal of Southwood High. When Rick came to the school, he discovered that the staff had managed to persuade the previous head to create three smaller staffrooms to replace the single large one. This allowed staff to spend more time with their like-minded colleagues: the humanities people corralled in one room, the sciences in another and the 'creatives' in a cramped space dubbed 'the sheep pen' by Julian Frisk, head of music.

Rick regarded this as one of the factors contributing to a disturbing lack of cooperation between the various disciplines in the school. With minimal consultation (but strong support from

Marcus Li), he insisted on re-establishing one large common room for all staff, with a couple of smaller spaces available for departmental meetings, as required.

Though he doubts he'll ever 'get sport and music on the same page', Rick has been pleased by the outcome. Morale has improved; relationships between teachers in the different disciplines are warmer and more sympathetic; timetable difficulties have been easier to resolve. Although some teachers still spend a lot of their staffroom time glued to their computers, that, too, has declined. Particularly at morning and afternoon tea breaks, the place is abuzz with conversation, and that's just the way Rick wants it.

Cowards' cyber-castle: The rise of online bullying

One of the most unpalatable facts about human society is that, for some reason or no reason, people occasionally take an active dislike to each other and, if they lack the maturity to restrain themselves, may express that dislike in aggressive and even violent ways. This may be based on nothing more than mockery of a person's appearance, as if the shape of their face, the colour of their skin or the style of their haircut were a symptom of some shortcoming in them.

The victims of bullying don't always understand why they are being victimised, and the perpetrators don't always know either: sometimes it's a perception of some physical or emotional vulnerability in another person that unleashes a mindlessly aggressive response. This is why young children will sometimes tease a child with a disability or some personal eccentricity, or pick on something as simple as wearing spectacles.

So perhaps it isn't surprising that bullying has emerged as a major problem in online communities. In fact, cyberbullying has become a problem of epidemic proportions, being experienced by one in three teenagers. Cyberspace has the potential to change the character of bullying and to increase the level of emotional distress, psychosocial trauma and humiliation inflicted on the victim.

Even if the bully is known to the victim and might have engaged in face-to-face bullying, the fact that hostile or humiliating messages have been posted online means they have the potential to be circulated far and wide.Victims are no longer being ridiculed, harassed or intimidated within a closed social circle: now they will feel they have been exposed to public ridicule, possibly on an enormous scale. In their 2012 paper, 'Online social Networking and the Experience of Cyber-Bullying' (in *Annual Review of Cybertherapy and Telemedicine*), Bridianne O'Dea and Andrew Campbell note that although cyberbullying may be less prevalent than face-to-face bullying, 'it created a stronger sense of fear in victims as bullies were able to transcend the school yard boundaries'.

The online space also makes it easier for cyberbullies to remain anonymous, increasing their power to intimidate their victim. If you don't know where the threat is coming from, this is in many ways more disturbing than if you do: 'I'm coming to get you' is nasty enough, but seems more manageable if you know it's the kid around the corner who is making the threat. If you have no idea who the perpetrator is, this increases the anxiety. O'Dea and Campbell note that 'unwanted stranger contact is a common experience' among teenage users of the internet, exposing them to the full range of cyberbullying activity, ranging from traditional harassment to online stalking and identity theft.

New Zealand has led the world in introducing legislation designed to curb and punish cyberbullies. Although some commentators thought that was an overreaction, it was a recognition by the New Zealand parliament that cyber-bullying adds some new and sinister dimensions to the age-old problem of bullying. The NZ legislation also includes the new offence of 'inciting to suicide', since the framers of the legislation had learnt of cases where young people had been so devastated by persistent online attacks that they had indeed taken their own lives or attempted to do so.

Nowhere is the beneficial power of our flesh-and-blood communities more evident than in their restraining effect on human nastiness. We are much less likely to behave badly towards people who know us – people with whom we share a neighbourhood – than we are towards total strangers. (Look how aggressive some drivers can be, in word and deed, when they are hidden within the anonymous capsule of a motor vehicle.)

∼

Jocelyn Hart is becoming worried about a noticeable shift in the character of bullying at Southwood High.

Bullying has been a problem in every school where Jocelyn has worked, but Southwood had managed better than most places to get it under control by the use of a very thorough training program based on the idea that bystanders play a crucial role in bullying. If you stand by and let it happen, you're complicit in the bullying – that was the key message. So the program was based on the need for a whole-school intervention designed to change the students' perceptions of what is acceptable behaviour, and equip them with the skills to intervene when necessary. The program has been very successful and is being adopted by several other schools.

To Jocelyn's dismay, the problem of bullying has returned in a more insidious and covert way. She is coming across students who are being intimidated online, rather than in the playground, and the cyberbullies are keeping their identities hidden. From the nature of the attacks, it's clear that the perpetrators are indeed students at the school, but there seems to be no way of tracking them down. Even though she has advised the victims to stay away from the online sites where the bullying occurs, they point out that other students know about it, and the word soon gets around.

Jocelyn is also dismayed by another effect of online communities, unrelated to bullying. She says that many students are now so active in online communities that they are spending more and more time at their computers – often well into the night – and she believes sleep deprivation has become a major cause of substandard performance at school.

'At least we don't have the problem one of my friends is having at Kentwell College,' Jocelyn says. 'She is an English teacher and all her students now use laptops. She has to teach from the back of the class so she can keep an eye on their screens. So much for eye contact as an important ingredient in the process of teaching!'

Our changing attitudes to privacy

Talking and listening are things we do with each other, whereas we read and write alone – which is one reason why a communication culture based on the written word encourages the idea of privacy. A print-based culture also creates the illusion that 'meaning' is in the words themselves, because writing separates the author from the message (whereas we know that, in reality, words are merely ways of expressing the meanings in the minds of the people who use them).

Influenced by the very patterns of printed words on a page, the print culture also privileges rationality and linearity, and that affects not only how we communicate but also how we think. To become readers and writers in an alphabet-based system, we have to submit ourselves to the disciplines of one word after the other, left to right, line after line. That leads us to talk about needing to 'see things in black and white'; we urge people not to 'read between the lines'. A culture – including an education system – dominated and saturated by written language even challenges our traditional (natural?) ways of scanning our environment. (Eventually we needed Edward de Bono to re-teach us how to think laterally.)

The cultural dominance of print in twentieth-century Western societies was gradually eroded by the advent of radio as a popular mass medium, and then, more comprehensively, by the arrival of television in the second half of the century. These new media reintroduced some features of the old oral culture (taking messages off the printed page and putting them back into people's mouths) and also began to place a higher emphasis on *shared* messages, since radio and television programs were consumed simultaneously by the members of their mass audiences in a way that was never true of print.

And now, the digital revolution. Because we are still in the midst of it, we can't yet see what's its long-term impact on our communication culture will be. But the early signs suggest a return to a more 'tribal' communication culture with a heavy emphasis on networks bound together by shared data, less attachment to the rationality and linearity of print (though, paradoxically, most digital messages are print-based), a new reverence for speed and brevity and, quite possibly, a declining interest in precision ... and privacy.

Already, a significant gap has opened up between attitudes and behaviour on the subject of privacy. Research conducted in 2013 by the Office of the Australian Information Commissioner (OAIC) shows that 78 percent of people do not like their online activities being monitored, yet they continue to engage with websites and social media platforms where they believe such monitoring is taking place. Perhaps we are witnessing the power of belonging in the online context: the desire to be part of the digital world and to belong to online communities (that old FOMO again) is so powerful that it may suppress our concerns about the security of the material we are posting, or the messages we are exchanging.

One of the most significant findings from OAIC's 2013 survey is this: 60 percent of people believe that social networking is a public activity. Given the teeming millions who are now using social media sites for the exchange of personal information, this figure points to some intriguing possibilities. Are we learning to adapt to a new communication culture that has some features of the oral culture of pre-media village or tribal life? Do we no longer care as much as we say we do about the fact that our personal messages are on public display? Under the influence of the digital revolution, are we resigning ourselves to a massive loss of privacy and deciding that, on balance, that's okay?

Jocelyn Hart, the school counsellor, is certainly coming to that conclusion.

I say to these kids, 'Don't you realise that everything you post on Facebook or Twitter is there for all eternity and, one way or another, it can be seen by practically anyone, including people you really might not want to see it – like a future employer, or a future partner, or even your parents?' They just shrug, basically. They know what I'm saying is right. They know they should be more careful. They pay lip service to the idea that putting anything on the net is like sticking it up on a public noticeboard. But they get caught up in it. They can't help themselves. And if everyone's doing it, I guess they don't really care. In fact, that's what they say: 'We're all in the same boat.' They are very tribal, after all, and there are some really nice things about that. They look out for each other far more than my generation did at school. If anyone's in trouble, they rally round just like a family. People say 'friends are the new family' . . . and it's true. They are endlessly hugging each other. I'd say they are generally a more cooperative bunch. I see it in the way they talk about sharing clothes, or even their enthusiasm for the idea of these new car-sharing services – they talk about 'collaborative consumption'. There are still plenty of rev-heads among our final-year students, mainly boys, but a surprising number of these kids are saying they're not going to be interested in owning a car. Maybe private ownership of things like cars is a bit like private information – just not as big a deal as it has been for the members of my generation.[9]

That view is confirmed by a European study of attitudes to social media among sixteen-to-eighteen-year-olds, reported in January 2014 by *The Guardian Weekly* (vol. 190, no. 5). The Global Social Media Impact Study, based on research conducted in eight EU countries, found that teenagers are typically unconcerned about how information about them is being used commercially or as part of surveillance practices by the security services.

The same European study points to another difficulty in trying to draw firm conclusions about the impact of information technology on society. Fashions change so quickly, the social medium that seemed to have captured teenagers last year may by now be dismissed as uncool. Facebook is a dramatic case in point: the Global Social Media Impact Study found that, among older European teenagers, 'Facebook is not just on the slide – it is basically dead and buried,' and privacy turns out to be one of the factors involved.

The anthropologist leading the study, Daniel Miller of University College London, found that as parents and older users saturate Facebook, its younger users prefer to go elsewhere – to Twitter, Instagram, WhatsApp and Snapchat. Although those alternative services may be less sophisticated than Facebook, this is of no concern to older teenagers who wish to dissociate themselves from a social medium that now seems to have become the province of younger children and older people, especially – *gasp!* – parents. According to Miller: 'Mostly they feel embarrassed to be associated with it. Where once parents worried about their children joining Facebook, the children now say it is their family that insists they stay there to post about their lives.' The seminal moment in a young person's decision to leave Facebook appears to be 'that dreaded day your mum sends you a friend request,' Miller writes.

Teenagers have long used a lack of communication – or highly selective communication – as a means of putting some necessary distance between them and their parents as they wage their personal War of Independence. Facebook was fine as long as it was a teen domain. Now it's become a playground for parents – and, worse, a way for them to invade their teenagers' privacy – it has lost its appeal for the older adolescent. (Echoes here of the death of blue denim among the young: once their parents adopted blue jeans as a sign of how cool and 'young' they were, their kids had to look elsewhere for their own fashion statement.)

Identity redefined (who are you falling in love with online?)

As some of the victims of bullying at Southwood High have discovered, one of the crucial ways online and offline communities differ is that the members of online communities can more easily hide their true identity. That problem is compounded in the case of internet users who find it necessary – or convenient, or amusing – to create several online identities, for use in different online settings.

In fact, some users of social media claim their online identity feels like a truer representation of who they are – more like *the real me* – than the person they present to the offline world in face-to-face encounters. That claim seems so preposterous, you wonder what they could possibly mean by it. Here's what a young single woman living in Southwood Central means by it:

⁶When I am online, I can control what I say more carefully than when I'm face to face with someone and possibly feeling flustered or intimidated. I can present a purer form of me – my thoughts, my attitudes, my values, my beliefs – without having them mixed up with how I look or how I sound. I'm happy to send someone a photograph, but I think you can get to know each other in a much more productive way if you stick to online contacts in the beginning. I even think I might be more honest online than offline – I'm able to respond to things more carefully and thoughtfully, rather than being distracted by how someone looks, or by what else is going on in a restaurant.⁹

Biology beware! Is this a new way of thinking about 'reality' – that I am more truly myself when I'm *not* face to face with someone? That the unique language of my body – my facial expression, my posture, my gestures, my tone of voice, to say nothing of the sex pheromones I exude – is a distraction from the real me, rather than being as we always used to think, absolutely integral to the real me? That personal presence is not essential to courting?

There are certainly times when we might need to consider our attitude to something or our response to another person coolly and carefully, and perhaps express ourselves in a more formal, linear way than is possible in the to and fro of conversation. But that's no different from saying that we sometimes need to write things down in order to be sure we have made our position clear (possibly even to ourselves). The love letter has always had a special place in romance precisely because it affords an opportunity to compose one's thoughts and set them down more formally – perhaps more poetically – than we can normally manage in the spontaneity of a face-to-face exchange. But a love letter is not more truly its author than the person who takes you in their arms.

Plenty of people now initiate romantic liaisons via the internet: dating sites, once stigmatised, have become commonplace and even fashionable. No one now feels embarrassed about admitting that they met their partner on a dating site. (Tyler Cowan, predictably, met his wife on match.com.) Many people go further and claim that they *fell in love* on the net, though there's plenty of anecdotal evidence to suggest that biology wins in the end and that many net-based prospective love affairs peter out when it emerges, after a few face-to-face meetings, that the crucial chemistry is missing.

Still, many romances that start on the net do end up in bed, or even at the altar (or, increasingly, under a tree in a park with a celebrant in attendance). Reliable statistics are hard to come by, but it looks as if at least a quarter of contemporary weddings may be between people who met on the net, and the claim is sometimes made that marriages based on internet dating will experience a lower divorce rate than others. We shall have to wait and see, but the claim does make some sense: if, like that young woman from Southwood Central, people sort out a lot of stuff (attitudes, beliefs, tastes and preferences) before they even meet, then a lot of the groundwork for a good relationship might have already been laid. And perhaps people who start with an internet dating site and an exchange of personal information are likely to be more cautious in choosing who they are prepared to meet and correspondingly less likely to rush into an unwise liaison with an incompatible partner.

However much our curiosity may be aroused by information exchanges online, it still takes the magic of a face-to-face meeting to sort out the deeper questions of attraction and compatibility. Even on the phone apps devoted to trawling for casual sex (either in fantasy or in practice), nothing can be concluded until the parties meet and any online deceptions are exposed: *He was forty, at least – there's no way he was in his early thirties like he claimed.*

If I belonged to an online community that also occasionally met face to face, my online persona would need to match pretty closely the kind of person my friends know me to be, or I would seem like a fake, a phony or a hypocrite. If I belonged to a community that existed exclusively online, I'd be free to play with alternative versions of me; I'd be free to explore what it would feel like to change my identity; I'd be free to pretend, to posture, to pose. (I would also, of course, still be free to present myself as closely to my offline persona as I could, even though my physical presence is excluded from the transaction.)

In Southwood East, Harvey Rendell is known as something of a recluse. He is not unfriendly, but he is rarely seen outside his small apartment; he does his food and grocery shopping online, and he often orders home-delivered pizza in the evening. He sometimes emerges at dusk in a tracksuit and walks to the Ponds and back. He works in the data-processing department of an insurance company in the city and travels by bus to the railway station. At work he is respected for his great efficiency and he sometimes lunches with another IT person who shares Harvey's love of computer chess. He never discusses his work with his neighbours.

Jim Glasson has got to know Harvey a bit, but even Jim finds it hard to sustain a conversation with him. Harvey is perfectly polite, but he generally seems anxious to scurry back inside his apartment after any such encounters.

Harvey has always been shy. He hated parties when he was young, never showed any interest in dating girls and, as a young man, quickly dropped out of the post-school social scene. He moved to Southwood East when he was in his early thirties and has been there for three years.

Look inside Harvey's apartment. It's all very neat and tidy. Very few books are to be seen, but there are three TV sets – one in the living room, one on the kitchen bench and one in Harvey's bedroom. There's an iPad on Harvey's bedside table and in the room he calls his study, there is a bank of three large monitors.

Online, Harvey is mainly Rusty and occasionally, for a laugh, Darlene. He spends several hours a night online, and comes to life in a way that would amaze people who only know him from their personal encounters with him.

Rusty was a farm boy who has come to the city to make his fortune, and he's doing brilliantly at it. He's taken a degree in economics and is making his mark in funds management. He's obsessed with cars and loves to travel. Plenty of women want to organise meetings with Rusty, but he always backs out after a few weeks of amiable flirtation.

Darlene is a very different proposition – cool, provocative, and living off the handsome settlement she received when she divorced a wealthy Texan whose identity she refuses to divulge. Darlene is a self-confessed good-time girl and is not reticent about recounting her exploits, though she's very discreet about the identity of her partners.

Rusty and Darlene supply all the excitement Harvey can handle. Both his online identities are witty, clever and popular. Harvey himself is witty and clever too, though few people realise it. Popular is the one thing he aspires never to be. Harvey finds socialising online, courtesy of Rusty and Darlene, safer and less emotionally threatening than his encounters at work or in the neighbourhood. It suits him very well to be thought of as reclusive; he likes to be left alone. No one who knows him personally has any idea of his private online adventures.

Harvey might seem like the kind of person you'd expect to become lonely and depressed, but the reality is quite different. His active engagement with online communities has been an emotional lifesaver, and who needs to know that Rusty and Darlene don't exist? One way and another, they give as much pleasure to others as they do to Harvey.

And yet, doesn't Harvey's case sadden you a bit? It's good to know that online communities can assuage the problem of loneliness for people like Harvey, but doesn't he seem to be missing out on something most of us would regard as precious, if not crucial?

After all, if we spend so much time interacting with online communities that we end up neglecting the face-to-face variety, we might need to ask ourselves all over again: What makes us fully human? What does it mean to say we are social creatures?

If (as suggested at the end of chapter 1) our moral sense is a social sense, formed and reinforced by the communities we live in, there's an obvious danger in spending too much of our time online: RSI (reduced social interaction) might not only diminish our social skills; it might also dull our moral clarity.

8

Shadows

Every community lives within the shadow of human frailty. Every community is weakened by the loss of the energy its members squander in the struggle between their competitive and cooperative natures. Every community is wounded by conflict, pettiness, insensitivity, infidelity and malice – just as every community is strengthened by people's willingness to take each other's needs and wellbeing into account and to live in a spirit of mutual obligation and respect.

Here's an odd thing, though: our need to belong to functioning, supportive communities can sometimes blind us to what is actually happening around us. When a community feels like home to us – the place where we belong – it's tempting to assume that everything is okay; that we don't have the problems other communities have to put up with; that we're lucky to be part of a 'good' community that doesn't require any particular effort to nurture it.

Yet the title of this book means what it says: belonging is an art – a process we have to learn to master. As with any personal relationships we value, a healthy relationship with a community needs to be tended, and that includes a willingness to face the problems that inevitably arise in any relationship and to deal with them in a spirit of kindness and compassion.

Here's a Southwood Fields parent, bewildered by the discovery of the extent of the drug problem in his teenage daughter's circle:

In a suburb like Southwood, you're inclined to think most of the social problems you hear about don't exist here. Crime isn't out of control. Our employment situation is pretty good, we're told. We haven't had shootings or knifings like you get in some parts of our big cities. A bit of binge drinking goes on . . . but as far as I was aware, there never seemed to be much of a drug problem.

I remember when someone was trying to organise a fundraiser for a kids' shelter – kids who'd run away from home or been kicked out or just needed somewhere to chill – the reaction was almost hostile: 'But we don't have that kind of problem in Southwood. Maybe a bit over in Southwood East, but not up here.' I was as guilty of that kind of thinking as anyone. We didn't want to admit that our lovely suburb could have such troubled kids, let alone homeless kids. *Us?*

Everything changed when our next-door neighbours' sixteen-year-old was carted off to hospital suffering a violent reaction to some dodgy drug he'd taken at a party right here in Southwood Fields. Everyone assumed he'd be okay, but after three days of the doctors trying to keep him alive while they worked out what had actually happened to him, he died.

That was a wake-up call, I can tell you. It shocked a lot of people, especially parents. When the full story came out, there was nowhere to hide – it turned out a lot of our kids were into it, one way or another. Underage drinking was the least of our problems.

A few of us got together and decided we had to do something about it. Something low-key – not a great campaign or anything, but just set up a place where kids could go for a bit of advice, a bit of support. Counselling. That type of thing. So we put together a committee and went to the council, and they were very supportive, I must say. They found us a space attached to the old Senior Citizens Centre – a couple of rooms no one was using – and said we could have that.

We had to start raising enough money to allow us to employ staff – even though we knew we'd have to rely on volunteers, we needed a couple of paid professionals to run the show, and train the volunteers. Well . . . what a different story from that last miserable fiasco. People knew this was happening in their own street, or just around the corner, so they were much more responsive. They knew there was a problem, although I must say there was some resistance to the project from people who lived near the place where we were going to set up shop.

Anyway, the place is up and running, and it's going quite well. Lots of kids are starting to use it as a general drop-in centre, so the staff and volunteers have opportunities to talk to them before there's a crisis. And we're all just more generally vigilant about what's happening to our kids. There's more of a genuine community spirit in the neighbourhood, I'd say. Definitely. More looking out for each other.

It took a death, though.

When groups fall apart

Ailsa and Imogen were members of the same book club. Ailsa and her partner, Jerry, were recent arrivals in Southwood and the book club had turned out to be a wonderful way for her to meet some interesting, like-minded women. She had been put in touch with the club's convenor though a contact at the library, and quickly felt at ease among the seven other members of the group. They were neither too serious nor too flippant, and they were always well prepared for the monthly discussions.

Imogen was a long-term resident of Southwood. She and her husband, Martin, had rented an apartment in Southwood Central shortly before their wedding, and had bought a house in Southwood Fields when they began to talk about the possibility of starting a family (though this had not yet happened).

Ailsa and Imogen hit it off from their first meeting. Ailsa was tall and blonde and built like a swimmer; Imogen was short and dark and struggled to keep her weight down. Ailsa was a rowdy extravert, Imogen quieter and more introverted, but they both laughed easily and had a similar sense of humour. They enjoyed the same books, the same music, the same movies. They both worked in city offices, Ailsa for a property development firm and Imogen for a marketing consultancy, and they soon began taking the morning train to the city together and meeting for occasional lunches. Ailsa was delighted to have established such a special bond with Imogen so soon after arriving in Southwood, and it helped her feel more fully integrated with the book club.

When *The Life of Pi* was about to be released as a film, Imogen suggested the members of the book club should plan to see it together when it came to the Lewis cinema, since the book had generated animated discussion and some major differences of opinion within the group. There was some debate about whether partners should be included in such an outing and it was decided that a party of sixteen would be too unwieldy. After some unresolved attempts to agree on a date, the idea lapsed.

Ailsa and Imogen were both keen to see the film, so when it came to Lewis they arranged to go with Jerry and Martin. 'A painless way of introducing our men to each other and to us,' Ailsa had said, always on the front foot. She told the other members of the book club they were going ahead with this plan, and made it clear that anyone else was welcome to join them.

On the night, Ailsa and Jerry collected Imogen and Martin from their home and they drove together to Lewis, the women doing most of the talking on the way.

The film divided each of the couples. Ailsa and Martin both enjoyed it immensely and were captivated by the special effects; Imogen and Jerry were too sceptical to enter into the spirit of it. They all went out for a meal in Lewis after the film and the conversation was lively and good-natured. The men seemed to get on well enough, and each of them established an easy rapport with the other's partner. As a social event, it all went off even more smoothly than the women had hoped it might.

Gradually, the pattern was established that the two couples would have an evening together at the movies about once a month. As time went by, the men showed no sign of developing an independent friendship, but they seemed comfortable enough together, and Jerry and Imogen found they had much in common, both having worked in marketing and knowing a number of the same people. Ailsa and Martin also found conversation with each other easy and relaxed.

A year later, with Ailsa and Imogen's friendship apparently as strong as ever, Jerry came home from work one night much later than usual and, when Ailsa embraced him, she recognised Imogen's rather unusual perfume on his jacket. It was possible, she realised, that it had been someone other than Imogen wearing that same perfume, but the coincidence seemed overpowering. She said nothing, afraid of what she might uncover.

The following morning, the two women met at the station for their usual journey to the city. Their conversation was sporadic and inhibited: both knew something was wrong. Ailsa felt she might choke on the smell of Imogen's perfume. (Had Imogen splashed it on more recklessly than usual, Ailsa wondered, or was

Ailsa now hypersensitive to it? It felt to her like an olfactory assault.) Imogen, reserved by nature, seemed to Ailsa to have become restrained to the point of reticence. Two stations before their destination, Ailsa asked Imogen whether she ever had to work late. Imogen seemed confused by the question and simply said: 'Of course. Don't you?'

'And last night?' asked Ailsa.

Imogen looked into Ailsa's face and then looked away.

Ailsa stared at her. 'You faithless wretch,' she said, barely audibly. 'You disgusting, deceitful bitch.'

Sitting in the aisle seat, Imogen started back as if she had been physically struck. She gathered up her belongings, turned to Ailsa and silently mouthed, 'Sorry.' Then she stood up, moved towards the carriage door and got off the train one stop before their usual station. Ailsa stayed where she was. That was the last time the women spoke to each other.

Jerry's confession came quickly, once Ailsa let him think Imogen had explicitly admitted everything. Yes, he had met Imogen occasionally for a drink after work, initially with a group of colleagues. Yes, one thing had led to another. No, he wasn't going to discuss 'where they went'. Yes, he felt it was serious. No, he would not say what he 'saw in her' and no, Martin didn't know about it. Yes, he would pack up and leave. Yes, he was sorry. No, he hadn't thought through the consequences, obviously.

Ailsa, furious, phoned Martin to explain some of the less savoury interpretations of 'working back'. He was not grateful for the call.

Ailsa and Jerry parted immediately. Martin and Imogen stayed together, but sold their home in Southwood and moved elsewhere, at Martin's insistence.

Both women left the book club.

The other six members of the club were shocked by what had happened. They felt almost as betrayed by Imogen and as deceived by her warmth towards Ailsa as Ailsa herself did. They lost heart. Imogen was their old friend; Ailsa was the newcomer. They were confused, sad, angry and disappointed. The book club dissolved. Three of them joined other groups; three gave away the idea entirely.

~

It is not uncommon for an acrimonious divorce to lead to ripple-effect estrangements within the divorcing couple's circle. If the female friends of the wife feel she has been shabbily treated, they may urge their partners to break off all contact with the husband. In the case of any fractured relationship, marital or otherwise, the other members of a network can hardly restrain themselves from taking sides. Though everyone acknowledges that 'there are two sides to every story', individual members of a family or friendship group usually accept only one of them. Having decided to support one of the parties involved, it's easy to swallow their version of events and to remain sceptical about any alternative interpretations. 'I'm *your* friend' usually implies that I'll accept your side of the story and that, in turn, implies an undertaking to put some distance between me and the other party. The integrity of the network is then threatened even more fundamentally by the fact that it has divided itself into two camps.

Love sometimes fades; friendships sometimes reach their use-by date; most partners disappoint each other in large and small ways; people lose interest in each other, for reasons that are not always easy to explain; even apparently committed spouses sometimes lose their way and wander into Lovers Lane. Occasional fractures and breakdowns are inevitable. Yet all our personal relationships, even of the most intimate kind, function within the context of larger networks – families, friendship circles, workgroups, neighbourhoods – and the termination of a personal relationship usually has a negative impact on the dynamics of those networks.

Such collateral damage is often painful, because it challenges the very basis on which the other members of a group have come to feel that they belong in this place, with these people. Most of us belong to more than one network – more than one herd – but the disintegration or loss of any one of them generally involves some adjustment, some loss of trust, perhaps even a period of feeling somewhat adrift or disorientated.

Depending on the importance of the group to us, such fractures can also create some emotional vulnerability. In just the same way as partners who have separated sometimes fall in love quite inappropriately 'on the rebound', so people bruised by their estrangement from a herd – being left out of family events after a separation or divorce, for instance, or coming to realise that a friendship group is no longer functioning as it once did – may respond too eagerly to fresh possibilities. Feelings of disorientation following such a loss of connection may make us more than usually vulnerable to the blandishments of commercial, religious or political propaganda, to say nothing of our responsiveness to other overtures, sexual and otherwise, we might normally have resisted. Alternatively, we may retreat for a while into our shell, withdrawing from social contact in order to protect ourselves from further hurt.

One way or another, when a group falls to pieces, its members will eventually need to regroup. That's the kind of creatures we are. If we allow the experience of one fractured group to inhibit our enthusiasm for belonging to others, we will be the losers.

In Southwood, we used to have a thriving men's choir. It grew to be quite a serious affair – we even competed in a couple of eisteddfods and male voice festivals. Our accompanist was the conductor's wife, and he treated her atrociously. Abused her in front of the choir, criticised her playing – it was appalling. Eventually a few of us were deputed to go and speak to him about it. We told him that Deirdre might be his wife but she was our accompanist and we were not prepared to have her treated like that at rehearsals.

The repercussions were terrible. He was furious with us, furious with her . . . lost the plot entirely. Rehearsals became intolerable. The tension was palpable and he continued to treat his wife badly, but now with a kind of icy politeness that reduced her to tears on more than one occasion.

Men started leaving. The choir was soon reduced to a rump of its former self, barely able to rustle up enough people for a performance. Eventually, we all packed it in.

A few men went across to Glee and seemed to integrate quite well, but most just lost interest in singing in a choir. They had been too badly burnt by that experience – me included. I still sing under the shower, but that's about it.

Friendships cool for all kinds of reasons and this, too, can cause ripples on the social pond. Mothers who have struck up a relationship based on their children's friendships with each other may become estranged as a result of arguments, rivalries or tensions between their children: *Did your son really say that to my son? Do you realise what your daughter has been saying about my daughter behind her back?* The knot of mothers caught up in such wrangles can quickly unravel, with some resultant strain.

Neighbours who have become close friends can experience a similar kind of awkwardness if, for some reason, their friendship wavers. They might find themselves on opposite sides of a neighbourhood dispute, or some tension may arise from a disagreement over how to deal with an overhanging bough or an ill-disciplined dog. Or they may simply come to recognise that the tricky, blurry line between neighbourliness and personal friendship should possibly never have been crossed in their case. Too much intimacy can become a problem when its basis is mere proximity rather than spontaneous friendship. When such a realisation occurs, it can be difficult to re-establish the less personal, less intimate relationship that is characteristic of good neighbours who don't aspire to become each other's close friends.

The things we expect — or hope for — from our neighbours are usually rather different from those we expect or hope for from our friends, though there's obviously some overlap. We want to know our neighbours well enough to be able to call on them for help when it's needed, and vice versa. We want to feel as if we are on sufficiently friendly terms to be able to do occasional favours for each other — look after our mail, or perhaps a pet, when we're away; take in each other's garbage bins; lend each other a tool, or a few plates for a larger-than-usual social event. We may also choose to socialise occasionally — Christmas drinks, street parties and perhaps an outing to a local cafe to mark some special event. Where children are involved, the links between neighbours can be quite strong, particularly if they have lived next door to each other for a long time and watched each other's kids grow up.

But there's still a level of intimacy between close friends that neighbours rarely want or need to achieve. (One sign of the difference: when one neighbour moves away from the street, the other neighbours rarely maintain contact, yet close friends stay in touch regardless of where they may roam.) The very fact that we are living in close proximity to each other is, for most people, a cause for some appropriate restraint: we have to continue to get along as neighbours, so we don't want to load the relationship with too much emotional freight. How often have you heard people praise their neighbours by remarking that 'we don't live in each other's pockets'?

Yet neighbours form one of the important networks that link us to each other and to the community. John Donne's famous line — 'No man is an island entire of itself' — applies as much to relationships as it does to individuals. Because of our interdependence and interconnectedness as members of a community, we need to recognise that no relationship – romantic, friendly, familial, professional, neighbourly – is 'entire of itself'. We are all like dots that have been joined, and when a relationship dies or undergoes some revision or upheaval, it's not just a matter for those two 'dots' to deal with: the wider network is inevitably affected. Pluck one strand of a spider's web and watch the whole web vibrate. That's what human group dynamics are like.

When neighbours become adversaries

In Southwood Rise, an explosive situation has developed between two neighbours. Alan and Sue Hermann live in Raven Close – a cul-de-sac that runs off Liesl Crescent – and Peter and Kate Ludwig live next door. They both have children and the two families have had a history of being socially engaged. They have had several backyard barbecues; Sue and Kate occasionally have coffee at Bruno's; the kids ride their bikes together.

Peter Ludwig has always had some reservations about the Hermanns. Kate thinks he imagines it, but he is convinced there's a touch of jealousy there. From what he can gather, Alan Hermann is a pretty accomplished funds manager in one of the major banks, though he's not in Peter's league, Peter himself believes, when it comes to income. Peter is a senior figure in what he describes as a 'boutique investment vehicle'. Some people, including Alan, are not sure what that means.

The Hermanns admired the Ludwigs and had always been pleased to have them as neighbours, until they discovered a new room was about to be added to the side of the Ludwigs' house. Without any consultation at all, the Ludwigs submitted a development application to the council to add a room that, from the beginning, the Hermanns realised would block a significant amount of light from their living room windows and overlook their back garden.

When they received a copy of the application from the council, the Hermanns were more puzzled than worried: they could hardly believe the Ludwigs would have gone ahead with a DA without consulting them first. Convinced there must be some misunderstanding, they knocked on the Ludwigs' front door and asked for an opportunity to discuss the application. Peter Ludwig glanced at the paper they were holding and failed to invite them in. He simply said he had been assured by the council that the application was perfectly straightforward and no rules were being broken.

'But what about the effect on our sunlight? What about your new room looking straight into our back garden? Couldn't you have discussed this with us first? Can't we negotiate something – a bit of compromise?'

'I hear what you're saying, but actually it doesn't hold water. We've had the architect do all the drawings – shadow diagrams, the lot. It's all perfectly legal. There really isn't anything to discuss. You have no grounds for complaint. You're free to lodge an objection with the council, of course, but I'm assured it won't stand up to scrutiny.' Peter was not smiling as he said this.

The Hermanns lodged their objection. They had a meeting with a sympathetic officer in the building department at Southwood Council who assured them the Ludwigs had indeed done their homework. There were no grounds for an appeal against the application.

'Didn't you discuss this with them before it got to the DA stage?' the council officer asked.

'We didn't know a thing about it until we got the notice from you.'

'Really?' he said, unable to hide his incredulity. 'Do you normally talk to them? Socially, I mean?'

'Of course we do. We thought we were quite good friends. It's just that they chose not to discuss this with us – not even to let on they were going to do it. What about them overlooking our back garden?'

The council officer shrugged. 'They've been very careful with their window size and placement. I recommend you plant a tree or two.'

The building proceeded with many delays and problems, one of which caused a section of the fence between the Ludwigs and the Hermanns to be demolished. The builder asked the Hermanns if he could erect a scaffold where the fence had come down, encroaching slightly on their side of the boundary, to allow his workmen easier access to the job. The Hermanns agreed – they had nothing to lose, they thought, and they hoped a bit of accommodation on their part might ease the tension between the two families.

It didn't. The Ludwigs showed no sign of appreciating the gesture.

The extension was completed two months later than the estimate. The scaffold was removed and a half-hearted attempt made by the builder to clear away the rubble from the Hermanns' side of the boundary. There was no sign of any attempt to replace the demolished section of the side fence.

Once again, Alan Hermann approached Peter Ludwig. 'I assume you'll be replacing the fence,' he said.

'I'll take it up with the builder,' said Peter. 'It will be covered by his insurance.'

Six months later, the fence was still not repaired and Kate Hermann could be seen, night after night, standing at the side of her house making hex signs in the direction of the Ludwigs.

From the Ludwigs' point of view, hostilities had moved to the other side of their property, where they were now defending their plan to enlarge their garage and put a media room on top of it. The neighbours on that side were threatening legal action.

'Why do people have to make life so difficult?' Peter Ludwig said to his wife one night as they lay in bed dreaming of a second storey.

'Maybe we should move to Lewis,' said Kate. 'Or Kentwell.'

'No – that would feel like a surrender. I refuse to give in to these people.'

~

There's no law that says neighbours must be nice to each other. And there's no law that says, when it comes to building extensions, noise, tree plantings, dog control or other encroachments on our neighbours' amenity, we should go beyond the requirements of the council's regulations. But the spirit of community says otherwise. Does anyone really believe that the legalities are the only considerations the Ludwigs should have taken into account?

Sometimes it takes much less than a building extension to turn neighbours' friendship into enmity – or, at least, into something cooler and more distant. Just down the street from the Ludwigs, another pair of neighbours fell out over a remark made by one woman about her neighbour's husband. 'He gives the bottle a real nudge,' she had said to a mutual friend. In the way of such things, that remark quickly found its way to ears of the drinker's wife, with full attribution, and that was that.

When the thread of connection frays

The prospect of being cut off from a community that sustains us is appalling. If we are suddenly retrenched from a workplace that had come to feel like a place where we belonged, the consequences can be catastrophic, at least for a while. Stories abound of men too humiliated to tell their friends or neighbours – or even their family – that they've lost their job, and who continued to dress as if for work, continued to take the usual bus or train to the city, and then spent the day wandering about aimlessly, trying to come to terms with what had happened to them.

Similar feelings of dislocation and disorientation have sometimes overwhelmed members of the armed forces, returning to civilian life after war service and finding it almost impossible to become reintegrated – not only with the neighbourhood but sometimes even with their own family. The Men's Shed movement began as a result of just such feelings among some Australian soldiers returning home from service in the Vietnam War: by offering them a place to feel secure and connected, and by providing opportunities for voluntary work that would gradually reconnect them to the community, Men's Sheds have played a crucial role in the lives of many men – including those newly retired – who might otherwise have struggled to find their feet.

Southwood Men's Shed has been operating for ten years, with financial support from two of the local churches and accommodation supplied by the council. The current president is Bill Hartley, a retired public servant.

'Some of our fellows are pretty cut up when they first come here. They are grieving over the death of a loved one, or maybe they've been divorced or taken some other kind of knock. Some of them are having trouble adjusting to retirement – particularly a retrenchment that came sooner than they were expecting. We don't offer counselling as such, though we do send some of the fellows off to a counsellor who keeps an eye on us – a local psychologist with a wonderfully light touch. But you'd be surprised how helpful it can be just to sit down with a few blokes who've been through the mill, and talk things over.

It's not just the talking, of course. The big thing is the work we do. We have a fully equipped workshop, and we can do all sorts of repair work on furniture, toys, bicycles, scooters, lawnmowers, you name it. Even old appliances, provided they're not too far gone. We're fortunate here – we've got a retired sparky in the group, as well as a couple of carpenters and a painter. But most of them are blokes like me: no trades background at all, but we'll have a go at anything. We don't take work away from the tradesmen or retailers – we're very careful about that. The stuff we repair would normally just get chucked out. And when we tackle a project like painting someone's house, or cleaning up a garden, it's for people who couldn't afford to pay a tradie to do it. So we're confident we're not eating into anyone's livelihood.

Once people get involved, you can see the change in them. They might come here for a bit of support and so on, but it's a working shed, I always tell them, and the work soon takes over. Before they know it, they're thinking more about the families we're helping – especially the kids. There's nothing like lending a helping hand to take your mind off your own troubles, and get you up and running. A bit of community service and – hey, presto – you're feeling part of the place again. It's not rocket science, is it?

Social isolation

Dotted around Southwood are people who, for a wide variety of reasons feel their sense of connection with the community is in danger of fraying.

The relentless demands of caring for disabled, sick or frail family members, or even for young children, can narrow the focus of daily life to the point where the carers find it hard even to hang on to the idea that there's a 'a life' going on in the community around them. If neighbours don't stay in touch – occasionally calling in to see how they are getting on, perhaps making a cup of tea and staying for a chat or offering to do some shopping – feelings of isolation and confinement can snowball into a miserable sense of exclusion.

Some people become socially withdrawn because they are crippled by grief, or other forms of sadness or disappointment, or because they lose their nerve: the erosion of confidence in their own social competence may not amount to mental illness, but it might be enough of a problem to inhibit their normal social interaction, perhaps by reinforcing their natural shyness.

A growing number of grandparents are unexpectedly finding themselves thrust into the role of full-time carers for grandchildren whose parents are both working and who don't wish – or can't afford – to use child-care services. In some cases, the circumstances are more dire: the children's parents might be barely able to cope with the care of young children because of their own emotional problems, health issues, drug addiction, criminality or other difficulties that may have rendered them temporarily incompetent as parents. Grandparents drawn into a second phase of parenting typically report that not only are they struggling to find the energy and patience to keep up with young children, but that their own social lives are put on hold for months or even years.

Single parents are sometimes at risk of social exclusion because of the intense demands of caring for one or more children without the support of a partner. Although children often act as the catalysts for social connections between families, single parents may feel that they simply don't have the time – or the energy – to devote to such connections, and they may also feel some awkwardness about trying to integrate with a group of parents who are all couples.

Whatever the cause, social exclusion is a major blow to our sense of identity. It also creates a challenge for neighbours. In some of Southwood's streets where neighbours have established regular contact with each other, people are alert to any problems of social isolation in their midst; in places where neighbours have not been quite so assiduous about keeping in touch, the very invisibility of the socially isolated means they don't attract anyone's attention. In the most tragic cases, social isolation has preceded a lonely, unnoticed death.

The art of belonging is not just about finding your own place in the networks and neighbourhoods that sustain you; it's also about creating space for others to join (or rejoin) the circle. Social exclusion is a crime against humanity. While it's true that people sometimes exclude themselves, our duty as humans is to ensure that they receive every encouragement to reconnect, knowing that the longer they remain excluded, the harder it will be for them to emerge from the shadows.

Shame

The thread of connection with the community might also be frayed by shame over a partner who strays, a child who gets into trouble with the law, a financial disaster that cripples a family. All such situations call for sensitivity and compassion from friends and neighbours, and sometimes the individuals who find themselves in the midst of such personal dramas actually do need a break from socialising: people temporarily crippled by shame will naturally wish to avoid the embarrassment of having to discuss a painful topic.

Shame is, after all, a social phenomenon. It's our reaction to the knowledge that other people have seen or heard something about us – something we feel sure they would condemn or be shocked by or at least disapprove of – and that makes us squirm. It's the humiliation of having our vulnerability exposed to the public gaze that generates feelings of shame. (Guilt, by contrast, is a personal, private matter: an alarm rung by our conscience, alerting us to the fact that we have offended against some moral code of our own, or contradicted some values we claim to espouse. You can feel guilty on your own, but it takes a social context to induce shame – and you can feel ashamed without feeling guilty.)

Eventually, friends and neighbours bear some responsibility for helping to ease the shamed person back into 'communion' – into a place where they feel able to accept the emotional nourishment that a supportive community offers.

Bereavement

For many people, the most dramatic experience of 'frayed connection' comes after the death of a spouse. In one moment, you are part of a couple, fully integrated with your family, your friendship circles, the neighbourhood and the wider community as an established pair.

Then, suddenly, you're on your own.

US novelist Joyce Carol Oates describes bereavement as shocking and surprising: 'You have some strong compulsion to do some weird thing, like set the house on fire. Or give away your cat,' she says, describing her own experience of new widowhood.

Even if your partner had been ill for a long time, even if the final stages of an illness were drawn out to the point where death came as a relief for all concerned, even if the quality of the relationship had deteriorated with the passing of the years . . . a pair is still a very different thing from a widowed sole survivor. And if your partner has been torn away from you by an accidental death or sudden illness, the shock is correspondingly more acute.

Molly Swift knows all about that. She and Stuart had moved around a lot during their thirty years of married life – he was a mining engineer and she was a doctor – and they had settled in Southwood Fields three years ago in anticipation of Stuart's retirement. Molly gave up medicine when they returned to the city, and she had begun to enjoy the suburban life. She was not long home from her art class when she received the news that Stuart had been killed in a light plane crash. It was a Friday morning; she'll never forget the day or the hour, or the ticking of the kitchen clock.

Everyone was wonderfully kind when Stu died. The kids came from interstate to stay, the neighbours rallied round, the funeral service was everything Stu would have wanted it to be. And then suddenly there was nothing. It was all over. The kids went back to their own lives, as they had to, a couple of the neighbours would drop in or phone occasionally, but I suppose they assumed that I was a reasonably competent woman, perfectly capable of getting on with life.

But there seemed to be no life to be getting on with.

I remember sitting by myself in front of the television a week after the funeral and thinking, 'I'm a widow at fifty-eight. This is what it feels like.'

Because we'd only been here for three years and Stu was on the move so much, the house hadn't really come to feel like his yet – we were looking forward to doing a few renovations and creating a proper study for him. That was all in the future. But he was a very gregarious person – much more than I am – and so the neighbours all knew him and he'd struck up a couple of really nice friendships with other men in Southwood, mainly through the golf club.

Now he's gone, I feel strangely reticent about socialising – not that I'm asked anywhere much. People only knew us as a couple and I suppose they have to adjust to the idea of me being on my own, the same as I have to. I've had some funny approaches from people, I can tell you. A couple of neighbours have been here – men, offering to do any odd jobs. One of them came quite late one night and I felt his intentions were not entirely honourable. And there was a woman who asked me out for coffee and she was trying to run the line that she knew how I felt – knew how it felt to be suddenly on your own. But her situation couldn't have been more different from mine. I discovered she had walked out on her husband – I have this from one of the neighbours – so I thought she had a real cheek suggesting that she and I had anything in common. I don't return her calls.

I know I'll have to ease back into some kind of social life. It's much easier as a couple, though. I think I probably always let Stu take the lead. Anyway, I've kept up the art class, but I'll need to do more. I'm not going back to medicine – I'm too out of touch with it now – but I think I might do some volunteering, if anyone wants me.

Funny how disconnected you can feel, right in the middle of a busy suburb like this – and a friendly enough suburb, I'm sure. I could move, I suppose, but I don't think I will. I think I'll see how life works out. It's a new phase all right. But it's all been so sudden.

Distressed children

Twice a month, a team of three therapists arrives in Southwood to work with seven or eight children who have been referred to them by teachers, social workers or other health-care workers. Their specialties are music therapy, art therapy and drama therapy, and the children they work with come from a wide variety of backgrounds, but have this in common: they are struggling to deal with some personal trauma.

Before they have even got through childhood, they may have found themselves the victims of abuse, neglect, bereavement through the death of a parent or sibling, unendurable domestic tension, family dislocation, relentless bullying or serious illness. Some have become uncontrollably aggressive; some have withdrawn into a private world where they hope no more trouble can reach them; some have developed an aching desire for someone to notice them, listen to them, play with them, hold them; some have already become cynical. In all cases, their sense of belonging has been diminished.

It generally takes ten sessions for the team to achieve its therapeutic goals. During the program, a workshop will be conducted for parents and carers, so they can better understand what is being attempted. As far as possible, it's made to feel like play. Talk is encouraged; tears are shed; paint is splashed and sometimes hurled; images of a brighter future begin to emerge; music does its healing work; fears and anxieties are acted out and dreams begin to be dreamed. Gradually, peace descends, and smiles appear on most of the faces (not all: these therapists are angels, not magicians). By the time the children are ready to leave the program, its effects are being felt not only in the children themselves, but in their families ('We didn't know he was capable of doing things like this') and in their schools. The therapists call their operation 'our little mobile village' and that's exactly how it must feel to the kids. 'I feel safe here,' says one of the nine-year-olds, and you sense she hasn't been able to feel safe anywhere else.

'Mental' illness

Although a warm, supportive family or a few close friends can help most of us weather times of emotional turbulence, more severe cases of emotional debilitation – including depression, anxiety or any form of so-called 'mental' illness – need the same level of specialist professional treatment as any other illness. The community is a place of healing, up to a point. But where the special skills of a psychiatrist or psychologist are required – in suicide prevention, for instance – it can be dangerous to assume that sympathetic friendship and loving support are enough. Several Southwood families have had to learn to live with the knowledge that their care and concern were not enough to save a teenage son or daughter from suicide.

The problem is compounded by the fact that mental illness can fray apparently well-established connections with family, friends or neighbours. People who suffer from even relatively mild forms of depression, anxiety, panic attacks or obsessive-compulsive disorder – to say nothing of more serious psychotic conditions such as paranoia and schizophrenia – often come to feel cut off, either because their state of mind renders them uncomfortable in social situations or because they feel they can no longer function as 'normal' members of the community. Sometimes this is due to an actual loss of social competence, and sometimes it's due to a kind of self-stigmatisation, where the person assumes that mental illness is so different from other forms of illness (or that other people might think it is), it would be best to keep quiet about it.

Many people regard the distinction between 'mental' and 'physical' illness as self-evident. Yet no one quite knows where to draw that line, and many philosophers, psychologists, biologists and neuroscientists dispute the whole idea of a mind–body duality. The more we learn about dementia, for instance, the more we realise that the 'mental' is physical, too.

The brain's biochemistry is particularly sensitive to fluctuating hormone levels. Any woman who has experienced the horrors of extreme pre-menstrual tension or the bleak depths of post-natal depression knows that hormonal changes in the body can alter our brain states in ways that feel decidedly 'mental'. Indeed, when you consider our wild mood swings, our unprovoked outbreaks of emotional and even physical violence, the insistent power of sexual desire and the countless examples of the apparently irrational behaviour of humans – including our notorious tendency to become cranky when hungry – it's probably fair to describe the brain as being more like a gland than a computer.

We talk confidently of 'psychosomatic' illness – as if the problem starts in 'the mind' (presumably meaning 'the brain') and then somehow expresses itself in 'the body' (presumably meaning some other, non-brain part of the body). Even if this distinction between 'psyche' and 'soma' were valid, it still wouldn't rule out the possibility that an apparently 'mental' illness might have arisen from a physical condition: is it a person's anxiety that causes their irritable bowel, or is it an irritable bowel that causes their anxiety? Or are they both manifestations of a third factor, like stress (from work, perhaps, or from a difficult relationship) or unresolved tensions arising from early childhood trauma, a poor diet, a lack of exercise, or some as-yet-undetected disease that attacks both brain and bowel? Or are the brain and the bowel in a symbiotic relationship?

This is not to rule out the category of illness we call 'mental', but simply to suggest that illnesses associated with particular brain-states ought to be regarded in roughly the same way as any of the other categories of human ailments (gastrointestinal disorders, cardiovascular disease or respiratory problems, for instance) requiring appropriate professional diagnosis and treatment. The original use of the word 'madness' to describe some forms of aberrant behaviour certainly hasn't helped, but in the modern world, to stigmatise such behaviour – even to stigmatise the experience of having dark and disturbing thoughts – is surely a sign of how little we understand the operation of the human anatomy.

The number of high-profile individuals who now refer as openly to their depression as they might to their respiratory ailments has begun to influence public perceptions of mental illness. Dr Geoff Gallop, the former premier of Western Australia, has been prominent among those prepared to discuss the impact of depression on their lives – in his case, leading to his resignation as premier and his retirement from politics. (Gallop has also expressed concern about a possible unintended consequence of this greater openness: that some people who are experiencing the natural emotional cycles of everyday life may become overeager to seek a diagnosis that will qualify for treatment, preferably via medication.)

As long as the stigma persists – in sufferers themselves, or in the wider community – mental illness has the potential to create social exclusion; to diminish our confidence that we are legitimate members of a 'healthy' community; to cause us to question whether we are pulling our weight as friends or neighbours.

The impact of mental illness – or any chronic illness – on family members and carers is well known. What is not often discussed is the impact on partners of the various forms of psychotherapy a sufferer may turn to for relief. In many cases, the therapeutic process is so intense, and so rewarding for the one experiencing it, that a partner may come to feel not only excluded but emotionally superfluous.

Walter and Marie Bilson live in Southwood Ponds. When Marie began showing signs of uncontrollable anxiety, Walter saw she was struggling and did what he could to support her. Eventually, he encouraged her to seek professional help from a psycho-therapist. Although he remained solicitous and sympathetic, Walter soon came to realise that he was to be excluded from the therapeutic process. At first, he would ask Marie how the session had gone, and would try to elicit some information about the sort of thing that was being discussed, or the kind of progress Marie thought she might be making. He felt this was a natural, normal response from a loving and supportive husband, but Marie would only ever say, 'Oh, Dr McKern is very good,' and leave it at that.

Gradually, Walter came to resent these meetings between Marie and her therapist and to feel as if the only intimacy left in his relationship with his wife was sexual, though even that was being affected by Walter's uneasy feeling that there was a ghostly third party in their bed – as though everything he did or said might become grist for the therapist's mill. He assumed that Marie's deepest and most significant thoughts – the kind of things they had once discussed openly with each other – were now being reserved for her sessions with the therapist.

Increasingly hurt and frustrated by this, Walter mentioned his concerns to his close friend Theo whose ex-wife had struggled with depression. Theo smiled knowingly. 'Tell me about it – I used to feel as if it was the equivalent of me going to see a callgirl: paying for a kind of intimacy you couldn't get from your marriage. I always thought my wife and I were on the same wavelength; she used to say we were like soul mates, but not after this happened. She clammed up totally – that was the thing that got to me. I was all in favour of her going to this fellow, but I assumed I'd get the odd progress report. Nothing. Zilch.'

This sounded familiar to Walter. 'I must say I had assumed a counsellor would suggest this is something you might like to share with your husband,' he said. 'You know, talk it over a bit, like Marie and I always used to do.'

'Oh, no. They run it like the confessional – everything you say in here stays in here. Well, it's a two-way street, isn't it? Eventually, I just backed right off. Then, guess what – my wife complained that I was bottling things up. You can't win.'

Walter was already regretting having raised this with Theo. He simply shrugged.

'Anyway,' Theo said, 'you have a choice. You can try to ignore it – go into denial, as the professionals say. It's not normally recommended, but sometimes it's a bloody good coping strategy.'

'Or?'

'Sign up with a therapist yourself.'

'I think that would feel weird,' said Walter. 'What would I say – I'm here because I need help coping with my wife's psychotherapy? I don't think so.'

Over the following weeks, Theo occasionally enquired how the process was going, but Walter eventually asked him not to mention the subject again. He was grappling with the uncomfortable feeling that not only had the therapeutic process created a barrier between him and Marie, but it had become the one subject he couldn't discuss with his friends. Even to raise it felt disloyal to his marriage.

Not all men and women whose partners are in therapy feel as Walter did. Some are relieved to have a qualified person take over the burden of listening to their partner on a subject they may feel has already been 'done to death', or where they have felt out of their depth: 'I'm all in favour of outsourcing – my wife gets a sympathetic shoulder to lean on, and I'm off the hook, basically.'

People who are uncomfortable with the whole notion of mental illness may be alarmed by a partner's willingness – even eagerness – to speak openly to family members or friends about their experience of therapy. Others, grateful for professional help that might reduce tension in the relationship, are happy to leave it to their partner to decide whether or not this is a process that should be shared.

Who is a 'burden' on the community?

The phrase 'a burden on the community' is often used to describe people who seem to be taking more than they give and who, through poverty, illness, misfortune or frailty, require more care and attention than the rest of us.

To use the word 'burden' to describe people in need is to completely misunderstand the nature of a community and to overlook the responsibility we all bear for the health and wellbeing of those less fortunate than we are.

In any case, the so-called burden keeps shifting. Let's take three examples.

Refugees?

In the early months or years in their adopted country, some refugees may be heavily dependent on welfare, public housing, health care and training in language and job skills. Then, as they find their feet, they are typically keen to work and make a positive contribution to the society that has welcomed them. That, after all, is why they fled their homeland and became refugees in the first place: to find 'a new life'. Even if they have arrived unconventionally, as asylum seekers, once their status as genuine refugees has been established, any civilised host country will offer them the support they need, unconditionally, while they adapt to that new life.

In the overwhelming majority of such cases, the outcome is positive: refugees and their children become fully-functioning members of the society, keen to make their mark and to repay the host nation for its humane generosity towards them at their time of greatest need, greatest vulnerability and greatest fear. 'Burden' hardly seems the right word to describe the early, post-arrival phase of their lives when they are being prepared for the more productive, more contributive phase. (We don't call our children a 'burden' on society while they are at school, do we?)

The elderly?

With the ageing of the population in all Western societies – a direct consequence of low birthrates and greater longevity – it's become fashionable to speak of the burden likely to be placed on the health-care system, in particular, by people who are no longer earning their keep via taxable wages. What a strange way to speak of the members of a generation who have spent a lifetime paying taxes; who may still be paying taxes on their investments; who are continuing in paid work for longer than any previous generation in our history. What a strange way to speak of the generation some societies might respect, even revere, as their 'tribal elders'. What a strange way to evaluate the distribution of a society's resources – as if the only way to do it is to take a snapshot at any given moment and decide that some are givers, right now, and some are takers, right now, without acknowledging what the net 'takers' might have already given, or, like refugees and children, might give in the future.

Quite apart from those quantifiable contributions, there's the vexed question of voluntary work performed by older people who may have left the paid workforce. In her hard-hitting analysis *In Praise of Ageing* (2013), Australian sociologist and educator Patricia Edgar explodes the myth that an ageing population is unrelievedly bad news for our social and economic future. She points out that, in Australia, the voluntary work done by 'non-earners' contributes significantly to the health of the economy – to say nothing of the health of the society. Drawing on a 2003 Australian Institute of Family Studies report by David de Vaus, Matthew Gray and David Stanton, Edgar notes that 'those over 55 contribute the staggering sum of $74.5 billion a year through caring for spouses and grandchildren and in other unpaid voluntary work. Women aged 65 to 74 contributed $16 billion in unpaid work inside and outside the home; men of that age, who are fewer in number, contributed another $10.3 billion.' What is productivity, Edgar asks, when our GDP 'fails to measure the significant dollar value of caring work, voluntary work, community work and creative work, without which our economy could not function, and none of which is a monopoly of the young?'

You only have to consult the members of the sixty-five- to seventy-five-year-old cohort to be rocked back on your heels by the vehemence of their reaction to any suggestion that they might have reached the stage where 'finished' is the right word, never mind 'burden'. The members of this generation typically regard themselves as healthier, fitter, livelier and mentally more acute than their parents were at the same age (if their parents had survived this long, that is). They look forward to a long and active future. We shall let Arnold Crabtree, a recent arrival in Southwood Ponds, speak for them:

I think I may go quietly bonkers if I hear another remark about the ageing population. Yes, we're all ageing, day by day, year by year, every last man, woman, boy and girl of us. We are all precisely one year older than we were a year ago.

I know what they mean, of course. The proportion of people over the age of sixty-five is rising rapidly, estimated to be 25 percent of the population by the middle of the century. That's down to a falling birthrate, of course, which is hardly our fault. I think I can confidently predict that I shall not be here to witness this demographic tsunami, though what with new hips and transplanted hearts and miracle drugs and what not, who knows? In fact, come to think of it, I'll only be 104 by then. A bit unlikely, I suppose – my wife says she's going to hit me over the head if I become a burden.

But seriously, at sixty-eight I'd say I'm still in pretty good shape. I went to the dentist for a check-up and he said, 'Your teeth are not bad, considering they're sixty-eight years old.' He was trying to be lighthearted, but I took exception to that. The doctor said the same thing about my feet when I complained about a bit of soreness in the heel. The wife of a friend of mine got worse treatment than that at the doctor: she was told she didn't need to have any more pap smears now she had turned seventy – as if there was no point: you're seventy, so you can sink or swim. What century are those doctors living in? Actually, I shouldn't be too harsh – there must come a point in life when expensive tests are a waste of money, because these things are probably not going to have time to kill you. That's what my doctor says about prostate cancer – you'll die with it, not from it. On the other hand, I remember my mother, at eighty-eight, being told by her GP that she'd have to get her cholesterol level down. She just sneered at that. 'I'll eat what I like at my age,' she said, which I thought was fair enough.

And then there was our friend who went to buy a rather expensive new coat and the sales woman said to her – actually *said* to her – 'Do you think you'll get the wear out of it?' Our friend is pushing eighty, but still . . .

I'm still working at the old firm. Only four days a week, but they still need me, and I still need them – they're a bit like family. I've told them it's down to three days a week next year and then I'm retiring fully at seventy. But that just means I'll be doing something else. Voluntary work of some kind – lots of charities need a bit of accounting help. Or I can do something useful up at the Ostara Foundation, or maybe coach the slow readers at our local school. I was a slow reader myself. My wife is already volunteering at the hospital – it's the older folk they rely on, of course, the retired ones, especially now so many women are working full-time into their late fifties and beyond.

We'll travel a bit. We'll spend some time with the grandchildren. We'll get stuck into the garden. But we won't be slackers. While we're fit and able, we'll keep making ourselves useful. We didn't come here to veg out. We came here to make a fresh start – to refocus, not retire. Why not? Seventy is the new sixty, or is it the new fifty? I've forgotten. Anyway, my own father was a broken man by the time he was my age. He died before he reached seventy. He'd worked hard all his life, retired at sixty-five and his health went. It was like the switch was turned off. I remember him as an old man.

I can't say I've never felt better – there are a few aches and pains – but I've got a bloody sight more life in me than you might think. I'm looking forward to having more freedom in a couple of years, and I intend to use it. I may learn to play the trumpet. I've always wanted to do that. Don't tell my wife.

Dr Aubrey Jones, the GP who worked with Jim Glasson to establish his singles club, gets angry when he reads about the strain on the health system created by an ageing population. 'I'll tell you the real strain,' he says. 'Obesity.' Aubrey sees obesity as a seriously under-rated problem that will cast a long shadow over Southwood's future, though he recognises it's hardly a local problem.

I'm not sure where this is going to end. People don't seem to understand the consequences of being overweight, let alone obese – it's a huge risk factor in cardiovascular disease, type two diabetes and some forms of cancer, to say nothing of arthritis. It's at least as big a health problem as smoking used to be. Yet there's no serious attempt being made to address it. We banned advertising for smoking and jacked the prices up, but there's no sign of us doing any of that for soft drinks, yet they are one of the main culprits. I talk to my patients about it, but it's very hard to get people to change the way they live – especially their diet – until they are actually sick. Even then, some can't kick the habits of a lifetime. We're supposed to be a caring society – well, sometimes that means taking stern measures for people's own good.

Makes me sad to see some of these young parents who mean well, but they're setting such a terrible example to their own kids by feeding them all this sugary processed stuff. It's like planting a timebomb inside your kids. When I give my talks to the singles club about the mating of primates – yes, I know, people call it Aubrey's eco-porn – I always point out to them that you never see an overweight chimp. Now why is that? I ask them. Everyone knows the answer, of course – diet and exercise – but we haven't reached the stage of being bold enough to change the social environment in ways that will encourage good choices. That's what we did with smokers: we actually made it easier for people *not* to smoke. You don't change people's behaviour by pleading with them – you have to modify the context. As long as we think of sugar as a pleasant, rewarding thing – the way we used to think of nicotine – nothing will change, and the nation's health bill will go up and up.

This is not anyone's personal, private problem. It's a problem for the whole community. We all have to foot the bill – just as with tobacco-related diseases. This idea that 'it's my choice' is bunkum.'

The poor?

Whenever there's talk of 'burdens' on society, the welfare-dependent are usually mentioned, as if it's their fault, though many of the factors that contribute to poverty are entirely beyond the control of the poor – underemployment, for instance. (In Australia, something approaching two million people are either unemployed or underemployed: our official unemployment figures are notoriously misleading, because they only count people who are registered as actually looking for work, and they disqualify anyone who has had at least one hour's work in the past fortnight.) A two-income family may be reduced to one income because of accident or illness and then find itself battling 'post-housing poverty' because too great a proportion of its income is being spent on rent or mortgage payments. Financial hardship may be caused by an acrimonious divorce or a commercial swindle, or disabilities, low intelligence or other accidents of birth.

I suggested in *Advance Australia . . . Where?* (2007) that we're so stuck on the question 'Why are so many people poor?' that we keep forgetting to ask the far more significant question 'Why are so many people rich?' The rapid rise in the number of rich Australians is directly linked to the rapid rise in the number of poor – and the same can be said for many other countries, most notably the US. Year after year, the Organisation for Economic Co-operation and Development has been pointing out that, in spite of its overall level of prosperity, Australia now has one of the most unequal distributions of income in the OECD. The expanding problem of poverty is not a problem in isolation: it's a consequence of a radical shift in the distribution of income that strongly favours the already wealthy.

Poverty will never be eradicated. But it can be minimised by more imaginative approaches to the taxation system and its impact can be reduced by a substantial increase in funds available for public housing, public transport and public education.

The poor do not need to convince us of their need for assistance: their poverty is eloquent enough, and any civilised society, driven by compassion and a respect for all its citizens, will say of the poor: 'They are part of us, too, and we must bring them with us, regardless of the cost.'

Post-school drifters

Like many other urban and rural communities, Southwood has a problem with unemployed young people – males somewhat more than females – who can't quite work out what to do when they leave school. In fact, about a quarter of Southwood's school leavers spend the first year or two in a kind of limbo where they are in neither tertiary education nor full-time employment. Some drift in and out of casual, part-time jobs; some decide to travel on a shoestring budget, perhaps trying to turn this into a 'gap year'; some simply hang around their parents' house, spending odd nights on each other's couches, drinking and dreaming up ways to fill in the time.

Here's one such nineteen-year-old:

This has been the most stressful year of my life. School was, like, okay, I guess, but I wasn't really into it. Not that I got into any trouble, or not much, but I just cruised, mostly. Apart from sport. I loved sport. And art, strangely enough. We had this awesome art teacher.

I had no idea in the world what I wanted to do when I left. I remember walking out the school gate on the last day and thinking: What the fuck now?

My parents split years ago, and I live with my dad, and he was, like, 'You'll have to get a job.' Not so easy, actually. You can stack supermarket shelves until you go crazy, and then what?

'Well, you'll have to do some course,' he said. 'Study something.' Yeah, right. Study what? If I knew what I wanted to do, I'd be doing it. I was going to enrol at the tech for some course or other, but I missed the cut-off point for filling in the form, so that will have to wait until next year.

Anyway, there's a few of us in the same boat, so it's cool. We sort of hang out. We probably drink more than we should. Smoke a bit of grass. But we have an alright time. We sleep late – we're, like, nocturnal animals.

It's funny, you know. I realise my dad means well, but every time we talk about stuff, we end up having an argument, so it's better not to talk, really. I get what he's thinking – *I'm the dad, I'm supposed to do something about this.* Actually, he's doesn't have to do anything about it. It's my shit, not his. I think he gets embarrassed about me. Some of the other guys say that, too. Their parents want to be able to say, 'Oh, my son's at university,' or some shit.

Sometimes we discuss bad-ass stuff. You know, you just imagine, what if we robbed a Pizza Hut, or nicked some old lady's handbag? Stuff like that. We're not going to do it, but you can spend hours working out how it could be done. Could be fun. Until you got caught.

It does my head in occasionally. I can hear myself saying stuff to my dad that I don't even really, like, agree with? You hear this shit coming out of your own mouth, and you're wondering, why am I saying this? But you're still saying it.

I've even been like that at the pub sometimes. I kind of wonder what it would be like to say something pretty outrageous to some punk who's, like, annoying me and I think, nah, that's silly. And then I hear myself saying it. I think that might be what happens when some people really go off the deep end – with guns and stuff. They imagine what it would be like to do something, and then they just do it, even if they'd already started to think it might be stupid. I don't think that makes sense, except it sort of does.

My dad keeps asking me when I'm going to do something. I say to him 'The dole beckons,' and that freaks him out. We both know it can't go on like this forever. If he stopped, like, asking me all the time, I might be able to think straight. The whole thing feels like pressure.

Rick Swanson, the principal at Southwood High, was acutely aware of the problem of the post-school drifter. His heart bled for the pupils who had only just scraped through school, often needing strong encouragement and support simply to hang on to the end. The thought that they might then drop out of sight and lose whatever sense of direction the school had provided disturbed him deeply. In fact, he saw them as a serious challenge to the quality and the value of the work he and his colleagues were doing.

Marcus Li, his deputy, came up with an idea that appealed to Rick.

'I think part of the problem is that it's all school, school, school, right up until the moment they leave, and then they're suddenly expected to be fully-functioning adults in an adult world. Most of them can handle that, but some of them clearly can't. Maybe we need to create a kind of transition year for these kids who struggle, where it's clear they have left school, and they're not subject to school rules, but they come here, maybe two or three times a week, to help out with coaching sport or playground duty or simple clerical work in the office. Meanwhile, we line up some people who can give them some skills – maybe something more specific than they were getting in their final year. I mean life skills. Time management, diet, cooking . . . I don't know. Health stuff. Job-seeking skills. Some regular sessions with the school counsellor. Even a spot of work experience. Volunteering. They could certainly spend some time in the community garden. Surely there'd be people around Southwood who'd help us construct a program like this, or at least steer us in the right direction.'

Over a period of three months, with lots of consultation with school-leavers themselves, local employers, health professionals and retirees, the Pathfinder project took shape.

It began slowly, with just eight people from the previous year being recruited for the program. They were wary; the school wasn't sure how to handle them; some of the final-year pupils teased the Pathfinder kids. But Marcus persevered and the project began to flourish. Within two years, about half the school-leavers who were unsure of their next step signed up for the Pathfinder team. Not all of them lasted the full year. Some got full-time jobs and left, some lost their enthusiasm, but most stuck it out and enjoyed their ambiguous status in the school community – no longer students, yet not quite staff; volunteers and learners, all at once. By the end of the third year, Rick and Marcus were convinced they had a viable project. It wasn't working miracles, but it was rescuing vulnerable young people from boredom and ennui and offering them a pathway for their transition from school to the adult world.

∽

Southwood is no Utopia.

There are petty criminals who steal cars and break into homes. There are hoons who disturb the peace by racing cars through the streets of East and around the Ponds. There are graffiti-writers and people who vandalise common property. There are peeping Toms who wander the streets at night, hoping for a glimpse of something exciting through a lighted window. There are bullies. There are binge drinkers aplenty, and underage drinkers too. There are people – mostly young men – who resort to physical violence when they are both drunk and angry. There are kids who occasionally light fires in the bush to the south of the Ponds. There are unplanned teenage pregnancies. There are drug dealers and their favourite clients: the addicts. There are reckless and irresponsible parents – and there are overanxious, overprotective parents who inflict a different kind of damage on their kids. There are householders who let their places fall into a state of neglect, with overgrown gardens and cars up on blocks in the front yard, to the irritation of more house-proud neighbours. Southwood has its share of poverty, but people respond generously when local charities appeal for support, including food and even cash, in cases of real hardship. The police in Southwood are generally seen as allies rather than mere enforcers, and they have done a good job of encouraging the residents to speak up if they see something that arouses their suspicions.

Walk the streets of Southwood and you'll find plenty of sadness, disappointment and grief in among the peace and progress. You'll find dysfunctional families and desperately unhappy marriages. You'll find people gripped by all kinds of neuroses. You'll find disordered personalities and flawed characters aplenty.

It's a human environment. It's all there.

The other thing that will strike you is that the community spirit is strong. Neighbours generally look out for each other. The council is keen to promote activities and events that foster a sense of community, and the mayor is not embarrassed about her vision for Southwood as a place that offers its residents more than somewhere to live. She may overplay her hand by her constant references to 'our village', but she understands people's need to belong.

She knows what Jim Glasson and the local clinical psychologists and social workers all know – that most of the shadows falling across the lives of people in Southwood are cast by the failings and frailties that all mortal flesh is heir to; these are rarely the bleak, black shadows of hopelessness and despair.

9

Sometimes it takes a
crisis . . .

When Jason and Victoria Ng's baby died in its cot, the residents of
Kendall Street were not only shocked, they were united in their
concern for the bereaved young couple. In the aftermath of the
tragedy, people made more of an effort to keep in touch with each
other. It wasn't as if they became best friends, but there was a new
camaraderie in the street, a new alertness to each other's needs and
a greater concern for each other's wellbeing.

A rather different kind of crisis united the residents of Pelham
Place in Old Southwood. It began when Joe Stuckey, long-term
and rather reclusive resident of the house on the corner, knocked
on his neighbours' door and said, rather too loudly, to the young
man who answered: 'Your wife has the most beautiful bottom
in Cairo.'

The neighbour, a recently arrived Cambodian who, with his
wife and young family, was still finding his feet – financially
and culturally – wasn't sure whether, in the Australian context,
this should be taken as a compliment. The reference to Cairo
confused him, as did the rather vacant look on Joe's face and

the lack of eye contact, as if Joe were attending to some other voice.

The neighbour, not wishing to give offence, retreated into the house without shutting the door, and Joe mooched off, apparently neither surprised nor offended by the lack of a response.

The following night, the residents of Pelham Place were astonished to hear a wavering voice raised in song at midnight. The sound seemed to be coming from outside. Lights went on and people appeared in their front gardens in dressing gowns and tracksuits. A baby was crying. There they found Joe, working through his repertoire of wartime songs. *Pack up your troubles in your old kit bag and smile, smile, smile*, he sang, word perfect, with uninhibited gusto, marching as best he could up and down the centre of their cul-de-sac.

A man who knew a little of Joe's background went up to him, walked beside him as he sang, and gradually persuaded him to go inside and get a little more sleep.

The next morning, there was concern up and down the street about what might be happening to old Joe Stuckey. Had he finally cracked? A couple of older residents had heard from even older residents, now moved on, that Joe had been badly shell-shocked in World War II and had never been able to settle to anything since he returned, still a young man, almost seventy years ago. He had apparently never married, and somehow he'd managed on his own, with a pension, all these years. It was generally agreed that he must be well into his nineties.

It soon emerged that only two men in the street had ever spoken to Joe, and a sense of shame descended on the little community of Pelham Place. They had always thought of themselves as a friendly street, with lots of waving and smiling, and occasional chats over the fence. They were proud of the immaculate appearance of their little cul-de-sac, too: Pelham Place had quite a reputation for its pretty gardens and well-trimmed nature strips. In fact, the only thing marring the beauty of the street was the neglected front yard and peeling paint of Joe's place – modest fibro amid all the brick veneer, almost obscured by a huge and undisciplined crepe myrtle that occupied most of his front garden. Because he lived on the corner, they had managed to think of Joe as belonging more to Dickens Street than to Pelham Place.

No one had ever volunteered to help him clean up his yard; no one had ever enquired whether he'd like some assistance, or even some company. No one had ever offered him a cup of tea or a glass of something stronger, even at Christmas. These admissions gradually came out in the concerned conversations about what should now be done.

Joe was rarely seen, and it was generally assumed that he had family somewhere – someone had once seen him being collected in a car driven by a woman – or that he spent most of his time at the pub. No one had the faintest idea how relatives, if any, might be contacted.

A week later, Joe knocked at the door of Simon and Rhonda Kinnear's place, apparently chosen at random. 'The privy calls!' he shouted gleefully. 'Latrine parade!' When it rather looked as if Joe might be about to squat then and there, Simon called for reinforcements from the people next door, who had come into their front garden to watch. Joe was led home once more, but this time Simon went right into Joe's house with him, with no protest from Joe. Simon had to squeeze his nostrils shut against the smell of the place, and was shocked at the mess strewn everywhere.

'Do you have family, Joe?' he asked. 'Anyone I could ring up to come and stay with you?'

Joe appeared to have no idea what he was talking about, or even any sense that a response was needed. He flopped down on a sagging sofa and began singing again, very loudly: *It's a long way to Tipperary* . . .

Simon looked around, checking first to see if there might be a list of telephone numbers by the old phone on Joe's hall table. Nothing. He asked again: 'Any family you'd like me to call, Joe?' Nothing. It was clear to Simon that Joe shouldn't be left alone in this mess. 'Come with me, Joe,' he said. Nothing. Then, in a moment of inspiration, Simon said: 'Smarten yourself up, Joe. Atten-*shun*! Pull those shoulders back. Head up. We're moving out.' And so they did.

As they left Joe's place, Simon called Rhonda on his mobile to prepare her for their arrival. She made Joe some tea which he drank with noisy enthusiasm, looking for more as soon as he'd drained his mug. She prepared some bread and cheese which he devoured with similar gusto, while tears of sympathy and concern pricked Rhonda's eyes.

Simon scoured the council entry in the phone book, looking for something like emergency services, but all he could find were references to wounded animals and fires. He looked at the state government entry and found departments with suitable-sounding names – 'community services', 'aged care' – but there were no after-hours numbers that he could find and, in any case, he blanched at the prospect of trying to explain all this to someone on the end of a phone. He thought of the police, but felt that was not fair – he didn't want Joe to spend the night in a cell. His wife, meanwhile, was scrolling through various sites on her smartphone, and came up with the name of Jim Glasson, pastor of Southwood East Community Church, with a number to call for 'all emergencies'. Worth a try, she thought, looking dubiously at Joe, who was still working his way through the slices of bread she had kept piling on his plate. She got him another mug of tea and made the call from another room.

Jim Glasson came in person.

Joe said: 'This woman has the most beautiful bottom in Cairo.'

Jim said: 'Doesn't she make beautiful tea?'

Joe nodded.

Jim said: 'Come with me, old soldier. I'll find you a clean warm bunk. Everything will look better in the morning. Listen. All the guns have stopped. It's over.'

Joe looked bewildered.

Recalling Rhonda's account of Joe's rendition of old army songs, Jim pointed to his own rather battered brown backpack, and said: 'Let's pack up our troubles in *this* old kit bag, shall we?'

Joe smiled, just a flicker, then crumpled, shaken by silent sobs. Jim helped him to his feet, put an arm around him, and together they shuffled to Jim's car.

Jim phoned the Kinnears the next day to thank them for contacting him and to assure them Joe was safe and well in temporary accommodation with a member of Jim's congregation. He would need institutional care, Jim felt, and that was being investigated. No relatives could be traced. Jim arranged to come to Pelham Place on the weekend to meet a few of Joe's neighbours and discuss what might be done, collectively, to clean up his house and yard. There was no prospect of Joe returning there to live, but the place would eventually have to be sold. In a brief flash of lucidity, Joe had confided to Jim that he was worried about the state of his house. (He had said his mother would be ashamed of him, letting himself go like that.)

A skip was hired and placed on the footpath outside Joe's fence. Over the following four weekends, teams of people from the street worked their way through the inside and outside of Joe's house, sorting through everything to see what might be worth saving – what might possibly have even sentimental value to Joe – and what was clearly junk. The skip was soon filled. The main task was cleaning: every surface was washed, every floor scrubbed, threadbare rugs taken outside for beating and hosing. Curtains were taken down; those that didn't fall apart were washed and re-hung.

Once the place was clean and clear of debris, it was decided the exterior paintwork should be done and several more weekends were devoted to that. The crepe myrtle was pruned, a trailer-load of weeds pulled from the front and backyards, and dozens of bottles and cans taken to the recycling depot. Those neighbours not actually engaged in these tasks were kept busy preparing tea and coffee and sandwiches for the workers. No one in the street hung back.

There was an air of sadness over the whole project. Why did it take a crisis for us to realise that Joe was in such a desperate situation? Couldn't we have guessed? Were we slightly afraid of him? Why? Aren't we better people than that?

~

Not all crises are tragic.

Humans can be strange creatures. We all live together, right next door to each other, and yet we don't always acknowledge each other the way we should. I think we used to be better at it than we are now, but that's another story.

You'd think Southwood Ponds would be different — the way our houses are clustered around the ponds makes it easier for us to bump into each other. And the paths by the ponds are ideal for strolling and talking. Well, we do a lot of strolling, but not so much talking. I'm as guilty as the next man. I'm more of a wave-and-keep-walking kind of guy, I suppose. My wife is better at the happy hey-hey type of thing.

Everything changed the night Debbie drove her Vespa into one of the ponds.

She's a nice kid, Debbie. Lives just a couple of clusters down from us, and we've been aware of her since she was going to high school. I think the family moved in when she was about thirteen.

So we were on waving terms with her and her parents. My wife knew the mother a bit.

We were also aware that Debbie had left school and was going to university. Next thing, she had acquired a motor scooter and was puttering around the Ponds on her L-plates. I had noticed she seemed a bit unsure of herself; a bit wobbly; a bit overcautious. I stopped waving to her – she looked as if she didn't need any distractions.

On the night in question, I just happened to be putting some garbage into our wheelie bin when I heard the unmistakeable pop-pop-pop of Debbie's scooter nearby – very close to our side fence, in fact, and I wondered why she was not on the road. Then I heard a very restrained little scream – more like a squeak, really – followed by a splash.

I grabbed a torch from the shed and ran down the side of the house. There was Debbie in the water, with the handlebars of her Vespa just visible above the surface of the pond.

The ponds are quite shallow – I knew she would be able to stand up alright, but I hadn't counted on the effect of her panic. She was floundering about and seemed unable to take the half-dozen steps that would have got her to dry land. It was a cold night – fine, but decidedly chilly, and I was wearing a few layers.

I tore off my jumper and shirt, took off my shoes and waded in, calling to Debbie to remain calm. She wasn't listening to me. The water was actually a bit deeper, and much colder, than I had expected, but I reached her without difficulty, grabbed her by the arm, and sort of dragged her to the edge of the pond.

She was soaked to the skin, poor girl, and shivering. Her teeth were chattering like a caricature of a cold person and I thought she appeared a bit wild-eyed. I looked at the Vespa and decided it wasn't going anywhere, so I took Debbie inside, called to my wife and she put Debbie straight into a hot shower. We threw her clothes into the dryer.

While all that was happening, I went back out to the pond to retrieve the Vespa. It had sunk beneath the waves, as it were. So I began feeling around with my feet, hoping to locate it. Which I did after a few minutes, lying on its side in the mud at the bottom of the pond.

Scooters are not very heavy things – easy to manage on a sealed surface with their engine running – but they are very difficult to manoeuvre when the operation is taking place under very cold water and the base of operations, as it were, is mud rather than tar. The scooter and I wrestled each other for a few minutes, until I was forced to admit defeat. I abandoned it where it lay.

Staggering back into the house, I explained the situation to my wife – Debbie was still in the shower – and went to our ensuite bathroom to get cleaned up and to find some dry clothes. I was freezing and actually a bit irritated. I was not sure what my wife was finding so funny.

It all ended well. My wife took Debbie home and her father, Doug, was not as angry as Debbie had feared he might be. The next day, he and I went back to the pond with a rope, but the salvage operation was not as straightforward as we had anticipated. The water can't have been as cold as it was the night before, but it was still freezing. The ponds were not meant for swimming – they were supposed to be decorative, and there were signs warning against swallowing the water – so it's not as if either Doug or I were used to this. The mud was slippery and we both went under at different stages of the operation. Our wives were lakeside, as it were, almost helpless with laughter, and I think it was the sound of their chortling that brought a little knot of neighbours to watch the fun.

One of them – a bloke I hadn't seen before – went and got another rope and waded in with us, showing every sign of knowing what he was doing. Between the three of us, we had the thing out in no time.

The Vespa was a sorry sight, but the bloke with the rope assured Doug he would help him clean it down and he seemed to know which bits would need special attention. Debbie herself was nowhere to be seen. 'Gone to uni,' said Doug. 'Typical.'

'That's not fair,' said his wife. 'I told her to go. She's got an assignment to do in the library.'

Quite a crowd had gathered. This was on a Friday, and the decision was made to have a celebratory barbecue at Doug's place on the Sunday. It was not clear what was being celebrated – Debbie's life had hardly been at risk, but I was nevertheless being slapped on the back by various hearty neighbours.

The barbecue was a great success. Debbie was again nowhere to be seen – wise girl – but there were neighbours I'd never spoken to before who were saying things like, 'Two heroes in one street!' – a reference to Dan Furness, the architect who lives nearby. It was Dan who had uncovered the shopping-mall scam. I decided not to protest too much. The attention was quite nice while it lasted.

What was even nicer was that everyone suddenly knew everyone else – we knew each other's names – and it was surprising how many of our neighbours had ridden motor scooters in their youth, had hairy tales to tell, and were determined to tell those tales.

Debbie never reappeared on that scooter, by the way. But she does give me a big hug whenever she sees me, as if I had saved her from drowning. It's possible, I suppose.

Although some people behave badly in a crisis – running away from danger that others need to be rescued from, or looting properties that have been flooded, or laughing at others' misfortunes – most people rise to the occasion; not just satisfactorily, but brilliantly. It's one of the characteristics of human beings:

because our sense of community is so deep and powerful within us, we respond almost unthinkingly to the needs of others when they are suddenly in our face. And the more acute the need, the more reflexive is our response.

That's not because we're born to be heroic; it's simply because we are social creatures. We know – viscerally rather than cognitively – that we are connected to each other; part of each other; bound by our common humanity.

When you look at the success of resident action groups in marshalling the support of local communities in a common cause – opposition to coal seam gas mining, for instance, or securing a pedestrian crossing on a dangerous street – you realise it can be done. When you see the response people make to appeals for disaster relief, locally or across the world, you realise the vein of generosity is rich within us, needing only to be tapped. When you see the way people band together in time of disaster – storms, floods, fires, the death of a child like Jason and Victoria's baby – you realise that it only needed a catalyst for the connections to be made.

The good news is that it doesn't always need a catalyst. Even without a crisis to face, we are naturally inclined to connect rather than disconnect, to engage rather than disengage. Look at the volunteers who give up precious evenings and weekends, year after year, to work with their local bushfire brigades, or to train kids' sporting teams, to conduct choirs and bands, to run drama groups or to clean up local bushland, and you realise the spirit of community is far from dead. And if you were to visit the parks of Southwood on a Sunday afternoon, teeming with people of all ages and types, interacting with each other via bats and balls, kites and dogs, you would realise that playing together – like eating together, working together and helping each other out in a crisis – comes naturally to us. Hermits are the exception.

But there's no doubt that a crisis sharpens our awareness of our interdependence. When a fire sweeps up a gully and threatens a rural community, the neighbours are as concerned for each other as for themselves, and the concern spreads – as soon as we hear of their ordeal on the evening news, we wonder what we can do to help. When the 2011 floods swamped the Australian city of Brisbane, how could you not have been impressed by the thousands of volunteers who arrived by bus, by car and on foot, mops and buckets in hand, ready to help total strangers face the heartbreaking task of cleaning up? In the same year, the rioting and looting that swept London, Birmingham and other cities across England was swiftly followed by the arrival of hordes of volunteers – strangers – offering to help shopkeepers clean up the mess and get back on their feet.

Sometimes the precipitating crisis is personal and internal. When people face the moment of retirement from a lifetime of paid work, that can feel like a crisis. And, like any other crisis, it can bring out the worst in us: self-pity, lack of motivation and a descending cycle of despair. But it can also bring out the best in us, leading us to decide to spend more time with the people who populate our lives – family, friends and neighbours – and to seek ways of remaining useful: volunteering to help out with slow readers at the local school; keeping the books for a charity; getting involved in Meals on Wheels or a Men's Shed; mowing the lawn or doing the shopping for an elderly or frail person who can no longer cope; delivering library books to the housebound; teaching English to refugees; mentoring or fostering disadvantaged youngsters; deploying the skills we acquired at work in ways that will benefit our local community. Relieved of the burden of having to earn a living, we may feel liberated in other ways – freer to contribute, to relate, to connect, to create.

The experience of a life-threatening illness is a crisis many of us will face and that, too, may have a dramatic effect on us – clarifying our values, reordering our priorities and stiffening our resolve to live the best life we can. (Nothing fuels our zest for life like the prospect of losing it.) In such circumstances, some people slip into self-pity and perpetual victimhood, but most do better than that. Recovery from an illness sometimes fuels a fresh resolve to start living well – and that means living more consciously for others; seeking to live in harmony with the community; being alert to all the ways we might be able to make life a little easier for someone else, or add to their quotient of personal wellbeing.

After all, the great paradox of 'the good life' is this: we are at our best when we are striving to give others the very things we ourselves most desire – respect, recognition, kindness and compassion. The Bengali polymath Rabindranath Tagore (1861–1941) wrote: 'We may become powerful by knowledge, but we attain fullness by sympathy.' The sad thing is that some of us only come to a full realisation of that when we are plunged into a crisis.

The all-too-predictable personal crisis that engulfed the Ritchie and Koutsoukas households was hugely destructive, but there were signs, even there, of the way communities instinctively reach out to help with the healing of their wounded members.

It happened like this. One of the lectures in the library's 'Industrial Revolution' series was cancelled at the last moment and so Petra and her group of friends, having already eaten together, went their separate ways. Michael drove Petra home, ninety minutes earlier than usual. He dropped her off in his driveway as he always did, and she walked to her front door. He drove his car into the garage, locked up and walked to his back door. He was puzzled that, apart from the outside lights, his house appeared to be in darkness. Petra was puzzled that, although all the lights were on, Bill was nowhere to be found in any of his usual places — not standing at the front window, not hunched over his computer, and not in the bathroom.

She heard raised voices coming from the Koutsoukases and moments later, Bill appeared in the doorway, trembling and dishevelled. Michael's voice could still be clearly heard, remonstrating with Angie, who was sobbing hysterically.

Petra looked at Bill and understood immediately. 'How could you?' was all she said. Given all she had been through with him, she found she was more disgusted than outraged. Michael, by the sound of it, was both of those things . . . and much more besides.

She packed a small bag and told Bill she would be back in the morning to talk. He began to object but was silenced by her look.

She called Grace, asked if she could stay with her overnight, and drove away.

Bill was even more shocked by her coolness than he had been, moments earlier, by the heat of Michael's rage.

The disintegration proceeded in slow motion. Both houses were put on the market. Michael and Angie moved to a city apartment where, Petra heard from Fran, their relationship soon dissolved, since Michael could not forgive Angie and she was, in any case, swept away by the distractions of the city now on her doorstep, and by the many men who stopped to stare.

Angie was a textbook narcissist — not merely self-absorbed, but fixated on herself, in love with herself, and preoccupied with her own reflection. Other people existed for her only as potential admirers or, even better, as helplessly devoted adorers. The community, for Angie, was not a network of human beings with the potential to sustain and enrich her in return for her engagement with it; no, the community was simply an audience (just as she felt certain Bill had been an audience when she undressed for bed within range of his window).

Michael was something of a lost soul: his unrequited devotion to Angie, having persisted in the face of so much discouragement, now appeared foolish to him, and he was embarrassed by it. He had rented a small city apartment for himself, but had mentioned to Fran that he would like to return to Southwood 'when things settled down'. He often joined Petra's Thursday evening group for dinner and attended whatever lecture was on the agenda. There was some awkwardness between him and Petra, but they both worked at overcoming it.

Petra never contemplated leaving Southwood, though she couldn't wait to get out of Liesl Crescent. She rented a cottage in Southwood Fields while the property settlement with Bill was being worked out. The World-in-Focus gang, as she still called them, became the foundation for her newly vigorous social life. Her friendships with Fran and Grace blossomed.

Back in Liesl Crescent, the shockwaves from that traumatic night were felt in many homes up and down the street. As the gossip become more lurid, neighbours became determinedly warmer and more open with each other, as if to say 'nothing like that could ever happen to *us*'. Bill had stayed in the house until it was sold, and the neighbours on the other side, determined not to be judgemental, befriended him. He and the husband began playing golf together, and Bill was surprised by how much he enjoyed the companionship, and the game. He missed Petra's energy, but knew that door was firmly shut. He made one attempt to contact Angie, but was rebuffed. Once the house was sold, he purchased a small flat closer to his work, but kept up the weekly golf game with his former neighbour. Emboldened by the success of that experience, he began to engage with the social life of the office, participating in more general conversation, and discovering that two of his colleagues were also keen golfers.

Thus were two marriages terminated, four new single-person households created, a community disrupted and, through it all, some social bonds strengthened.

~

Among the many kinds of crisis that might challenge us, workplace redundancy – like illness or the breakdown of a relationship – generally seems like unrelievedly bad news when it happens. Yet redundancy is becoming increasingly common in the developed world, where economies are undergoing radical restructuring and, in many cases, shifting their emphasis from production to transaction.

Here's the experience of one Southwood resident, initially traumatised and later energised by having been made redundant at his workplace:

❝No one likes to be told they're redundant, and I was shattered the day it happened to me. It's such an awful word, isn't it? 'Redundant.' As if you're left over. As if the world can get on perfectly well without you.

It was hard hearing it. It was hard facing my colleagues as I packed up and left the building. It was bloody hard telling my wife. But she was wonderful. She gave me a hug and said I was overdue for a holiday anyway, and we shouldn't even think about what to do next for at least a month or two. She had her own full-time job in IT and she just carried on with that – never missed a beat.

It took a while to get over it. At first I was in a rush to find another sales job as similar as possible to the one I'd lost. That was what I was trained for. That's where my experience lay. But nothing was presenting itself and one day my wife said: 'Why don't we think outside the square? If we're honest, you weren't really enjoying that job, and I don't think you'd been enjoying it for years. You often looked like a condemned man when you left for work in the morning. Why not think about what you'd really like to do?'

Well, of course, we both knew what I'd really like to do. Carpentry. I was good at it. I loved it. But I'd always thought of it as a hobby. Anyway, it's a long story, but the short version is, I enrolled at TAFE with a whole lot of blokes who were ten years younger than me – they were terrific, by the way – I got a job, took a fairly big pay cut, and I've never felt more useful in my life than I do now. I'm still going to tech one night a week, I work with a great group of guys and I enjoy what I do.

The question I ask myself is this: if I hadn't been retrenched, would I ever have thought to make the switch? Scary, isn't it?

It is scary. And here's another scary question: Why does it so often take a crisis to bring us to our senses, to help us decide what's important in life and clarify our sense of meaning and purpose?

And another: Do we really require the trigger (or the threat) of pain, trauma or loss to remind us that we are part of a larger whole; that communities can only support us if we let them; that disengagement is not an option if we are to fulfil our destiny as social creatures?

10

The Southwood Festival

On the very dot of two o'clock on a hot and steamy summer Saturday, the pipes and drums of Southwood City Highland Band (the brainchild of a Scottish immigrant who is its pipe major) led the centenary festival procession out of the marshalling area in the carpark of Southwood Central Mall. Immediately behind the band was the figure of Judith MacGregor, swathed in a MacGregor tartan shawl and pleated skirt, in spite of the heat. She carried a mace to which was attached a large placard saying 'Parade Marshal'.

Judith had been practising this moment for months. Under the tutelage of the pipe major, Hamish Johansson (Scots mother, Norwegian father), she had learnt to march with the best of them, perfectly in step, shoulders back, chin jutting, mace held aloft in her left hand, her right arm swinging ferociously.

Behind her stretched a procession fit for a festival ... acrobats somersaulting and leapfrogging; a Pilates group going through its paces on the back of a truck; a yoga class, testing the limits of its capacity for mindfulness, striking meditative poses on the back of another; the bicycle club out in force, ducking and weaving in formation like counter-marchers; a group of actors from Southwood Players modelling the military uniforms of World War I; a vintage fire engine; a horse-drawn milk cart with 'Hereford Street Dairy' painted on its sides; a couple of members of Southwood Gamers, bent over their digital consoles in the back of a ute, with images of death and destruction displayed on two giant video screens ('We need new as well as old, Judith,' Marcus Li had insisted); ten members of the advanced dog-obedience class, their charges on leashes, just to be sure; a group of boys and girls proudly holding kites and model aircraft aloft, impatient to get to Dysart Park to fly them; twenty garden club members dressed in straw hats and overalls, some carrying baskets of flowers, some brandishing garden tools; a group of little girls in tutus, cleverly combining dancing with marching, accompanied by music amplified through the sound system of a sports car leading them; cricketers and tennis players swinging bats and racquets and tossing balls to each other; police and ambulance officers marching gamely, too far from either of the bands to be sure of the step; Marcus and his community gardeners pushing wheelbarrows filled with vegetables; members of the Historical and Heritage Society dressed in the fashions of a hundred years ago; jugglers, unicycle riders, clowns on stilts and pogo sticks scattered through the procession, and the Southwood High concert band bringing up the rear playing tunes of the period, heavily dominated by the songs of World War I (no doubt gladdening the heart of Joe Stuckey, now confined to a wheelchair and buried somewhere in the crowd in the care of Rhonda Kinnear). All this had been personally sorted and marshalled into its correct order by Judith in the hour between one and two. When the parade was being planned, Judith had agonised briefly about whether she would prefer to be on the dais with the other members of the steering committee or at the head of the parade, but when she imagined that magic moment when the pipe band would sweep out of the carpark and into the main street, it was a no-brainer.

～

The celebration of Southwood's centenary had been set for the first weekend in December. After months of wrangling, the steering committee had agreed that a concentrated burst of activity over two days would have more impact than a protracted program of events.

The Saturday morning had been devoted to a garden ramble with several of Southwood's loveliest gardens open for inspection, and a display of suitably themed work at the primary schools and Southwood High, mainly attended by dutiful parents. But everyone had anticipated that the Saturday afternoon parade and the Sunday afternoon street parties would be the highlights of the weekend.

～

The head of the procession swept into Heywood Place, past the official dais, around the corner and on towards E.K. At that point, Judith ducked into an alleyway where her husband was waiting with a costume change inside an improvised cubicle. Off with the tartan and on with the straw hat and overalls, then a scurry around the block to join her colleagues in the garden group, Judith herself now positioned at their head, waving a bunch of gladioli as the midsection of the parade approached the dais, a phalanx of cameras recording every moment for posterity.

Once again, Judith stayed at her post only until her section of the parade had rounded the corner, out of sight of the cameras, and had passed E.K. Then it was back into the alley, her husband still patiently waiting to assist, off with the overalls and into formal attire, vaguely historical, with flowing skirt and plumed hat, and another dash around the block to catch the other members of the Historical and Heritage Society at the tail of the procession – 'the climax', Judith had assured them. A collection of six vintage cars of questionable reliability followed at a safe distance, where it was felt that any mechanical difficulties would cause the least disruption.

The procession swung into Hereford Street, on the way to its destination in Dysart Park. Judith MacGregor had correctly guessed that most spectators would assemble in the Heywood Place area, and so she was content to remain with the historical group for the rest of the journey. There were a few people hanging over their front fences as the procession went by, but the excitement, so palpable at the beginning, had largely subsided by the time the leaders were halfway down Hereford Street. Much to Judith's displeasure, a number of the groups peeled off and disbanded, in search of shade and refreshment, well before the park had been reached.

After cold drinks had been provided for the survivors, there was a brief display of model aircraft and kite flying – a combination not fully thought through. Several planes became entangled with kite strings and plunged to the ground, their owners' fury fanned by the heat.

At four o'clock, a small crowd had assembled back at Heywood Place for the unveiling of a commemorative plaque by the mayor, Mary Kippax. This is what she said:

I know we're supposed to be commemorating the centenary of the establishment of Southwood but, as you probably know, it wasn't some great historic event. An enterprising real estate developer simply saw his chance and went for it. It wasn't even an auspicious time – the world was on the brink of war and many Australians would be lost.

What I want us to celebrate is the character of the place one hundred years on. I want us to celebrate the fact that, over this period, so many thousands of people have not just made Southwood their home, but have enriched the place by engaging with it. People complain that some of our streets are less friendly than others, and I suppose that might be true. But the remedy lies with us, not our neighbours. In all the important ways, friendliness comes from us, not to us.

My dream for Southwood is well known. It is that no one would live a lonely life here; that each of us would bear some responsibility for sustaining the life of this community; that our watchwords would not be growth and prosperity – though who doesn't want to grow and prosper? – but kindness and mutual respect. My dream is that those will come to be recognised as the hallmarks of life in Southwood.

Why don't we let this plaque symbolise our commitment to making it happen? Here's to the next hundred years!'

As the mayor unveiled the plaque with a flourish, someone in the crowd yelled, 'Three cheers for Southwood,' and received a spirited response.

After the unveiling, the members of the festival steering committee and an assortment of dignitaries and other guests disengaged from the crowd and wound their way to the mayor's reception room on the first floor of the council chambers. Mary Kippax was flushed with happiness. The local members of state and federal parliament were there. The mayors of both adjoining municipalities were there too, making mental notes of shortcomings in the Southwood Festival they aimed to avoid in their own looming celebrations. School principals, clergy, the senior officer from Southwood police station, Harry Goodman the stationmaster, the council's senior executives, Roslyn Kennedy from the library . . . even Laurie Griff, the chairman of Southwood Central Mall's holding company, was there, keeping his distance from Mary.

Dom Fin, deputy mayor and chair of the festival committee, was in a reflective mood, astonished by how well everything had gone but acutely conscious, yet again, that a deputy is a mere deputy, and that Mary Kippax's name would be forever on that wretched plaque. But he was ready for his own big moment – making the speech Mary had graciously asked him to prepare for this VIP occasion. The sight of Judith MacGregor, now changed back into her Highland garb and revelling in the persona of parade marshal, briefly irritated him, but he was determined not to let himself be distracted by that.

'Have you seen Jim?' Marcus Li was at Dom's side, looking anxious. 'He wasn't on the dais, I noticed, and I didn't see him on any of the floats.'

'Knowing Jim, he'll be off binding up someone's wounds,' said Dom, not unkindly, but evincing zero interest in the possible whereabouts of Jim Glasson.

Marcus moved around the room, checking with the other members of the committee. No one had seen Jim. A call to his mobile produced only a recorded message.

'Mary, will you excuse me for a minute?' Marcus said when he was able to manage a quiet moment with the mayor. 'I'm slightly concerned about Jim Glasson. No one seems to have seen him all afternoon, and he's not answering his phone. I think I'd like to slip over to Southwood East and makes sure everything's okay.'

Mary was a great fan of Jim's and had recently decided she was going to make a special presentation to him at the next council meeting: a mayoral award for Good Citizenship, or some such thing. She knew it would have to be low-key and unpretentious or Jim would run a mile. Mary had lost count of the number of people she had met who felt, for reasons large and small, that they were in Jim's debt.

'Take my car,' she said to Marcus, handing him the keys to her mayoral Mazda.

Marcus slipped away, found the car in the basement and edged his way through the crowd and onto Hereford Street, picking up speed as his anxiety grew.

Within ten minutes he was parked in the grounds of Southwood East Community Church. A couple of youngsters were bouncing a ball on the basketball court at the rear of the hall. There was no other sign of life. 'Seen Pastor Jim about?' he called to the boys, both of whom he recognised. They shook their heads rather tentatively, as if they thought they might be in some kind of trouble for having failed to show up at the parade. Marcus knocked on the door of Jim's study. No response. He tried the door. Locked. He walked around to the front door of the church, which was always open, went inside and hurried down the aisle to the other entrance to Jim's study.

Suddenly fearful, he knocked. No answer. He tried the door. It was unlocked. He swung it open and looked into the study, gloomy in the early evening. The blinds were drawn and no lights were on. And then Marcus saw Jim, sitting at his desk, his head tilted forward and his chin resting on his chest.

'Hello, Jim,' said Marcus in a quiet voice, not wanting to alarm Jim if he was asleep. Then, a little more loudly: 'Jim?'

No sound from Jim. Absolute stillness. Absolute silence, apart from the bouncing ball outside. No rising and falling of that barrel chest. Marcus approached the desk, reached out and took Jim's hand. It was cold. Up close, Marcus could see that Jim's eyes were open but there was no life in them.

Marcus stood silently for a moment and then, without thinking, took a step backwards, bowed his head and recited some lines he had learnt as a student, from a translation of a Prudentius fourth-century hymn:

Take him, earth, for cherishing
To thy tender breast receive him.
Body of a man I bring thee,
Noble even in its ruin.

Marcus remained still for several minutes, quietly repeating the phrase that had so captivated him when he first encountered it: 'Noble even in its ruin.' That was precisely how he felt about the man before him: ruined, finished, yet noble.

Feeling strangely calm, Marcus called Aubrey Jones, his GP, who, he knew, was also a close friend of Jim's and probably his GP too. Aubrey said he would come straight over, and asked Marcus to call the police. Marcus went and sat in a church pew while he waited. Within ten minutes, Aubrey arrived, squeezed Marcus's shoulder as he passed him and went into Jim's study. He emerged after a few minutes, sat in the pew beside Marcus, took a deep breath, and filled out a death certificate.

'I'd say his heart finally gave out,' Aubrey said, dabbing his eyes with a handkerchief. 'He was supposed to have been on medication, but Jim was the least compliant patient I've ever encountered. He simply wasn't interested in his health. Some people aren't.'

A police officer arrived, inspected the corpse, took statements from Marcus and Aubrey, expressed his condolences and left.

Aubrey mentioned that he had also called Simon Kinnear. Since the episode in Pelham Place involving old Joe Stuckey, Simon and Jim had struck up a close friendship and Simon had found himself acting increasingly like Jim's de facto assistant.

'Simon and Jim were up all night trying to sort out a family who were being threatened with eviction. Simon thinks Jim probably got no sleep at all,' Aubrey said, 'which was not all that unusual.'

When Simon arrived, Marcus excused himself. Badly shaken, he drove back to the mayoral reception, parked the car, ran up the stairs and was met by Mary Kippax in the foyer of the reception room. Over her shoulder, he noticed that the room was now tightly packed with dignitaries. He could hear the resonant tones of Dom Fin, making his speech to the gathering.

Mary read the expression on Marcus's face and knew at once the news was bad. 'Tell me,' she said, gripping Marcus's arm.

'Jim is dead,' Marcus replied. Then he added, almost inaudibly, 'Noble even in his ruin.' Mary absorbed the first statement, but failed to catch the second. She led Marcus away from the open doorway and he explained in a trembling voice what he had found and what he had done; what Aubrey had said; what Simon had said. Mary nodded and closed her eyes, struggling to compose herself.

There was a ripple of applause at the conclusion of Dom's remarks, less hearty than he would have liked, but most people were holding a glass in one hand, and some merely slapped their free hand against their thigh.

Mary pushed her way back through the crowd, moved to the front of the room and held up her hand.

'Thank you, Dom – and thank you for all you and your committee have achieved. Today has been a wonderful success and I'm confident tonight's choral concert and tomorrow's Meet-the-Street parties will be equally successful. And now I'm afraid I must bring you some sad news. Some very sad news. Our dear friend and colleague Pastor Jim Glasson has passed away.'

There was a shocked intake of breath followed by complete silence. Everyone either knew Jim or knew who he was. Everyone respected him and many of the people in the room loved him.

'Marcus Li was worried by Jim's absence from this afternoon's events and went out to the church. He found Jim at his desk. He had apparently died peacefully. We don't know precisely when, but probably early this morning. We do know that Jim had been up all night sorting out a family who were being threatened with eviction. How characteristic of Pastor Jim that that should have been his final act.

'Thank you all so much for coming. I think perhaps we might disperse now. Many of us will want to be alone with our thoughts of Jim.'

~

At seven o'clock, the choral concert conceived and presented by Julian Frisk took place in the crowded assembly hall of Southwood High. The enthusiastic audience consisted mainly of the families and friends of the performers, including many parents who found themselves involuntarily mouthing the words as their offspring sang.

Petra Ritchie's year one class from Southwood Fields took the stage first with great panache, charming the audience with an Australiana medley. Next, a huge choir from Southwood Central Primary School surged onto the stage, barely fitting, and presented an exuberant if slightly chaotic rendition of some assorted Beatles, Abba and Percy Grainger numbers. Their parents loved it.

It took the choir a long time to leave the stage and get settled in their seats, by which time the audience had become restless. Julian was suddenly fearful of the reception his rather refined high-school madrigal group might receive, and wondered whether including them had been a miscalculation. But from the moment they opened their mouths, even the most musically unsophisticated members of the audience were astonished by the purity of their sound. The program concluded with Southwood Glee's first public performance of 'Dancing in Heaven', dedicated to the memory of Jim Glasson. Its seventeen-year-old composer, Lucy Nguyen, took a bow.

It was over in exactly an hour. The audience spilled out into the hot night and people seemed reluctant to disperse.

~

At midday on the Sunday, street parties were scheduled to take place all over Southwood. Mary Kippax had dubbed this the Meet-the-Street project, and was encouraging anyone who still hadn't met their neighbours to make sure they took this opportunity to introduce themselves.

In Liesl Crescent, it was more like a series of private soirees than a street party, though care had been taken to ensure no one was left out.

In Raven Close, the Ludwigs and the Hermanns were observed speaking to each other for the first time in months.

In Southwood Ponds, the event took the form of a communal picnic, with rugs spread on the lawns surrounding the ponds, and people sharing their food and drinks.

Not every street in Old Southwood joined in, but little groups of neighbours did congregate in front gardens and, in the spirit of the occasion, people who had been meaning to make themselves known to the newcomers in their street finally did so.

Molly Swift found that she was not the only widow in her street.

In Kendall Street, Jason and Victoria brought smiles to many faces when they announced at the street party that Victoria was pregnant again. 'Only just,' said Victoria, and the women laughed, delighted to be let in on the secret.

The students in the rundown Hereford Street cottages rose wonderfully to the occasion, setting up a table on the nature strip and offering food and drink to anyone who cared to come and join them. Many of their neighbours, previously wary, wandered up to say hello. A few of the students had formed a rock band and were playing with more restraint than usual, in deference to the occasion.

In Pelham Place, the residents had been careful to make themselves known to the new owners of Joe Stuckey's old place on the corner as soon as they had moved in, but the street party was the first time anyone had told them the full story. Rhonda

Kinnear had fetched Joe from his nursing home and brought him to the party in his wheelchair. He recognised no one and showed no interest in his old home, but seemed to be having a whale of a time nevertheless.

Reg Blakey finally introduced himself to the young couple who had moved into 12 Railway Parade. Their three-year-old daughter, recognising a surrogate grandfather when she saw one, had attached herself to Reg and showed no sign of letting go.

∾

In Southwood East, all plans for street parties were quietly abandoned as word of Jim Glasson's death spread. Instead, people started winding their way to the church hall, carrying food and drink in baskets, backpacks and coolers. By one o'clock a huge crowd had gathered, with people standing around in groups or sitting on the grass. Kids ran between them, chasing each other and panting in the heat. The church grounds soon filled; the basketball court was covered in rugs and it, too, was quickly occupied. Some people moved out of the hot sun and into the hall, others into the church itself, filling the pews and offering their food and drinks to each other. People who had never set foot in this church before wandered up and down the aisles, chatting to friends and introducing themselves to strangers. Picnic rugs were spread on the floor.

The afternoon wore on, and people showed no sign of moving. Some walked back to their homes to rustle up some more refreshments, returning to add their contribution to a common table that Aubrey Jones and Simon Kinnear had set up outside the hall. By dusk, the sound of voices had subsided to a murmur and many people were stretched out on the ground, dozing. The children had fallen quiet.

Three cars drew up, and a dozen members of Southwood Glee climbed out, found a spot on the roadside, and began to sing.

First, they reprised a couple of numbers from the previous night's concert and then, with Christmas just three weeks away, led the crowd in the singing of some familiar carols. Even those without a skerrick of religious faith, even those who didn't know the words beyond the first line or two, hummed along and there rose a great sound – not particularly tuneful but unmistakeably celebratory.

When they had finished, the choristers were offered food and then they too fell silent.

Some families with young children began to drift homewards. Most people didn't move, relieved by the falling temperature, and pleased to stay right where they were; pleased to be where Jim had been.

Seated in the darkness of Jim's study, Aubrey and Simon were lost for words. Eventually, Aubrey said: 'You know, Simon, we had a lot to learn from Jim, including one lesson he didn't intend to teach us. You can't just give, give, give, or you'll burn yourself out, and then you'll be no use to anyone. Everyone needs to take regular breaks, and Jim never did. The rest of us might think of Sunday as our day off, but it was the busiest day of Jim's week. He used to tell me he took Mondays off, but I never saw any sign of it.'

Simon nodded, conscious of his own singularly unsuccessful attempts to get Jim to ease back. 'Can I get you a cup of tea or coffee, Aub? The urn in the hall has been working overtime. By the way, I saw Harvey Rendell out there a few minutes ago, standing in a group. He wasn't saying much, but he was there, and he had a drink in his hand.'

~

Petra Ritchie had her feet up on the coffee table and was nursing a glass of wine. Her friends Fran and Grace had joined her after putting in an appearance at their own street parties. Michael Koutsoukas was expected at any moment: he was collecting Fran to take her out for dinner. Marcus Li had promised to drop by later in the evening.

The mood was subdued. None of the three women had known Jim Glasson personally, but the news of his death had saddened everyone.

'Marcus was the one who found him apparently,' Petra said. 'He doesn't want to talk about it. Understandable, I guess. I think they'd become quite close, working on the festival committee together. He had an enormously high opinion of Jim, even though he didn't share a single one of his religious beliefs.'

'It's not about that, is it?' Grace replied. 'It's never about whether we believe the same things. It's only ever about whether we know how to rub along together. Kindness and respect – those are the magic ingredients, just as Mary Kippax said yesterday. I don't know what any of my neighbours believe, and I don't need to know. They're good people, and we all get along perfectly well. I know I could call on any of them if I was in a jam.'

'Anyway, religion isn't the great divider it's sometimes said to be. Most wars are about territory, not religion,' Fran said. 'That's one thing we learnt from the World in Focus lectures.'

'Marcus reckons we'll never see another Jim Glasson in Southwood,' said Petra. 'That's a grim thought, isn't it?'

'I'm not sure that's the right way to look at it,' Grace replied. 'Just this week, I was listening to a young American civil rights campaigner on the radio, bemoaning the fact that people kept saying the civil rights movement needed another Martin Luther King. She strongly disagreed. She admired King's leadership for having given the campaign the momentum it needed, but her point was that if the movement was to be a long-term success, it needed everyone to get on board, not just another charismatic leader. Maybe that applies to Jim's work, too.'

The three women lapsed into a comfortable silence.

After a few minutes, Grace said: 'May I say something else?'

'Since when did you need permission?' Petra replied with a smile.

'Well, you'll think it sounds sentimental, but I mean it quite seriously. I'm very grateful that you two ended up in Southwood. My neighbours are wonderful, but I never expected to find friends here as well.'

'You'd find friends wherever you went, Grace. But thanks for saying it.'

There was a knock on the door and Fran got up to answer it.

Postcript

Every community has its quota of outsiders, non-joiners, passengers . . . people who choose to remain aloof from the life of the neighbourhood in a kind of permanent retreat, while enjoying the benefits of living in its midst. The more reclusive they become, the more likely they are to experience isolation as exclusion and even alienation; the more likely they are to become bitter and cynical, and to develop an unrealistically negative view of the rest of us. Nothing is easier than standing back and mocking those who are having a go.

Every community has its differences of opinion, its social divisions and its cultural tensions, which is simply to say that every community is both diverse and, inescapably, human. If you want to master the art of belonging, you'll need to accept the imperfections and deal with them. And the best way of dealing with them is to overlook them. There's a lot of tolerance – a lot of forgiveness – in the art of belonging.

What's in the art of belonging for you? Why should you bother trying to master it? Three reasons, at least. First, the experience of belonging to a community enhances your feelings of physical safety and emotional security, and enriches your sense of identity. Second, you'll benefit from the mental stimulation of unplanned social encounters and interactions that are characteristic of life in a community. (Indeed, as you grow older, frequent social interaction is the best way of keeping dementia at bay – more effective than that daily crossword!.) Third, the 'state of the nation' starts in your own street, and your own workplace: the way we interact with the communities we belong to ultimately determines the kind of society we will become.

We are all driven by our most cherished beliefs, and by our personal ideals. As social creatures, there is no loftier ideal than a determination to nurture the communities that sustain us. On a global scale, this is the dream of peace. At the local level, it is the dream of a fair, just and equitable society in which we all place our commitment to the common good ahead of our own petty ambitions and fantasies of personal glory.

The local neighbourhood – our street, our apartment block, our suburb, village or town – is the acid test of our commitment to the idea of belonging. Because we have chosen to make our home in an area where other people also live, we have some responsibility (call it our 'social destiny') to be good neighbours.

Not everyone who moves into a neighbourhood will accept that responsibility. Some will want to confine their social connections to a circle of friends located elsewhere, and offer no more than a curt, keep-your-distance nod to their neighbours. Others will obsess about their privacy to the point of actively resisting any attempts to draw them into the life of the neighbourhood, as though this might diminish their security rather than enhance it. Some will have decided that 'being' is more important than 'belonging', and will prefer to focus on their individuality (*Who am I? What will become of me?*) rather than their communality (*Who are we? What kind of society do we want to become?*). Some will convince themselves that 'this is a club I don't want to join' – where 'club' might mean anything from the local neighbourhood to the entire structure of a Western capitalist society. Not liking what they find, they may decide to opt out rather than try to exert some positive influence.

Okay.

But we are still social creatures by nature; that can't be denied. We are still born to cooperate as well as compete, and we are not at our shining best when we retreat into the self-serving, arrogant (sometimes narcissistic) position of the outsider. There's a place for us, somewhere, even among a loose affiliation of surly solipsists who want to deny their connection with anyone.

It all depends on how you choose to make sense of your life. For most of us, life's richest meanings spring from our personal relationships and connections. That's why the desire to belong is a throbbing urge that won't be stilled until our hearts find safe lodgings.

Acknowledgements

I am grateful to Ingrid Ohlsson, my publisher at Pan Macmillan, for her sympathetic guidance, encouragement and support throughout the writing process. I also want to acknowledge the support of the rest of the Pan Macmillan team, particularly Paul O'Beirne's editorial skill.

I have benefited, once again, from the astute and sensitive editing of Ali Lavau.

Stephen Barnett introduced me to his research on the use of online communities to alleviate some of the problems of isolation experienced by medical practitioners working in rural and remote areas. Helen Christiansen, director of the Black Dog Institute, was helpful in discussing several issues canvassed in the book, particularly the danger of relying on 'community support' to address mental-health problems that require professional treatment. Keryl Collard, Maitland City Librarian, gave me valuable insights into the range of activities and services being provided by contemporary regional and suburban libraries. Andrea Selvey, Director of Creative Communities at Geraldton City Council, assisted me with background information on the participatory budget process. Elizabeth Coombs, NSW Privacy Commisssioner, put me in touch with research on changing attitudes to privacy.

The work of Margo Ward and her colleagues at KidsXpress inspired my reference to therapy groups for distressed children in Southwood.

The sign behind the counter at Eine Kleine Caffeine was borrowed from the Gertrude and Alice bookshop in Sydney's Bondi.

Several friends and colleagues helped clarify the themes of the book – sometimes through explicit advice and sometimes through conversation: John Bennett, David Dale, Geoffrey and Pamela Duncan, Richard Eckersley, Tracey Green, Bruce Kaye, Keith Mason, Robert McLaughlin, John Shepherd, Julian Wood and Pamela Young.

My wife, Sheila, has been a source of unfailing support through her research assistance, constructive criticism and constant encouragement.

Starting with Miss Hedges (my earliest memory of a next-door neighbour), I have been blest with many neighbours who have shown me how to balance friendly support and mutual trust with respect for each other's privacy. The book is dedicated to them, with gratitude.

Index

Index

Index

Index